CATHEDRAL OF THE WILD

CATHEDRAL
of the
WILD

An African Journey Home

BOYD VARTY

RANDOM HOUSE | NEW YORK

Published in the United States by Random House, an imprint and division of Random House LLC, a Penguin Random House Company, New York.

RANDOM HOUSE and the HOUSE colophon are registered trademarks of Random House LLC.

Photos courtesy of Londolozi Library unless otherwise noted.

Library of Congress Cataloging-in-Publication Data
Varty, Boyd. Cathedral of the wild : an African journey home / Boyd Varty.
pages   cm
ISBN 978-1-4000-6985-9
eBook ISBN 978-0-679-60485-3
1. Londolozi Game Reserve (South Africa)—History.
2. Varty, Boyd. 3. Varty, Boyd—Family. 4. Londolozi Game Reserve (South Africa)—Biography.
5. Wildlife conservation—South Africa—Londolozi Game Reserve—History. 6. Wildlife conservationists—South Africa—Londolozi Game Reserve—Biography. I. Title.
SK575.S5V37 2014
639.9096827—dc23   2013022706

Printed in the United States of America on acid-free paper

www.atrandom.com

2 4 6 8 9 7 5 3 1

FIRST EDITION

Book design by Casey Hampton

For my mother, who has been so quietly supportive, innovative, and steadfast.
Not everyone knows the immense contribution you have made,
but those who do are nothing short of amazed!
With love.

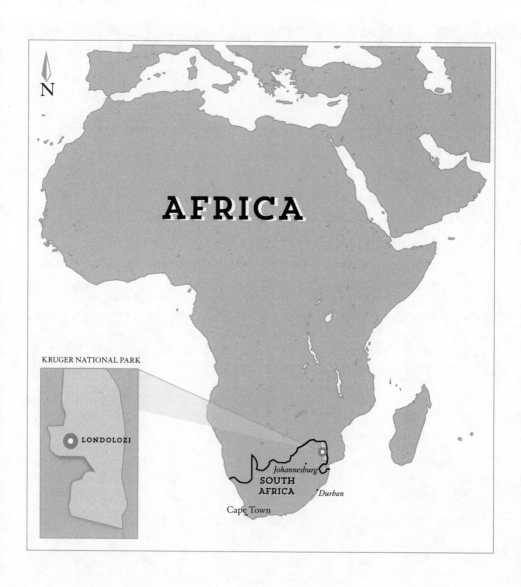

CONTENTS

AUTHOR'S NOTE

In writing this book, I've assimilated my memories as best I can. I've also collected stories from various people who were present at the events I describe; each recounting was slightly different, so I've had to decide for myself what the truest version is. So many of the stories of the early days of Londolozi, before I was born, have been told so many times that they have made the transition to fireside legend. I have tried my best to capture them. In a few instances, I've compressed events that took place over several years into a single scene. Out of politeness, I have also changed some names and other identifying characteristics. South Africa is, in the end, a village, and not every home wants to have its doors flung wide open. I have re-created dialogue as closely as I can remember it, and I have at all times tried to be as accurate as possible. This story is a very personal one and so is told from my own viewpoint. This is the nature of all stories; you can recall them only within the frame of mind you are in during the recollection. I am a particularly messy human. This book is a by-product of mucking around in all that messiness, and it's as honest and authentic as I know how to make it. I hope you will enjoy going on this safari with me.

Welcome to my campfire story.

INTRODUCTION

THE SNAKE WAS SLIDING over the backs of my legs, in slow motion but with purpose, like an army general inspecting his barracks, knowing that someone has been out of line. "Don't move, Dad," I kept whispering. "Don't move, don't move, don't move." The slightest motion and the snake would rear up and strike.

I was eleven, on a hunting expedition with my father. It was an overcast morning in September, early spring, and the rains had just arrived after the characteristic dry winters in the South African bushveld. The marula and acacia trees were just starting to flush green, and Dad and I had decided to stalk a herd of impalas grazing on the slope. After a few hours, we found ourselves entrenched on the side of a termite mound nearby. I'd fired a shot but couldn't tell if the impala had gone down. "Stay in position," Dad advised. "Keep a lookout through the scope of the rifle. If the impala's still up, you can finish it off."

I loved being out with Dad. I'd been going out with him almost every day of my life. When I was a baby, Mom would hold me in her arms as she sat next to him in the front seat of the Land Rover. As I got older, Dad would take me on short walks into the clearings around the house. Later, we went on longer walks into the bush that turned into hunting expeditions. These were my favorite times of day. As excited as I was, Dad always seemed even more enthusiastic.

At eleven, I was a rickety, gangly kid, more like a newborn wildebeest, all legs and arms. Dad, in contrast, had a profound ruggedness, as vital as the landscape around him, as if his body were battling to contain his energy. He was the outdoor cliché of the game ranger: clear blue eyes, lean legs in short shorts, a thin khaki work shirt over his broad shoulders, and slip-on Jesus sandals. I always knew that so long as I was with him, I would be fine.

When I felt something sliding over my legs, the coffin-shaped head was the first thing I noticed, followed by three yards of black mamba draped over and around me as if someone had thrown a fat black garden hose out of the sky.

I grabbed my father's arm. "Oh shit, Dad, there's a mamba. Don't move."

The black mamba's sheer size and mobility make it one of the most dangerous snakes. And its venom is exceedingly potent: if a mamba bites you, you will almost certainly be dead within thirty minutes—sooner if it strikes an area rich in blood vessels. A guy I knew who had miraculously survived a bite told me that he could taste the venom in his mouth almost the instant the snake's fangs sank into his leg.

I willed my body to stop pumping adrenaline, so that my heart wouldn't beat right out of my chest. The snake was now between my legs, making its way up the termite mound, toward our torsos. I didn't know if our nerve would hold if the snake made it to face height. The strain thickened the air, and in my peripheral vision I saw a line of red flowing from Dad's mouth. He'd bitten through his cheek out of sheer fear.

At chest height, the mamba turned back in what seemed a taunting way. Again it crossed my legs, heading for my father's feet, nearly naked in his sandals. As the snake's scales touched the bare skin on Dad's instep, it changed course once again, gliding away from us, slowly, slowly.

The only escape route was up over the tall termite mound, which was crowned with a thick tangle of brushy buffalo thorn. I saw Dad begin to weigh it up in his mind: Was the mamba still too close? Could we get through the razor-sharp spikes of the thorn in time?

"Go!" he screamed. The mamba's tail was still on my foot as we exploded up the mound. Dad pulled me in behind him and punched a hole in that thorn bush with his bare hands. It tore him to pieces. I came through without a scratch. He turned to me with blood coming out of his mouth and branches of thorn attached to his head. "Shit, that was a close one," he muttered, almost to himself. "Boydie, shit—you all right?" My old man is tough as nails, but he was rattled.

Dad told Mom the story as soon as we got home. "It was a bad one," he said.

Mom pulled out her go-to article from the first aid kit: a bottle of homeopathic Rescue Remedy. She gave me four drops instead of the usual three, in acknowledgment of the magnitude of the trauma. "There you go, Boydie, you've been through a shock." She slung a huge jacket around me. "You've got to keep warm when you've got shock."

Next they told Uncle John, Dad's brother and a famous documentarian. "Did you film it?" he asked. "It would have been a good action sequence." He was predictably disappointed in our failure to take advantage of such a rare opportunity.

That was it. We were bush people. We moved on.

———

At the end of a long day, we Africans love to gather by firelight with the flames the only wall between us and the wilderness. *Tsama hansie,* the Shangaans would tell me during my childhood, when they could see that I was exhausted in body or soul. *Put down all you have been carrying.* Rub the city's neon glare from your eyes and let in the soul light of these orange embers. As the night grows darker, we kick the logs bit by bit into the fire, giving the solid wood to the flame, keeping its warmth in our bodies as our gift from the trees. And we tell stories.

This is the story of my life so far.

My family was loving. My friends, who came in all shapes, sizes, and colors, had in common the qualities of kindness and idealism. Everywhere around me was the ferocious, dazzling gentleness of nature. Elephants grazed outside my bedroom window. Monkeys chattered on the roof. The beasts of the field and the fowls of the air were mine to name, love, and tend.

My childhood was largely set in Londolozi Game Reserve, a paradise populated with wild and astonishing creatures, many of whom were related to me by blood. My loved ones lived to tend their part of the garden—land that has been in our family for four generations, and that Uncle John, Dad, and Mom painstakingly reclaimed from its status as a failed cattle farm. Working side by side with the Shangaans, distant cousins of the Zulu, they restored its wetlands, took down fences to encourage the great predators to return, and created a beautiful, sustainable resort.

This was the playground where I and my sister, Bronwyn, grew up, raising lion and leopard cubs, piloting Land Rovers around at a tender age while simultaneously acting as production assistants for whatever nature documentary crazy Uncle John was making. I apprenticed with master Shangaan trackers, learning to read the land, to see the ghostly trails of lives passing across it. I became a tracker and ranger, sharing my knowledge and joy with guests from all around the world.

Our upbringing was also filled with the hazards of an unconventional life. Our parents never set out to put us in danger, of course; they would have defended us from anything, died before they let us be harmed. But they would not shelter us. To shelter us where we grew up would have been to fail to prepare us. They walked that line as best they could, and all too often they got it wrong. But in the end we survived all we ever faced, and we came out strong and largely unafraid of life, with the full knowledge of its dangers.

Confidence that comes from never having been burned is different from confidence that comes from having been in situations where it all went wrong—dodgy aircraft, unguided motorboats, uncharted bush— and we were lucky to survive. The second kind of confidence is all you need for life in Africa, where things pivot from day to day.

Uncle John took us places on a wave of his own confidence. He knew, even when my faith waned, that he would get us through whatever was put in front of us, whether it was a charging elephant or a wayward wildebeest. Uncle John was made for Africa, certain that all things were uncertain, solid on a foundation as wobbly as the ocean.

"We treat you like adults," our parents told me and Bron often when we were growing up, making us privy to things far beyond our youthful understanding. If safari means "journey," we went on one hell of one. Yet for all the explosive brushes with danger I survived in the bush, the greatest threat came not from any animal, natural disaster, or mechanical mishap, but from other human beings. A devastating encounter precipitated an even greater spiritual crisis for me. Surrounded by everything and everyone I loved, in a life of privilege and adventure, I woke up one day feeling like a stranger. As the weeks went by, I felt more and more alone. The hopelessness that crept into my heart was dense and anesthetic.

Though I still lived in Eden, I had to cast myself out of it and venture away from the place I loved in order to find myself again. From that self-imposed exile in other lands and countries, I learned that you find family members with whom you share no blood in the most surprising places. And I learned to follow that still, quiet track within, the trail to my true home and the restoration of my inner peace.

Reading over this manuscript, a sheaf of loose papers anchored by stone in the quiet of the front garden, pulls a blurry lens into the sharp focus of hindsight. I heard Dad muttering quietly to himself as he turned the pages among the sunbirds and robins on the front lawn: "What was I thinking?" His innocent vitality was more veiled now. He looked like a warrior who had become an elder, in whom the folly of youth wanting to go to war has given way to the wisdom that values peace above all else.

From the time I was a child, I walked on the wild grounds of my family's home on the western boundary of Kruger National Park, in South Africa. Like a small tree, I dug my roots into that soil of extremes, where the wet season paints the grass and trees green overnight and the dry season scorches the earth to powder-dry bones. It was a joy to hear the sound of an aviating dung beetle after the first rains or witness the emerald green of a cuckoo wasp amid the summer grass. My youth was a giant meditation on the perfection and layers of nature. And once I had put my own demons to rest, the reserve became a place I could retreat to, where I could restore myself whenever life pulled me too far from the landscape. On those nights, I'd lie alone on the ground, feeling not lonely but at home beneath a gift of stars. That very terrain became a part of my soul.

The gift I want to give the world is that which nature gave me.

Tsama hansie.

CATHEDRAL OF THE WILD

ONE

NOT FOR ANTS

I T'S FIVE-FIFTEEN IN THE MORNING, and my father is waiting outside my door. As I open it, I'm struck by his size. In my late twenties, I'm now bigger than Dad, but I don't feel it. In my mind, I still come up only to his shoulder. He has the weathered quality of a lifelong outdoorsman, his skin like tanned leather—a bit worn, but hardened by the elements.

"Bushveld morning. Best thing in the world," he says with a smile. Dad passes me a shotgun and a handful of shells, and we casually begin our morning stroll upriver, toward the safari lodge. At this time of year, it's best to be at it early, as by midmorning the heat will make further work impossible.

The dawn is just beginning to break into the pale blue that is precursor to the gold of the rising sun. Already the urgent cackle of the partridge-like francolin—what the bushveld locals dub "government chicken," as they're a ready source of dinner—can be heard from the riverbed. The air is fresh and cool, and the grass has been dampened by heavy dew that wants to crawl up my pants. The sun peeks over the horizon, catching the dew as it sparkles in the light.

The game path runs along the bank of the river and has been well worn by heavy animal traffic. Lions, leopards, elephants, and hippos use it for easy access to the river. A large, steaming, splattery pile of Cape buffalo dung is dead center.

"Whoops, look sharp here," my father says. Also known as "Black Death," Cape buffaloes are one of the Big Five—the most prized and deadly prey of big game hunters—all of whom reside at Londolozi Game Reserve. (The other four are lions, leopards, rhinos, and elephants.) It's been said that buffaloes look at you like you owe them money. Armed with prodigious swooping horns, they've been known not just to attack but to track and ambush hunters and gore them to pieces. They can even run lions up trees. I notice a buffalo track pointing toward us; the buff has already moved past. If we were going to bump into him, it would have happened already.

"You're losing your touch a bit," I tell my father. "Too much time in the city, not enough time in the bush."

"Tell me about it." He's smiling.

Dad looks up ahead. "The guests always say, 'I'm going back to the real world' when they leave. But as far as I'm concerned, this is the real world, and back where they're going is the fake one."

Far off, a lion starts to roar. We can hear the distant baritone boom as he winds up, the sound carrying miles in the cold winter air. The glorious rumble, however, is quickly drowned out by the cough and growl of a nearby Land Rover as someone revs the engine. Really, Land Rovers are useless first thing in the morning, until they warm up.

For a rare moment, the lodge is calm and relatively quiet. The guides, who will man the Land Rovers, are on the main deck drinking coffee, preparing to take guests out on safari. Early mornings are the best time to find animals, as they like to move in the cool of the day. Tracks from the night before are still relatively fresh, providing critical clues to their whereabouts. Soon the guests will join the rangers on the deck. This takes some time, as each guest must be escorted from their room by an armed guard, lest they bump into a lion or leopard strolling down the path. It's quite common for animals to come right into the confines of the camp. We once found a muddy set of leopard tracks on the bar counter. The guests will arrive on the deck dressed like they're ready for an alpine experience and be stripping down within an hour, as the sun rises. That's August in the bush for you.

The trackers are chatting quietly in the car park, listening for that lion's roar, a bushbuck alarm, or the sharp snap of elephants breaking branches. These signs will help them situate the day's main viewing attractions.

I'm feeling a little sleepy, as I've been up most of the night repairing a two-strand electric fence that runs around the lodge to keep elephants out. Yesterday morning a young bull elephant discovered that he could use his tusks to snap the wire and gain access to the lush gardens inside, the ones the generations of women in my family have so painstakingly planted. This is a new occurrence, and as far as we can tell, only the one elephant, whom we have dubbed "Night Shift," has worked out how to do it. Once inside, he was a gleeful vegetarian at a giant salad bar, pulling out the flowers, snacking on trees, helping himself to long drinks from the pool, and passing wind so loudly outside some guests' room that they phoned the night receptionist and claimed a lion was growling outside their window. He also managed to terrorize some kitchen workers by charging at them as they returned from serving dinner at Tree Camp in the beat-up old Land Rover that only turns left.

The gardens are an oasis in the dry season right now, as the rains won't arrive for another few months. We recycle gray water, filter it, and tip it onto the garden. The results are amazing. Clivias bloom a deep orange in the flower beds, and the scent of the plumbago's tender blue clusters hangs thick in the air. The aloes are putting out their long segmented flowers of red and gold, the nectar attracting droves of sunbirds, which flaunt their red, turquoise, and bright yellow plumage. My grandmother planted the aloes, and each one stands as a little shrine to her. The gardenia trees are dropping their fruit, large thick-skinned apples that the nyalas will pick up and chew on like giant gobstoppers, their jaws working furiously beneath the bold slashes of white splashed like war paint across their faces. The flush of all this green amid the drought has also caused the ebony trees to fruit early, attracting hordes of baboons into the camp to scamper up the trunks and pick the tempting brown berries. This wouldn't be a problem if these furry paparazzi weren't always spying on us like we're celebrities, not to mention breaking into the guests' rooms, destroying our coffee and tea stations, rifling through suitcases, ripping open minibars, and occasionally stealing off with objects they've mistaken for food, like the one caught gorging on a tube of toothpaste. I once spotted a baboon heading off with a brassiere and a handful of cookies, perhaps to gratify some unknown fetish. Yesterday one ran off with a woman's passport; maybe he was planning on some travel.

We've been in a spirited arms race with the baboons for years. We put latches on the guest room doors; in a matter of weeks they figure out how to pick them. We upgrade the latches; in a short while they've outwitted the new devices. The fact that the baboons know how to open doors is unnerving. There you are, innocently sitting on your couch, when you see the latch of the door slowly, slowly lower, as in a horror movie—and then in strolls a baboon!

I know which tree the baboons will be roosting in. Creeping up on it for the last three hundred yards, I pop a few rounds over the baboons' heads as they scream and fling themselves out of the tree. They bark indignantly as they run off. My father laughs. "So *this* is what the Great White Hunter routine is all about!" I may have won this battle, but the baboons have the edge on us in the ongoing war. They'll be back in time for afternoon tea, perched on the eaves and in the branches of the ebony tree growing up through the veranda, where they'll wait impatiently for the chance to thieve a slice of mango or a crumpet.

The fine lines that separate animals and humans are blurry. In the summer afternoons we occasionally discover the baboon troop lounging around the pool. They've taken to having naps on the large mattress Mom put out in the shade of the knobthorn for people to loll on in the heat of the day. As I've walked past the baboons lying with their heads on the pillows, legs outstretched, I've half-expected one of them to order a cocktail.

———

Just at this time I sight Phillip, the butler, handyman, and all-around bard for our family, barreling across the front lawn toward the maintenance shed. As he gets closer, I notice that he's carrying a bucket. This means the bull elephant is back in the camp, having found a new way through the electrified fence I repaired so painstakingly last night. I'm not sure how Phillip came up with the idea that the best thing to chase an elephant with is a bucket; perhaps this is a venerable Shangaan tradition. His technique is to stick his head into the bucket and use it as a sort of amplifier. He suddenly runs full bore toward the elephant, screaming into the cavern of the bucket while slapping its base. The elephant, casually destroying a tree by the maintenance shed while depositing a large pile of dung as his smoldering calling card, is completely unperturbed.

I prefer rubber bullets, and so when the elephant finally turns around and presents his ass to me, I shoot him. His hide is so thick that he is simply annoyed and lumbers out through the broken fence, into the veld. The Great White Hunter strikes again. I feel just a bit smug; I've spared the gardens a great stomping and our guests a fantastic ruckus. My radio crackles.

"Would the station using the shotgun please be advised that there are guests in camp," Bronwyn reminds me from the main office. Translation into Safari Lodge Speak: Will the uninformed idiot recklessly popping off shots please stop before I take time off from my normally calm persona to kill him? My sister's voice has a touch of acid in it, as she knows that later she will have to explain to guests why the camp looked like the beaches of Normandy this morning.

I meet my staff at seven in the old tractor shed to plan for the day. This meeting is with some members of the habitat team: a ragtag band of twelve Shangaan men and women whose job is to keep the park in tip-top order. Alien plant removal, road maintenance, firefighting, and all manner of odd jobs fall to them. In keeping with Shangaan tradition, only the men attend this meeting; later they pass along instructions to the women on the team. They've been issued uniforms over the years, but they wear them in unusual combinations, no man dressed the same. Their ability to create a large number of original looks given limited fashion options is unparalleled. Lucky Mkanzi has even managed to cut two eyeholes into his woolen cap to turn it into a makeshift balaclava. These Shangaan men speak barely any English, have no formal education, and are just the most wonderfully practical bunch. They are, however, easily hijacked when one of their own presents a problem that requires the group's attention. On one occasion, Cry, the tractor driver, had shown up with one purpled eye narrowed to an angry slit.

"Why is your eye all swollen?" I'd asked. There was a long silence as Cry began to smirk, looking away. The assembled group started to chuckle. Finally Cry said, "My wife she was hitting me with a pole." The men fell apart. This was the funniest thing that had ever happened; in Shangaan tradition, tales of women besting their men always are. Lucky laughed so hard he tumbled off a small wooden seat. This fired up another wave of hilarity.

I turn to Isaak, the *induna,* or chief of the team. He is the elder, which means he has standing in Shangaan tradition. In fact, Isaak is older than I am, so I respectfully tell him the day's chores and ask him the best way to go about doing them. He relays assignments to members of the group.

This morning a few trackers join the meeting. I learn that Sandross, one of the most experienced guides, is stuck with six guests in the Sand River. They were out on an early morning game drive when a leopard wandered into the riverbed. Sandross thought the ground was more stable than it really was; before he knew it, his wheels were thoroughly wedged into the thick sand. We'll need the tractor to pull him out, which wouldn't normally be a problem, except that no one will go near the machine because yesterday a goshawk landed on its hood, a snake gripped in its talons. When the crew arrived, the bird flew off, leaving the snake behind—in Shangaan tradition, a sure sign of witchcraft. Shangaans are raised on stories of mythical serpentlike creatures such as the brain-sucking Mamlambo and the deadly water serpent Inkanyamba. They are particularly afraid of dangerous snakes. No one will drive the tractor until a *sangoma,* a Shangaan medicine man, lifts the curse.

The *sangoma* is going to cost me. I will have to pay his transport, buy him some food, and then get someone who has more *sangoma* experience to negotiate his fee; *sangomas* are notoriously good hustlers. I will ask Solly, who is a close friend and tracking buddy, to make the deal for me. The Land Rover is going to be stuck there till later this afternoon, so I better send someone out in another Landi to fetch Sandross and his guests.

More worms begin to wriggle out of the daily can. Robert Sithole, the skinny second-in-command, announces, "There's a problem with the golf cart." This is troublesome; we need the golf cart to ferry fine linens, food, liquor, and a thousand other essentials around to all the camps. Robert's grin is a surefire way of telling me there is foul play involved.

Robert is a Shangaan. He grew up at Londolozi because his father was a chef here. He and I have loved each other from the time we played soccer together as five-year-olds. But there's no getting around it: race relationships have a complicated and horrific history in this country. Though neither of us could care less about the color of our skin, here we are, still having to negotiate our way through the baggage of our country's history. Even after two decades of freedom from apartheid, the fabric of South African society remains frayed. The incredible potential of its people is still crippled by those appalling ideologies. Robert and I are part of a born-free generation that is trying to move forward and yet is still shaped by problems of the past. He doesn't want to be seen ratting out another black guy lest he be called an *impimpi,* or informer. We've developed a code for talking in groups.

"I'm sure it crashed," says Robert.

"Sure." I'm an unhurried shrink awaiting his patient's next confession.

"Ya, sure," says Robert, shaking his head.

"Which camp was it coming from?" I ask.

"Maybe Pioneer," says Robert. "Maybe" actually means "definitely."

"Shame it was dark last night," I venture. This is the issue that will establish accident or violation.

"Yes, but then the moon came out," he says. Definitely not an accident. In Safari Lodge Speak, this means that Elphas Ntuli, the only butler at Pioneer Camp, was drunk and crashed the cart. We know he was drunk because he is always drunk.

"Just make a plan," I tell Robert. Making a plan is Robert's forte. Later that day I will see the fancy cuisine lovingly prepared by the chefs, including smoked hams, freshly cut papaya, mango, and melon, and trays of cucumber sandwiches, being transported to Pioneer Camp in a garden wheelbarrow.

Robert continues his report. Enoch, the rubbish man, who seems to have as many different personalities as trash cans, tried to stab Dudu, one of the chefs. Something about her cheating on him. Trek, nicknamed Shrek for his unfortunate appearance, won't go into the pool filter room because a cobra was seen there in 1968, so the pool is going a shade of green usually reserved for algae. The lady who lost her passport to the baboon yesterday is in a rage because her toilet is blocked; the bloody bull elephant who snapped the electric fence fell into the septic tank. "That elephant smell like shit!" someone cracks, and the entire meeting falls to pieces. It's now seven-fifteen.

I move on to the main office for my second morning meeting, which is with the lodge's more senior management—the camp managers, the general manager, and the head ranger—to plan the day and talk about any problems that have come up. Linky Nkuna, one of the stunningly beautiful camp managers, with her high cheekbones and dreadlocked hair, has a concern.

"Boyd, I know why the ice machine is broken," she tells me.

"Why, Links?" I ask.

"I have discovered a grave in front of my camp. The ghost has been unhappy for some time," she tells me. This ghost is apparently also responsible for the bits and pieces continually going missing, like the small bottles of gin for the minibars, the bewitching of Elphas Ntuli—hence the crashing of the golf cart—and the general destruction of any electrical appliance.

"Links, you don't think that maybe it's just old Henkie Muller's wiring?" I ask. Henkie, our local electrician, is known more for the creativity of his wiring than its effectiveness.

"*Hey, wena ndzi vonile spoko,*" Linky reprimands me in Shangaan. Hey, you, I saw a ghost.

I sigh. Linky is adamant, and the *sangoma*'s coming anyway, so he may as well exorcise the ghost, too. Even if the reality is probably that drunk Elphas keeps losing things and the wiring has always been dodgy. But who am I to know for sure?

Sandross and his guests return, raving about their adventure. As they drive past, I hear a heavily accented voice saying excitedly, "Ve could not believe ziz! Ve vere imbedded und za leoparden vaz right beside us!" A misadventure often proves to be the best part of a safari. . . . True of life, too.

Tom pops his head into my office. Tom, big and bearish, has been the head ranger for three years. He and his wonderful wife, Kate, provide a calming influence in the lodge. Kate is one of the few women I know who can silence the titanic clashes of a rangers' meeting with a stare. We have about seventeen rangers, men and women. They've had to master an incredible amount of training, and their job requires them to command an experience, to show guests the most amazing wildlife while keeping everyone safe. After doing this for long enough, they tend to believe their own press when guests give them high praise.

"We've just found the tracks of a female leopard and her cubs," Tom tells me. "I want to send a tracking team out to find them."

This is great news. Londolozi has been famous for its leopards since the eighties, when one female allowed Uncle John into her world and raised all her cubs in proximity to Land Rovers. She and her offspring developed a trust around the people of Londolozi. Visitors from all over the world come especially to see our famous felines, with their honey-dipped pelts stamped tip to tail with black-and-tan rosettes. A mother with a brood of cubs in tow is the ultimate prize of a photographic safari.

By now the *sangoma* has arrived, clad in his red straw wig, with beads around his neck, earrings made of pangolin scales, and a ceremonial wildebeest's tail. First he rids the tractor of evil. Then he's ready to exorcise the spirits from the ice machine. Linky has decided to turn that exorcism into a cultural experience, inviting the guests to come and watch him work. Afterward, a couple asks if they might have a reading. The *sangoma* agrees to "throw the bones."

He pulls out his small reed mat and an old leather binocular case that contains the bones and teeth of various animals, along with some cowrie shells. The couple sits down opposite him, and he simply stares at them until Linky coaxes, "Put some money under the corner of the mat." Once they've done this, the very financially aware spirit starts to come through. The *sangoma* shakes and bobs briefly, then begins to speak rapidly in a high staccato voice. Each time he pauses, the husband and wife are supposed to say *Siya vuma*—"We agree." They can't quite get their timing right, so the spirit grows agitated and the whole reading becomes a large reprimand from the spirit about not *siya vuma*–ing enough. The couple balks when the spirit indicates that it would like the *sangoma* to make tiny cuts on them with his knife so that he can rub *muti,* traditional medicine, into their bodies.

This ceremony is not something we would ordinarily do. We're opposed to "cultural shows," in which tourists are led around re-created villages where residents quickly shed their T-shirts and jeans and don various animal skins and other traditional clothing for the display. When this couple asked for a reading from the *sangoma,* they got the real deal, probably a bit more than they bargained for.

I'm about to check on Tom and the trackers when my radio crackles to staticky life again. "Gladys is not well," says Trevor Lubisi, one of the butlers from Founders Camp. This is extremely bad news. Shangaans are notorious for understatement. Gladys is a sous-chef at Londolozi, a large woman, rotund and fierce. In the complex hierarchy of the kitchen, she is highly respected for both her sweet center and her fiery exterior.

I brace myself. Whatever it is, as we say in South Africa, "It's not for ants." This phrase is reserved for things that merit respect: the gaping wound where a lion's claw missed an artery by millimeters; repairing the migratory patterns of a million wildebeests; a three-day trek out of a scorching desert carrying a wounded German shepherd.

I mean an actual German shepherd, not a dog. A dog—please. That's too easy.

That's for ants.

When I get to her, Gladys is sitting on the golf cart Elphas dinged, a blanket thrown over her. She's very quiet, her eyes downcast.

"How are you, Gladys?" I ask.

"Not so well," she replies.

I take the blanket off. She's been mauled by a hippo. Her wounds are horrific; the flesh of one arm seems to have been torn almost clean away. Hippos, for all their Disney caricatures with tiny ears, stubby legs, and wide, toothy grins, are in fact among the most dangerous animals in

Africa, aggressive and ferocious in certain circumstances. The biggest danger is to get between a hippo and its safe place, which is the water; it simply runs for the river, snapping its big chopper jaws at you if you're in the way. Gladys was fetching water for her church, Trevor tells me, when she startled the hippo and got a good chomping for her sin.

We try to organize an evacuation using our air band radio to see if a plane flying over or in the area would be willing to pick Gladys up. No luck with that. It takes precious hours to organize Gladys's care and treat her injuries. It'll be dark all too soon, so we call the paramedic who lives in the reserve. He is ex-military and very good; he'll get her to the hospital in his Land Rover, which has been converted into an ambulance.

I'm doing my best to bandage Gladys and note with horror that I have her fat on my hands. In these kinds of situations, I go on autopilot. Trauma isn't an unusual event in the bush; you just have to be ready to deal with it effectively and, above all, calmly. Burns from the kitchen, a maintenance worker spat in the eyes by a venomous cobra, a woman slicing her elbow wide open after tripping over a rock—we've all been trained to deal with these everyday injuries. I'm lucky to have a crack team helping Gladys: John, another guide, and Hailey, the operations manager. John's doing an especially effective job; he was trained by his mother, who used to teach first aid. We all talk continuously to Gladys, trying to calm and reassure her. Through all this she sits dead still, looking away from the wounds. The blood loss seems to be contained; I just hope the doctors will be able to repair her arm.

I pull Trevor aside and ask him to tell me more about what happened.

"Gladys was at the small pool in the river in front of Founders Camp, where she was collecting water for the church," he says. "That's when the hippo just attacked her."

Something doesn't add up. I know that pool. I've never seen a hippo there. In fact, it's a little small for them. And I've never heard of any staff members going there to get water for the church. I decide to take Richard Siwela, our master tracker, down to the site of the accident. If you want to find the truth, first you've got to find the tracks, and then you've got to follow them.

Being with Richard is like starring in a scene from *CSI*. Although the sand is soft, he finds no human tracks there. In fact, he doesn't find any human tracks at all. When you don't have the tracks you're looking for, you've got to work with what you've got. In this case, it's a hyena's tracks along the riverbank. (Richard knows this, but I do not.) He painstakingly follows the hyena's tracks, which lead to a trail of muddy human footprints and broken vegetation, which, in turn, leads us to the gory scene of the crime; as a scavenger, the hyena must have followed the scent of blood. We find river grass stained with Gladys's blood and low-lying branches festooned with chunks of the fat from her arm. Look closely enough, and the tracks will always tell the story. By pointing to the tracks, Richard becomes a fluent storyteller without having to say a word.

No staff member is allowed to venture down into the thick reeds of the river without an armed escort because it's extremely dangerous in the dense undergrowth. The tracks suggest that Gladys wasn't telling the whole truth about walking only as far as the pool. Richard begins to imitate how she would have moved through the terrain beyond the pool, showing me where she bent over to recuperate after her attack and how a puddle of blood is congealing there. "Look here!" He finds her fishing tackle and more than one rod. "She was with someone else," Richard tells me, showing me the second set of footprints. Gladys hadn't simply been fetching water; she'd unwisely and illegally gone deep into the riverbed and had been fishing in some thick reeds, where she had no visibility. A hippo had been sleeping on the bank behind her and was startled, when he then came ambling down his path toward the water, to discover that she was blocking the way.

Richard follows the second set of footprints and shows me where Gladys's companion had thrown a bucket of worms to hide the evidence. We find them lying in the high grasses. Richard's a true chauvinistic, hard Shangaan man. At one point he suggests, "Gladys's too fat one; maybe that hippo thinks, 'Another nice hippo for me.'"

Gladys had been asking for trouble, all for the sake of a few free fish. I'd have to ask around the camp to find out whom she'd been with and give them a stern warning about the dangers. All I can do now is make sure Gladys has the best of care. Everyone in the camp will be updated about her progress. We dissect every incident so that it won't happen again.

As we leave the scene, a three-foot-long monitor lizard explodes out of the reeds. With hippo attack on the brain, I leap straight into the air. Richard thinks this is very funny and walks off shaking his head.

I go back home to shower so I'll be ready to welcome the guests when they return from their afternoon drive. Afterward, I dress in a crisp new uniform of khaki shirt and pants and walk down in the fading light to the *boma,* a large circular area hemmed by a tall wooden fence to keep out the animals. A fire is blazing in a large, low-slung brazier. It's in the same spot where my great-grandfather made his first fire when he arrived on the property, cold and tired, in 1926. I am the fourth generation to sit around this fireplace, and every time I do, I'm with my ancestors.

All around are brown paper luminarias, the candles inside making them glow like orange butterfly cocoons. The three chefs in crisp white jackets stand behind a buffet of smoldering roasts and a fine cheese platter. The twenty guests take their seats at the tables, which are meticulously set with crisp white linens and sparkling silverware. The whole setting is framed by the stars above. I move from table to table, listening to each guest recount the adventures of the day.

Sandross's group is celebrating having survived their marooned morning with a few bottles of wine.

The ghost of Pioneer Camp has been exorcised. "It was an interesting experience, but we decided to call it quits when he got his knife out," says the couple who had the reading, their eyes widening slightly.

A message comes through from the night receptionist that Gladys is in the hospital and stable.

The elephant is back in. I can hear him munching on the bougainvillea my gran planted behind the *boma*. I better tell security to look out for him when they escort the guests back to their rooms after dinner. The elephant's stomach is rumbling in the darkness.

We have a name for days like this: Tuesday.

TWO

HUNTING AND HACKING

WANT TO TELL YOU how I came to be here.

The first bath I was ever given was in a turkey roaster. Once again, my family had failed to connect me with even the simplest conventions that go with bathing. I was bathed in the kitchen because at the time our bathroom had no plumbing. It probably would have made no difference if it had; in my family, bathrooms are considered places in which to gossip during parties rather than sites in which to engage in the tedium of ablutions.

I know this because my mother tells me this story every time she takes out the roasting pan. Ours is a family of storytellers. Virtually every object in our home was handpicked by Mom, and each has its particular origin story. Scrapbooks and photo albums are scattered over every surface. The stories passed down from generation to generation are as treasured as my grandfather's Rigby .416 rifle, my grandmother's leather journals, and the Varty recipe for impala stew. Of course, the story with which I was raised, with which my own story is intertwined, is the one told to me around countless campfires when I was growing up: the story of how Londolozi came to be.

———

Doing things the right way round has never been our family's strong point. In 1926, most landowners were absconding from the bankrupt farms adjacent to Kruger National Park, about four hundred miles from Johannesburg, a wasteland affectionately known as the lowveld. Malaria was so rampant there that it was said that a man had died from it for every railroad tie laid down. Cattle had overgrazed the land, leaving behind a dustbowl over which clouds of tsetse flies hovered, waiting to spread sleeping sickness.

My great-grandfather Charles Boyd Varty, however, was something of a maverick, and he saw the land through different eyes. When most people turned their back on this area, Charles and his good friend Frank Unger were magnetically pulled toward it. Frank, a Dutchman, was fascinated by the wide-open spaces of the bushveld.

The two were Johannesburg business associates who were also passionate about hunting lions; the lowveld was filled with hundreds of them. One of the reasons why cattle hadn't thrived there was that prides of marauding lions had picked them off.

Hunting lions through the bushveld was a pursuit reserved for madmen. Hours spent walking through thick thorny scrub would be followed by a few seconds of absolute blind fear and pandemonium as a wounded lion snarled and attacked. Those fleeting seconds during which you could easily get your throat ripped out were what lion hunters lived for. But if genetics is anything to go by, I put it to you that while Charles Varty might have loved hunting, what really drove him ran far deeper: a longing in the spirit for something wild and with teeth. A longing to be away from the confines of the city.

Londolozi, the central defining feature of my life, came into being almost on a whim. One night, Charles and Frank got greased up on gin and tonics at a tennis party at a friend's house in Johannesburg and decided to buy a vast tract of that lowveld land, sight unseen. It was not common in such a major city to purchase a piece of real estate in such hostile wasteland.

Surprising how life is; one seemingly controversial decision can tip the hand of fate against years of hard grind and the desperate human need to have a plan. My great-grandfather Charles, an agricultural and water pump equipment manufacturer, set out for what all perceived to be a dank hellhole on a leap of faith. His friends were astounded that he should want to go there, but to his mind, he was setting off for Eden.

Charles and Frank made their first visit in June, which was winter in the bush. The dawns and nights would be cool, the days wonderfully warm, and the scarcity of standing water would minimize the chance of getting malaria. They caught a train from Johannesburg Park Station and managed to convince the driver to stop en route to let them off in the middle of nowhere, on the endless stretch between Komatipoort and Pietersburg, on Siding 61, a kilometer marker. There they'd arranged for some donkeys to be left for them by the game warden in the area. From that unpromising spot, they walked into the unknown veld with nothing but a compass to guide them.

They arrived in early evening, set up a tent under a huge ebony tree, and put into motion the routines that the family would follow from then on. They would normally go for the month of July. The property had not a single outhouse or piece of infrastructure, no phones, no running water, no means to communicate with the outside world. The land was far too harsh for year-round living, so every year the family would come down by oxcart to camp out. They took goats for milk and cupboards full of root vegetables, laying wet cloths over the protective chicken wire so the breeze would keep the produce cool. My great-grandfather, Frank, and their friends dedicated their days to hunting lions, which were considered vermin at the time, a threat to the impalas, wildebeests, and other game—not to mention humans. "Bagging a lion" was a rare occasion, but family legend is stuffed with such stories. First my father and uncle and then I were raised on the tale of the time my grandfather held the lantern high so my great-grandfather could see the lion's eyes—reflecting silver coins in the darkness—and shoot it as it leapt onto the lead ox of the team of six pulling the family wagon into camp.

Even today a certain patch of scrub or hill will launch Dad into a tale of a lion hunt gone wrong. Charles and Frank eventually built old mud huts, or *rondavels,* erected in the Shangaan style of piling sticks in a heap and packing wet earth over them. Today these huts have been converted into a wine cellar, staff rooms, and a place where guests can watch Uncle John's movies. Their presence at Londolozi naturally draws my father and uncle into stories about their past uses. Every gully or boulder in the river is not just earth or rock but the home of some event, as if the land has absorbed the stories of the men who went before and my father is a radio tuned to their frequency.

Charles Boyd's son Boyd, my grandfather, continued the family tradition of spending winters at the hunting camp. Dad and Uncle John toddled around the mud huts. The routines remained the same for each generation: early morning hunting, midday swimming in the Sand River, and evenings around the fire. The camp diet likewise remained unchanged for three generations: impala meat for breakfast, lunch, and supper. The camp was peaceful and intoxicatingly still, and the winter sun perfect for napping.

My grandfather instilled his love of the bush in Dad and my uncle. He was a gruff man, uninclined to social niceties. A childhood bout of rheumatic fever had weakened his heart; unable to exercise strenuously, he'd had to give up cricket because he couldn't run between the wickets. He liked hunting because it was mostly slow moving. He wasn't terribly social. In fact, he refused to repair the dirt roads on his property, to discourage visitors. He loved kids, but he was of the more military, older school, not given to broad displays of affection. Dad always said he showed his love by how he spent his time with his boys: playing catch, rooting for them at their cricket matches, and going into the bush.

Singing was an old staple around the campfire at night, when the cold, crisp air pulled the ceiling of stars down around the family. My grandfather would ask my gran to sing, her voice, to him, rivaled in beauty only by the roar of the lions.

My paternal grandfather, Boyd Varty, had met my paternal grandmother, Madeleine, a.k.a. Madie, before World War II, although they didn't get married until afterward. Madie was a tennis prodigy who would have starred at Wimbledon had it not been for the war. She was the social foil to my taciturn grandfather. Where he was grumpy and reclusive, she was incredibly outgoing, arranging endless tennis and dinner parties.

My gran would sing the wartime songs he couldn't, the ones too close to home, slicing too finely near the heart—songs like "Comin' In on a Wing and a Prayer," which he'd last sung as he and his crew had flown a lumbering old bomber over enemy territory in Poland. As he told it, the missions were a grueling ten hours and forty minutes long, and the planes carried only enough fuel for eleven. Flying at high altitude over Warsaw, the planes made easy targets for the anti-aircraft guns. So my grandfather's captain conceived of a plan to fly low over the Vistula River, making them an extremely difficult target that seemed to come out of nowhere. They were dropping supplies for the Polish Resistance. You have to understand the nerve it took to fly a four-engine Liberator low over blacked-out Warsaw, using the light from burning buildings as your only source of navigation. My grandfather was the navigator. I often read his flight journals from that time. Countless names of other crew members have a simple "DNR" written next to them: Did Not Return. It must have taken tremendous courage to fly to Warsaw every single night, knowing before you took off that so many of your mates would be dead before you returned. My grandfather told my father that only two things would make men out of boys: wartime flying and hunting lions.

"Comin' In on a Wing and a Prayer," a rousing World War II ditty, described the joyous sighting of a missing bomber limping through the air "with our one motor gone" yet still managing to hit its target. In my grandfather's experience, the song rang all too true as his plane's fuel gauges read almost empty and the drone of the engines complemented its lilting tune.

But once he was safely home, finally grounded after the war, those lusty songs lost their appeal for my grandfather. He preferred the wistful tunes Gran warbled instead; "Where Have All the Flowers Gone" became a later favorite.

Boyd's head tracker was Winnis Mathebula, a Shangaan man who possessed immense character and a prodigious knowledge of bushcraft. Winnis was the survivor of countless encounters with animals. He'd been gored by a Cape buffalo in the reeds and survived. He used to pat his ribs and say, "Ya, the buffalo got me in my choppies." After my own encounter with Africa's largest, most aggressive, and deadliest snake, Dad told me the story of how Winnis and Simeon, my grandfather's chef, were out in the bush when they were attacked by a black mamba. The mamba reared up and bit Simeon four or five times in his midsection, staining his pants dark with venom. Then it turned and bit Winnis. Simeon lifted his shirt and realized that the snake had bitten his belt, leaving the skin unbroken. Everyone sat around waiting for Winnis to die, but Winnis hadn't gotten the memo and just kept on living. The snake must have spent all its venom on Simeon's belt.

My father considered Winnis a second father to him. Winnis, along with my grandfather, taught my father and uncle the ways in which the bush speaks to you if you can learn the language. How to listen for the harsh, rasping call of oxpeckers, the birds that pick ticks off large animals, so they wouldn't bump into one in the bush. How to read the fresh tracks of animals. How to listen for various animal alarm calls, like the squirrel's chatter that tells you there's a snake in his tree. Or the baboons' barking calls warning of a leopard passing by. Or a guinea fowl's high-pitched shriek when a martial eagle is looking for its next meal. The boys were taught to honor the land and the animals they hunted. One night my father threw an entire log into the fire only to be scolded harshly by Winnis: "Ya, you put just the tip of the log into the fire. Use only what you need for cooking and heat."

Winnis had such an intimate knowledge of the land that if a lion roared, he could cut off the track and take you onto its game path to wait in ambush. On cold mornings my dad and uncle would always try to get Winnis to tell stories so they could spend more time in the warm camp. If he took out his snuffbox, they knew they had him. Most of the stories featured Winnis as the hero, and he'd never hesitate to call out others who didn't meet his high standards of bushcraft. For instance, Steven Roach, a friend of my grandfather's, shot a lioness at sixty paces through the heart. She turned and charged straight at him and his party. As she got close, another tracker and backup rifle, Tie, stepped forward with his side-by-side Webley & Scott shotgun. The spray from the shotgun was meant to drive the lioness back, allowing the hunter to reload and get a second shot in. However, in the excitement of the moment, Tie had left the safety catch on, so the shotgun didn't go off. The lioness powered forward, smashing into the two men, knocking them sprawling. She then died in a heap almost on top of them before she could do any damage. Winnis thought this was hysterical, but an utter disgrace. "Winnis Mathebula would never have made the same mistake," he sniffed. Winnis was so attuned to the elements that his house was almost a skeletal stick structure; the wind howled through its walls. When one of Sputnik's cousins appeared overhead in the late seventies, Winnis got into his cups and asked to borrow the old .404 so that he could shoot the offense against nature out of the sky.

Grandpa Boyd likewise believed that hunting lions was the ultimate pastime. He thought nothing of sending his two young sons deep into the bush with Winnis to hunt lions. Dad went out for the first time when he was only five years old—a sign of my grandfather's incredible respect for and trust in the man. Dad and Uncle John shared that respect. Hunting with Winnis and the other Shangaans showed them how accomplished these men were at bushcraft.

My dad always used to tell me that Winnis had no fear of lions whatsoever. If he found a pride gorging themselves on a zebra or giraffe, he wouldn't think twice about running straight at them with a spear to chase them off the meat; he'd then cut himself a hearty fillet for his camp dinner.

My father claims that he was never a very good hunter; he said he lacked the attention span and disliked the way the cold, dewy grass would soak his pants through on a winter morning. If he let out a stifled cough on a hunt, Grandpa Boyd would spin round and give him a chilling stare. When they found lion tracks going into thick bush, they'd circle the area to see if the tracks came out on the other side. Once they'd established that the lions were still in the thicket, they would wait for the heat of the day to lull the cats to sleep, then crawl into the bush on all fours, sliding on their bellies alongside the tracks until they could spy the sleeping lions through the leaves. Then they would open fire as a hell of growling, snarling, and lashing exploded around them, lions bursting in every direction, some keen to escape, others on the attack as gunfire rang in the air. These moments of complete pandemonium and danger were what my grandfather lived for, what made him chuckle to himself around the fire. And the stories of those exploits, told around a different fire, were what I lived for.

I carry my grandfather's name, although I never had the honor of knowing him. The stories my father has told me about him are the stuff of family legend. One of the most stirring tells of how, in July of 1969, for the very first time, my grandfather brought the family accounts with him down to the farm that would become Londolozi, an act that he himself had up to this point considered sacrilege. To him the wild and hunting were sacred and were not to be tarnished by the calculation and blandness of business requirements. Prior to this trip, even the mention of work while in camp could elicit a severe reprimand.

But on this trip, to the bewilderment of the family, each day after the early morning hunt, Boyd Varty would pull Uncle John off to a sunlit spot at the "lookout," a flattened-out section overlooking the Sand River where the main deck at Londolozi now stands. Father and son would meticulously go through the accounts. Over the course of that trip, he taught my uncle bookkeeping.

Later that season, with sections of the camp already packed up in preparation for the epic journey back to Johannesburg, my grandfather and father drove out on the single dirt road that ran down to Winnis's *kraal,* or village, to say their last goodbyes to their old friend and tracker. On the way, my grandfather parked his ancient American Plymouth in an open clearing, and they both sat on the hood dressed in old tweed coats and hunting boots as the sun went down, enjoying the silence and that beautiful evening cool as the sun dropped below the escarpment miles off to the west.

As the light faded, an impala stepped out onto a patch of white sand way down in the clearing. My grandfather picked up his old .30-06 Springfield, the one he had built himself with the characteristic peep site that he preferred to all others, and threw it into his shoulder. I know what the action looked like and I know the distance of that shot because I've often driven out there with my dad and parked in that same clearing while he told me the story, irresistibly acting it out as the words and emotion of the moment came tumbling out of him.

The impala went down with the first shot. My grandfather worked the action of the rifle open, and as he handed it to my father, he said with an uncharacteristically satisfied grin on his face, "Always remember your old man could shoot." He wasn't joking; in fact, looking at the range of that shot with an open sight, I would go so far as to say there are probably only a few people in the world who could make it. My grandfather considered being in the wild and hunting a great honor, so I know that he was also saying, "Remember how deeply I honor this land." He gave the impala to Winnis and his family and left early the next morning; Dad had decided to stay on a bit longer.

My grandfather, the first Boyd Varty, died of an apparent heart attack a few days later. His ashes were sprinkled in the river around a large, dome-shaped granite rock that marks one of his favorite spots in which to stop and rest while the sun rose on an early morning hunt. On the place we call Plaque Rock, black letters on dark brass read:

BOYD VARTY
HE LOVED THE BUSHVELD

Uncle John was eighteen years old when his father died; my dad was fifteen. The two boys were told by their mother's financial advisers to sell the land that my great-grandfather had been "so damn romantic over" and "knuckle down" to university degrees and conventional lives in the city. Why not sell mining equipment, the family business? They tried; then they squirmed; then they threw down their toys and refused. Led by intuition, as well as their love of their father and of the wild, they decided they would hold on to the land. They had nothing but the idea of a home and a dream out in that wild landscape, and a determination to build them both one brick at a time. We call my gran "the mother of Londolozi," because when her teenage boys pled their case to her, she never hesitated: "If you want to keep it, just keep it."

It's difficult to convey the vastness of this undertaking. The land was situated in a wilderness roughly the size of Switzerland. The previous tenants had fenced out the wildlife and drained the wetlands. Dave and John were just kids; how on earth could they hold on to the land and support their newly widowed mother? A neighbor had started a game camp, so they just figured they'd go into the safari business too, leading groups who wanted to hunt or do wildlife photography. They had no real plan. They simply pulled the name Londolozi, which means "protector of all living things," out of a Zulu dictionary and set to work.

It's at this point in the story that I always stop my father. "But weren't you worried?" I can't imagine being that young and shouldering so much responsibility.

Dad always gets a faraway look in his eyes when I ask that. "We just knew we couldn't sell," he says, and then he goes quiet, as if back in that moment.

Dad seems to have created his life philosophy from a baker's mix of two mottoes: "Hack it through from the ground up" and "Hope the ball bounces your way." The safari business was practically brand-new. Dad embraced a light-on-your-feet, make-it-up-as-you-go-along style when facing unforeseeable challenges with neither money nor resources. He employed both to full effect in bringing Londolozi into being. My father has told the whole story beautifully in his own book, *Full Circle,* but from what I gather, Dad and Uncle John basically built Londolozi using impala skins. Dad would buy them at a discount from the guys who ran a tannery on the farm next door, load them into an old truck, and drive them to Johannesburg, where he would sell them for a profit to the fancy shops there. Dad always managed to sell just enough skins to bring in just enough capital to keep the creditors at bay and the business running. He and Uncle John would also sell crayfish door to door to get money for petrol for the truck.

Young upstarts that they were, Dad and Uncle John realized—not so much in a political as in a practical way—that the best way to make Londolozi work was to have the Shangaans working beside them, and to hell with apartheid, the law of the land instituted in 1948 that segregated blacks and whites. Under apartheid, black people were denied the vote. They were issued identity cards according to the color of their skin; sometimes family members were separated. Interracial marriages were outlawed. Most horrifically, blacks were forcibly removed to resettlement areas, including the infamous township of Soweto, which became the direst of slums.

Uncle John was born in 1950, Dad in 1954. They grew up in an all-white suburb in Johannesburg where ignorance was standard operating practice. Black people did all the hard labor and cleaned your shoes; this was the norm, and as children they simply accepted it. White people all over South Africa were complicit in the crime of segregation through their silence and acceptance.

Yet out in the bush, the law of the land didn't exist. When Dad and Uncle John hunted a wounded lion in thick bush with Winnis, all playing fields were leveled. If the hunter doesn't shoot or the tracker doesn't track or one of the party tries to run away instead of defending the group, someone can get his throat ripped out. When men face danger together, they lose the frivolous definitions of the world and simply become people who must work in harmony in order to survive. In the bush, the two brothers' view and experience of race simply didn't align with South African law.

When they began to bring Londolozi into being in the early 1970s, Dad and Uncle John employed blacks and whites alike because it was simply the most practical way to coax the land back to life. Dad and Uncle John are first and foremost advocates for nature. The Shangaans shared their reverence for the earth and the desire to reclaim it. It was a given that everybody would work side by side.

Although to this day Dad would never describe himself as political— he and Uncle John believe all politics to be flawed—he nevertheless traces his awakening to the 1976 riots in Soweto. He started to see how apartheid was damaging the entire country. Soon after, he and Uncle John met Enos Mabuza, who had a great influence on their thinking. Enos was an activist who later supported the ANC, or African National Congress, the political party that rose to power in 1994, abolishing apartheid. He told Dad and Uncle John to "pour the cultures together," and this is what they tried to do.

The Londolozi Club House, where blacks and whites gathered to enjoy a beer, watch a rugby match, and play pool, became Dad and Uncle John's favorite place to "pour the cultures together." This was a surefire way to bring a warning from the Special Branch—the police unit dedicated to suppressing black resistance to apartheid. They were constantly told, "We're watching you."

At the same time, Dad and Uncle John became wildlife activists. They believed that the promotion of wildlife should have benefits for all people. In the seventies, there were almost no private game reserves that charged admission to look at wildlife. If people wanted to see animals, they went to national parks like Kruger, which were bastions of the old apartheid regime. Dad and Uncle John's plan was to create an "economy of wildlife"—to make it economically feasible for people to make their livings not by destroying the land by raising cattle and sheep on it, but by conserving the land, encouraging wildlife to spread across it, and helping everyone living there to enjoy its benefits. A game reserve would return the land to its natural state. It would also employ locals—everyone from rangers and trackers to chefs, maids, and hospitality staff—affording more opportunities across the board for everyone. A poor community could prosper. Dad and Uncle John saw this as the only thing that would encourage people to conserve the land, but they were constantly being accused of exploiting nature for profit. Their "radical" belief—now a model for ecology—got them branded as Communists and outsiders, which made it that much harder for them to bring their vision into being, but it failed to deter them in the slightest.

At first Dad and my uncle worked at their fledgling safari business part-time. They'd make a booking from town, then double back to the camp to lead an expedition. Their tracking lessons from Winnis stood them in good stead. Word got out that two mustached hippies out in the bush could find game. At a time when the safari business was still quite new and guests might typically see not much more than a herd of impalas, this was a real edge.

Dad had no model for guiding or for finding game. The Varty brothers told guests, "Bring a musical instrument—and a Land Rover if you have one." They had three levels of service. "Luxury safaris" meant the guests didn't have to bring their own food; they got their impalas cooked for them. "Regular safari" guests had to bring their own food. A "walking safari" meant the Land Rover was probably broken and you got around on foot and slept under the stars. On the day of their first "canoe safari," there was so little water in the river that they could barely get the canoe over the rocks; then someone sprained their ankle on a hippo's head. The first canoe safari was also the last. They were always running out of food, so they'd just get the guests drunk and hope for the best. Inevitably, visitors would end up catching the spirit of these two outrageous adventurers.

Everything I've learned from my father comes from two premises: You've got to know your way around the bush, and have faith that whatever comes your way, you'll figure it out.

––––––

Dad and Uncle John realized the next step in their mission to restore the land and protect its inhabitants. They decided to focus first on a species even scarcer than leopards. "The biggest endangered species in Londolozi was the cheetah," Dad told me. "We decided we needed to save the world by raising money to save it." The logo of the Endangered Wildlife Trust at the time—a cheetah with the tagline "The cheetah . . . racing to extinction"—had made a huge impression on him. Dad and Uncle John formed the Londolozi Game Trust. They'd read that cheetahs were going to be shot in Namibia, so they decided to raise the funds to rescue three. They managed to attract enough attention that by the time they brought the cheetahs to Londolozi, the press was waiting to cover the hoopla. Dad and Uncle John were ecstatic, convinced that the publicity would bring attention to the plight of the animals and help build their safari business. With great fanfare, they raised the gates on the cheetahs' cages. The cheetahs shot out and bolted the area, never to be seen again. The Great Cheetah Rescue was a huge bust.

Why had they fled? Why had the sable antelopes likewise disappeared, while wildebeests, waterbucks, and elephants were also declining at Londolozi? Dad and Uncle John went searching for information, and one person's name kept cropping up again and again: that of the pioneering environmentalist Dr. Ken Tinley. Tinley was a tall, wiry, self-confident Clint Eastwood look-alike. He was also a high school dropout who had gotten himself enrolled in university after he drew a picture of a butterfly with such profound detail and brilliance that the leading professor of natural sciences there allowed him into the course without a diploma. He became one of the original game rangers and conservationists who worked with Dr. Ian Player, the famous South African conservationist, to restore the rhino populations in the Hluhluwe Game Reserve. A genius naturalist, Tinley got dropped into the greatest wildernesses in Africa by various conservation groups and worked almost exclusively by himself for months at a time, mapping the ecology and biodiversity of these areas. He'd been instrumental in fighting the South African government when officials had wanted to put a fence through the Damaraland and Etosha reserves in northern Namibia. Later he went to what is now Gorongosa National Park, in central Mozambique, and spent months mapping its waterways. It was there that he developed his profound understanding of the importance of preserving the moisture content of the soil in a reserve, information he would later bring to the restoration of the land at Londolozi. In the late 1970s, when civil war broke out in Mozambique, the Renamo rebel group shot up Tinley's research camp, and he literally ran for his life. An open-minded thinker, Tinley was always talking about incorporating the local people holistically into any conservation project. That irritated pro-apartheid scientists. He was also a generalist, whereas most scientists insisted on narrow fields of specialization.

"Don't listen to that radical," Dad and Uncle John were told. "He's way out of the mainstream." Naturally, they sought him out. When they eventually got Tinley to Londolozi and walked out onto the land with him, he was able to show them how animals and the land were intricately interconnected. Drawing on his knowledge of the water courses and soil types, he could explain why a certain tree grew in a certain area. He was an artist of the landscape.

Tinley scoffed at the cheetah project, however: "The trouble with you guys is, all you want is to get your picture on the social page by doing these glamorous relocation projects. They're all a bunch of bullshit. You're not really into conservation. You're pseudoconservationists."

Dad and Uncle John rose to their full heights and said, "No, we're not!" Tinley harrumphed and walked them around Londolozi and said, "Look at the scrubland. Why do you think you've got that here?"

"Because that's how it is," Dad said.

Tinley frowned. "Follow me." He walked them to the lowest point of the land, where all the water would flow down to because the grass cover on the slopes was gone; cattle had overgrazed the grass and trampled it. Without grass, rain hit bare soil and ran off. Only deep-rooted shrubs could survive in that arid soil, so the animals that used to feed on the grass, and the animals that fed on those animals, including cheetahs, had left the area. "Cheetah hunt in open grassland. No matter how many you bring in, they'll simply bugger off," Tinley told them. "You've got to partner with the land." They needed to clear the scrub and stick some of the uprooted bushes into the knickpoints, blocking them like a plug stoppers a bathtub drain, to hold some of the water back. Once they fixed the water, the grass would grow back naturally. "Make nature your partner; follow her master plan. If you fix the land, the animals will come," Tinley promised them.

Tinley changed Dad and Uncle John's lives, widened their vision. They slowly began to restore the wetlands that had existed before the cattle farms destroyed them. They tore out alien plant species. They rebuilt microcatchments. And they did it side by side with the Shangaan because Tinley had told them that unless local people see benefit from the wildlife, they have no reason to protect it. A lot of people attacked Dad and Uncle John's vigorous approach to repairing land as too heavy-handed because they used a bulldozer to clear thick scrub, but years later they have been proved right. And when Nelson Mandela visited Londolozi, he endorsed the brothers' vision of harmony between people of all races, animals, and the land.

Something amazing happened: the animals started to flow back onto the restored land, just as Tinley had promised. They began to lose their fear. Early visitors to Londolozi had been lucky to see a scrub hare. As a result of the hunting, game was extremely skittish, and the land was a brushy, matted mass of thorn trees. But by the time I was a toddler, guests were heading out in open Land Rovers—Dad and Uncle John couldn't afford ones with roofs—and seeing lions, elephants, rhinos, leopards.

When Dad told me the cheetah story, we were standing in a beautiful clearing where the land falls away for miles down to the river. All across the plain, impalas and wildebeests freckled the land. "This used to be a thick mat of thorn," Dad said. "If we saw a bird out here, it would be exciting. Now look at it!" I gazed at a land restored, and it made me see my father differently. To me, a little boy obsessed with nature, he was no longer the great hunter; he was a great healer.

———

Dad taught me to shoot a rifle when I was five. He had precisely three subjects for which rules were absolutely nonnegotiable: guns, vehicles, and women. "Those three things are mostly what get people killed in the bush," he told me. "It's not animals out here in the bush that are dangerous; it's people getting drunk and driving Land Rovers too fast, guys trying to show off to women, and people not concentrating and handling their weapons incorrectly."

Dad schooled me stringently on proper rifle safety: Never point a rifle at another person. Always personally check that the rifle is safe—no round in the chamber—even if someone checks it in front of you and hands it to you. Never leave your rifle unattended. After any high-adrenaline moment—say, an elephant charge—stop and make sure your rifle is safe before debriefing your guests.

I was taken out hunting from the time I was six. Dad made sure I could successfully shoot five rounds into a target from a thirty-yard range; that was the marker of readiness. I moved on to hunting guinea fowl and francolins. From then on, I was going to be doing game hunting—a man's job—and I better act accordingly. My father and uncle never said anything about this; I just knew it. The gravitas of the situation was apparent. We were going to go out into the bush. Walking three or four hours was rather a lot for a six-year-old, but there was no whinging or complaining about being tired or asking for food. I'd done it once and received the most withering look from my father. I learned that I didn't have to have my needs gratified just because they arose. That gave me a sense of toughness; I couldn't say, "I can't go on," because I knew I could.

Dad taught me Winnis's method for dealing with the heat. You started out in the morning with a full canteen of water, but you never glugged it. You took only the tiniest of sips, enough to moisten your mouth, throughout the day, so that you'd have an almost-full canteen of water by the time the sun went down. You drank most of your water at night, away from the day's heat. "Only townies need to drink all their water," Dad told me. We were bush people. Bush people tramped around on sore feet with no water. Some people might say we were thick; we said we were tough.

If I was too tired for a long trek, however, I would sometimes deploy the number one tactic Dad would use to get out of hours of fruitless walking with Winnis: to try to bait him into telling hunting stories in the quiet of a dry riverbed. I felt it was quite foolish of Dad to let me in on this strategy and think that I wouldn't try to use it. "Didn't something happen here once?" was the line that could spark Dad into all manner of storytelling.

Like a fine wine, the stories seemed to get better with age and on occasion change completely. If we were around the campfire later, the best was when you could get a few people who were there to add their comments, all throwing in extra threads like a cackling group of village women weaving a mat.

Of course, each person has his own way of attacking a story. In my father's tellings, he's always the bumbling observer who got in over his head, then miraculously managed to survive, turning hero in the end. Uncle John, naturally, is always a hero straight off the bat. My grandfather and Winnis are flat out heralded as the greatest, carved from stone and without a single insecurity.

I didn't question these stories when I was little. Later I began to appreciate the power of the storytelling itself: there's what happened and then the telling of it, which everyone had a view on. The stories became entities in themselves, and at first I didn't perceive the real people beneath them. The tales, seen through the lens of hindsight, often failed to convey what people felt in the moment and simply became the markers of the dramatic, the funny, the terrifying. Only later did I begin to realize that the stories could leave as much untold as told.

Huge portions of my youth were dedicated to the endless walking and endurance that come with the pursuit of impalas with Dad. I was really out there because there are few better ways to get the undivided attention of your father than hunting: the ultimate form of male bonding, with a bloody full stop. We are a heartless species.

Hunting impalas gives you such insight into predation. Thinking like a predator teaches you what it takes to survive in the bush. "That's the good thing about hunting," Dad told me. "It makes you more alert. It attunes all your senses." The minute you decide to hunt, you have to accept that you are no longer an observer. The rule of "If you leave it alone, it will leave you alone" no longer applies. You're in the system and had better behave accordingly. When Dad and I were out together, everything was information. If we heard an impala alarm—a rasping bleat—Dad would help me work out the best way to stalk in close. "Don't look around a bush, Boydie; look through its branches. Something could be standing behind it." He also taught me how to use high, rising ground or deep ravines for cover. Predators have a natural sense of the land's topography. They know how to read the land. Dad taught me how to do that as well.

Sharing his philosophy was as important to Dad as the finer points of tracking. He needed me to learn how to make decisions under pressure in the bush. For example, in every hunt, there comes a moment when you have to decide whether to shoot an impala or not. Dad never intruded. By handing me the responsibility, Dad told me he knew I could handle it. We never killed senselessly. If we shot an impala, we were going to eat it. Every part of the animal would be used.

In line with family traditions, I was six or seven when I shot my first impala. I was with Dad and Elmon Mhlongo, a legendary Shangaan tracker who was Uncle John's best friend and partner in filmmaking. We'd crept down into a gully. When an impala peered over the lip, I shot him in the neck. We ate him for dinner that night. Uncle John was a huge believer in the medicinal benefits of impala liver. I choked it down.

Sometimes on our impala hunts we'd cross paths with a buffalo or a lioness with her cubs. Dad would quickly grab me by the back of my khaki shirt, so that I was connected to him. He was thinking for two, and I could feel that. When I was with him, I always knew he would keep us safe. He knew how to operate under pressure in a dangerous situation and how to create the space for us to get out of harm's way.

He was always so calm; this was the foundation of the hunter. Once I went for a walk with him and a friend. It was late evening, and the three of us strolled casually through the clearings. A single elephant stepped into view, followed by the rest of the herd. Dad noticed something off in the way the lead cow threw her head and curled her tail. She swung sideways and locked onto us in a threatening way.

As calm as ever, my father turned around. "Run this way" was all he said. He sprinted; we followed. We made it into the thicket with the entire herd in angry pursuit. My father spoke quietly on his two-way radio while simultaneously charting a route for us. Mindful of the elephants flanking us, he would stop for a few seconds to listen, then reroute, basing his course on the sound of the elephants crashing through the bush. It was an awesome display of his strong hunting instincts.

My father and I have been to the wire together. Nature gave us that. So many fathers consider their duty to be clapping from the sidelines. In this domestication, fathers and sons miss out on that male bond that can be formed only in real adversity. You can enforce mutual respect, but there's no place to genuinely forge it without those pressurized situations. I worry that fathers and sons today are facing a new danger: a danger of no danger. There's an element of the male bond that is formed where things are unpredictable. Being in the wilderness is a wonderful environment in which to find connections that a lot of modern life doesn't allow for.

———

While city kids were at the mall, I was out hunting with Dad or Elmon. Elmon's bushcraft tutorials had a Shangaan flair. He used his tracking skills to find and rob carcasses from leopards and lions; he fished with the poisonous bulbs of the xiranzana as bait. He showed me how to snare francolins with bent-branch noose traps.

My parents happily allowed me to go anywhere with Elmon. A tall, handsome man with thick forearms, he was incredibly strong and resilient, unbelievably resourceful. I learned by watching his reactions on our walks how to check the wind, spot game paths, predict which way animals were heading.

It was Elmon who taught me how to hunt warthogs. Spears in hand, we'd approach the hog mound just before dawn and look for fresh tracks. If we spotted them, one of us would stand on top of the mound and stamp his feet, then stick the warthog as it came out of the mound to investigate the intruder. This was a very high-stress operation for a small boy; a disturbed warthog was a 160-pound beast burning for a fight. If the hog didn't come out, Elmon would disappear into the bush with his sharp panga, a sort of fierce machete. In a matter of minutes he'd be back with a stick braided with dried grass, which would be smoking from a fire he'd started with a hand drill. He'd thrust the burning end down into the hog hole to smoke the beast out. As soon as the hog appeared, he'd stab it with the spear, whereupon the hog would commence its horrible high-pitched squealing, alerting any predator for miles. Elmon would dispatch the hog quickly—hyena, lions, and heaven knows what else would be on the run for us—then cut out a bit of stomach and spread it all around the area. Then he'd hoist the carcass onto his back and we'd hightail it out of there. Whatever predator arrived would be distracted long enough by the bits of meat Elmon had scattered for us to make our getaway.

———

Hunting was an opportunity to be with my icons. I worshipped Dad, Uncle John, and Elmon. They were rugged. They were heroes always having adventures. I wanted to be like them. But by the time Dad took me out hunting, he was already seeing nature more clearly, more deeply as kin. Looking back, I recognize the impasse; I was largely hunting to impress him and be with him; he was doing the only thing he knew. Both of us were walking the steps of our ancestors, but both of us wanted a new path. Uncle John did, too.

Hunting had its place, and we learned that. And then one day it no longer did. As the two brothers worked the land in the early days of building Londolozi, they started to feel it responding. Dad and Uncle John saw more game, and their mind-set shifted toward conservation rather than hunting. They would occasionally see leopards, which would flee immediately. Then, at the end of a day spent clearing a thick snaggle of bush that encroached on the land, Dad saw a leopard calmly walking in the road. It looked at him but didn't bolt. "It felt like that leopard was almost carrying a message to me that I was on the right track," Dad told me. "My reward for all that work that day was the chance to see her for a few minutes." Uncle John, meanwhile, met a different female leopard and slowly began developing a relationship with her while filming her. He, too, lost his desire to hunt.

Once Dad and Uncle John started to see the benefits of partnering with nature, they could no longer separate the well-being of the animals from their own well-being; they were bound together. They felt what

everyone would feel given the time and the chance: that we are ultimately no different from the other creatures. Our survival and welfare
depend on theirs, economically as well as spiritually.

My great-grandfather, grandfather, father, and uncle at some point
all tested themselves in the pursuit of a lion. I am the first in the line not
to hunt one, something of which I'm personally proud. I don't think I
would be able to bear the horror of killing something so magnificent. It's
hard enough knowing that I have killed as many antelopes as I have. But
at least with antelopes, we were hunting for food; hunting lions was only
about collecting a trophy. Even so, I wouldn't have traded my hunting
experiences for anything.

If I could go back in time, I would spend a night in the original hunting camp, the four mud huts my great-grandfather built in the 1930s. I
would wake at dawn to walk with my grandfather and Winnis. As the
heat of the sun built, I would spend midmorning down in the river
swimming and lolling, the excitement of mornings in the wild now replaced by the calming effects of cool water and hot sun. In the evening,
as the nightjar began to call, we would light the fire and gather together,
bathed in silence and firelight. I still love the simplicity and wildness of
where hunting led us.

———

Londolozi was running well by the time I came along. I often wonder how
my father must have felt staring down the barrel of so much responsibility
at age fifteen. There must have been days when he would sit out in the
bush by himself, Londolozi's reservation ledger glaring up at him, its pages
as empty as the hollow in his stomach. During the moments when he felt
at his lowest, through the silence of that blue African sky would come the
bateleur eagle, its stumpy tail pivoting unsteadily behind its squat body
and black-and-white wings, its red beak jutting beneath a ruffled black
hood, totally at ease with its own instability, elegant in it. In that bird, my
father felt his father's guiding presence watching over him.

The bateleur eagle became the first emblem of Londolozi. With a name derived from the French word for "acrobat," these birds pump their short wings like walkers steadying themselves on a tightrope. Dad taught my sister, Bron, and me to treat the bateleur eagle as sacred, to honor it and to let it guide us. This is the magic of my father: he's practical to his core, yet with a deeper vision and wisdom. He imparted to me and Bron at a young age an almost mystical sense of the animals as our ancestors and family. What I learned from my father and uncle is that you don't always have a clear road to your goal; in fact, you hardly ever do. But that's no reason not to start. Have the confidence that you'll hack it out along the way. That confidence allowed their mission to evolve from hunting to creating and helping others build a spiritual connection to the land.

Nowadays, as we drive along and the bateleurs fly overhead, my father will look up and say, "Boss man," in simple acknowledgment of that connection to the animals and the land we call our home.

THREE

THE ROCK

THE YEAR MY SISTER WAS BORN, a drought swept Londolozi. The earth was red with dry resolve; the dust hung in the still air as if magnetized by a great dynamo in the sky.

My mother incubated Bronwyn through the hottest part of the year, working all day helping Dad get the safari business off the ground and spending the nights in a veil of heat on her sweat-soaked bed. The newly built house had no electricity at that stage—it was gas lamps until I was one or two—so my mom would rise by candlelight when the heat became too much and wallow whalelike in the water from her evening bath, now cool, moths floating on its surface like sailing vessels at sea. I can only imagine how she felt about the monumental task ahead—becoming a new mother, raising an infant—even as she and Dad floundered about, trying to make Londolozi work.

Shan Watson, who would become my mother, was fifteen and Dave Varty seventeen when they met at a seaside resort on a family holiday.

Sparks didn't fly then, although Dave was doubtless attracted to Shan's long, slender "Wednesday legs" (as in "When's dey gonna break?"), hazel eyes, and long brownish-black hair. She was drawn to his intensely blue eyes, tousled mop of brown hair, and beautiful singing voice when the families gathered around the campfire at night. Mom says she loved his enthusiasm in all manner of games, but I'm told he was rather solitary on that holiday, taking himself out every night to sit in the dunes alone and stare out at the sea. When she learned that he was mourning the recent death of his father, she tactfully gave him space. A few months later, though, he invited her to a movie in Johannesburg and the courtship began.

After a protracted and ultimately successful negotiation with Brian, Mom's father, Dave managed to get permission for Shan to come to Londolozi. Dad told me about that long, fateful evening. Brian kept trying to get a very young and callow Dave to join him for a few beers; Dad wanted to keep his wits about him, so he stuck to Fanta. After hours of sparring, Brian finally agreed to allow Shan to join Dave at Londolozi, but only if Mom's sister Diane came along as chaperone.

Mom fell in love with the place, the man, and the vision; she was in. Upon returning home, she promptly set up Londolozi's first reservations office in the attic of her parents' house in Johannesburg. Her home phone number was the reservations line for a weekend in the bush.

For a time she commuted between Johannesburg and Londoz—then a ten-hour drive on rough roads—catching lifts down to the lowveld, squashed into various delivery trucks with all manner of motley crew heading that way. Often she would arrive with guests coming down for the weekend, which might have undercut just a tad the professional veneer Dave and John were working hard to establish.

"Hi, this is Dave from Londolozi. Just checking that you'll still be coming down this weekend. . . . Great, great. . . . We look forward to it. Quick question: Could you take my girlfriend in your car?"

At first, Dad, Uncle John, my mother, Howard Mackie, who was the mechanic, and a revolving door of one of John's girlfriends lived in a one-room prefab trailer home that squatted in the middle of the bush, just behind the four mud huts that served as guest accommodations. Nothing worked. The water pump was always broken (a problem that exists to this day at the lodge). Their only Land Rover's gearbox had fallen out one day when they went over a bump in the road. The roofs of the guests' huts, which were made from river reeds, leaked like a sieve with the slightest precipitation.

By the time Mom was living full-time in the bush, she had, in usual Shan style, expanded her résumé to include receptionist, chef, housekeeper, hostess, scullery maid, chambermaid, bartender, driver, human resources director, doctor, counselor, chemist, midwife, nurse, and gardener. Nine years later, Mom's father called her in for a talk. "I need to ask you a question," he said. "Do you think that guy's ever going to marry you, or are you going to keep investing all this time and all this work?"

Mom must have been wondering the same thing, because the next year, twenty-five-year-old Shan Watson at last drew a line in the sand. "I have had enough," she told my dad one morning. "This is now ten years of me doing, giving, creating, being the bloody backbone, never getting any of the glory, standing and cooking when everyone else is having fun. I've had enough. I'm out of here. But before I leave, I'm going on a few game drives. In fact, I am going on one tonight!"

Dad said, "But you can't."

Mom was flabbergasted. "Why not?"

"Well, I've got a full Land Rover, and it's very important people."

"Well, you tell them to get off that car because I'm going on a ride."

Dad looked at Mom with big eyes. She stomped off and told all her mates, the unsung female support staff—by that time, there were two other women—"I've had enough, I'm out of here."

Late that afternoon, she climbed into the back of the Land Rover for her game drive, giving one of her friends an earful: "I am up to here—" At drinks time, they stopped at the beautiful watering hole called Winnis's Wallows. A full moon was rising. Dad came around to the back, reached up, and grabbed Mom's hand. "Will you marry me?"

She looked down at him, thoroughly startled. "What?"

Dad said it again: "Will you marry me?"

"If you are serious, get on your knee and ask me properly."

He got down on his knee and said for a third time, "Will you marry me?" He got no answer. They drove back to camp.

In all those ten years, Dad had never told Mom that he loved her. She was his best friend, his this, his that. But a declaration of love was something he reserved for a wife-to-be.

That night he held her hand. "So?"

She looked at him with grave hazel eyes. "Are you serious?"

"Yes, I'm serious."

Mom came to a decision. "Well, Davey, if you're serious, we'll go down to the office. I want it in writing."

At this point in the story, Mom is likely to break out the actual tourist's disclaimer form and turn it over to read: "I, David Varty, would like to marry you, Shan Watson, on"—at that point they had to go to the reservations book and come back and fill in the date—"15th of August, 1980."

Once Dave had signed the form, Mom said, "Done." She went back to all her mates. "So, Shanny," they asked, "did you tell Davey you're leaving us?"

She said, "No, we're getting married."

———

More than anything, visionaries need believers, people who keep them connected with the earth. That's what my mom has been for my father. From the start, they complemented each other's strengths. He could put the building up; she could invest it with feeling by adding the perfect touches. He could muster the group; she would make each individual feel cared for. The funny thing about leaders is that everyone sees them as leaders except for the people closest to them, who see them as human. It was my mother to whom my father turned for reassurance in the middle of the night.

In the face of all the hardship of getting their small safari business off the ground, Shan never blinked. "Be a chef? Well, I've never cooked a damn thing, but no prob." "Oh, you want me to prepare this warthog with bristling jowl hair for Christmas dinner? Well, why not? I'm sure the guests will love it." Once she tried to cook a warthog on a spit, but by the time it was ready to serve, hours later, the flies had gotten to it and it was teeming with maggots.

Mom remained unflappable. For a time, a landowner in the area banned the reserve from using a section of road, throwing up a wire fence that made it impossible to ferry guests from the nearby airstrip to the lodge. Mom's solution was to pilot the Landi full of guests up to a section of the park fence, haul out a large pair of secateurs, cut through the fence, drive the guests through, hop back out to mend the fence with some wire improvisation, then be on her merry way—all the while smiling innocently at the guests like this was the most natural procedure in the world.

Her equanimity was shattered one day when Dad started experiencing chest pain so massive that everyone assumed he was having a heart attack. Even Dad thought he was going to die. They flew him to nearby Nelspruit—some seventy-five miles away—where he was put in the ICU. Mom, then his terrified bride-to-be, accompanied him. When Uncle John found out, he too was frantic. He drove like a bat out of hell to a nearby lodge and buttonholed the helicopter pilot there, screaming, "You've got to fly me to Nelspruit!"

"Listen," the pilot told him, "I don't even know who you are! I'm not taking you." John decked him. When the pilot revived, Uncle John persuaded him to fly the helicopter despite his own rash behavior. They landed in the hospital garden. Mom was relieved to have Uncle John on the scene; it meant she could fall apart a bit. But then John worried that he, too, might be having a heart attack. He started doing jumping jacks and toe touches on the tarmac, "to get his blood flowing" to ward off the nonexistent attack. Then he flew into action, storming the hospital corridors. "Where's my brother! Where in damnation is Dave Varty! Get me Christiaan Barnard! I want him flown here *now*!" In a crisis, Uncle John can sometimes be more of a liability because he screams and shouts, but if you need a door kicked down, he's your man.

It turned out that Dad had a serious case of pericarditis—inflammation of the sac around the heart—and pleurisy. When he awoke in the ICU with Mom by his side, he told her, "I love you. I don't ever again want to wake up without you by my side."

They were married on August 15, 1980, with John as best man.

————

It has always amazed me that Mom was Londolozi's first executive chef. The kitchen is not her strong point, although she can take a tough impala leg and turn it into a creditable breakfast, lunch, or supper. And she's an absolutely brilliant manager, commanding Spook Sithole and Simeon, Londolozi's gifted but wildly unpredictable resident cooks, with amazing results.

Back then, Dad and Uncle John raced through life with their heads in the clouds. Mom was the more practical one. She provided a semblance of order beneath all the chaos.

The Shangaan people loved her. It wasn't unusual to find her unpacking and repacking a metal outdoor storage container five times on a scorching day. The Shangaans would stare at her in awe; they'd never seen a white woman work this hard.

My sister, Bron, was born in May 1982. Becoming a new mother did little to slow Shan down. Practically speaking, she couldn't afford to, anyway; the business was in such a precarious state. Guests had graduated from mud huts to chalets with running water and en suite bathrooms. A swimming pool had gone in. There was a growing infrastructure and influx of guests to oversee. In the tradition of white South African mothers, Mom handed Bron over into the care of Lucy, a Shangaan nanny, and went back to work.

In midmorning, Dad would sometimes come back from taking guests on a game drive and assume child-care duties for a few hours after Lucy had gone home, so that Mom could have a nap. He would zip an infant Bronwyn into his large bush jacket, which smelled thickly of him and rain and soil. She would bake in his warmth while he lay on the bed, allegedly to rock her to calmness, but in minutes he'd fall fast asleep while she gurgled at him, alert and content, as galaxies of dust particles drifted through the beams of sunlight that cut through the cracks in our air-brick house.

I came along eighteen months after Bron. My parents had plucked a name for me out of the ether: Craig. In Shangaan culture, they say that a child will sometimes cry for his name, ceasing his wailing only when he is taken to the *sangoma,* who will then tell the parents that an ancestor's name is trying to come through the child. When my mother looked at me, she could never call me Craig. My ancestors cried through me and I was eventually named Boyd, after my great-grandfather Charles Boyd and my grandfather Boyd. A hint of my father's father's adventurous spirit has walked with me ever since. I wonder if he, too, noticed the arch of the ebony tree's black bark above the greenery of the Sand River or how the paleness of the midwinter light makes you feel as if nature is whispering intimate secrets to you.

Mom attacked motherhood in the bush the same way she attacked everything else: with an enormous sense of practicality and flair for improvisation. You couldn't just run to the local pediatrician—the closest one was seventy-five miles away—so she kept a scale upstairs to weigh us every fourteen days, and she'd phone the doctor with the results. "Are we making progress? Are we on the right track?" She set up smart, practical structures and routines, which I found enormously comforting. As a small boy, I'd come into her room at five or six in the morning, when she'd still be in her jammies, with a tea tray waiting. "Come in, my chicken," she'd say. I'd jump on the bed, telling her, *"Maga teea"* in Shangaan, as I'd learned from Lucy. Make me tea. After breakfast I'd play with the sticks and rocks I always carried in my pockets or haul around my model stegosaurus while she pottered around. At ten, Bron and I would have juice in the garden and she'd hand us off to Lucy.

Mom and Lucy trusted each other completely. Lucy was a large woman with a broad smile, a gap between her teeth, and a laugh that gurgled out of her. She was solid in a way that is uniquely African, the fat of her body firm as an inflated pontoon, her hands amazingly strong from years of manual labor. When I was very, very small, Lucy would tie me onto her back with a towel and sing to me: *Tula tula tula, tula tula tula.* The lilting tune had no beginning or end and was as soothing as a comforting balm. With one cheek pressed against her back, I might have had a limited perspective, but wrapped warmly in a towel, drifting off to sleep, I felt as safe as when I was tucked into bed by my own mother.

Lucy was part oracle, part enforcer. If Bronwyn wanted me to do something, she had only to place "Lucy said" in front of it and I'd hop to it. (She once told me, "Lucy said you could use the cardboard center of the toilet paper roll" because she was too lazy to go fetch the toilet paper I'd requested.) Anytime the smile faded from Lucy's face, the stark contrast to her usual beaming grin made Bron and me concerned.

Lucy watched Bronwyn, and Bron, in turn, had the responsibility of looking out for me. In Africa there is nothing unusual in putting a small girl in charge of a very small boy. I still love to sit in rural villages now and watch the hierarchy of care play out in direct proportion to height. Survival here is about everyone contributing, no matter their age; the environment is too harsh for coddling. I once came upon an eight-year-old Masai boy shepherding his cattle, with no adult for miles around. We were all expected simply to get on with it.

Bron and I were left largely to entertain ourselves while Mom or Lucy busied themselves nearby. In the summertime in Africa, November through April, it's bright and hot by six-thirty in the morning. The cicadas would be buzzing in the trees, and pearl-colored butterflies already making the rounds in the garden. It would be months before we could even think of a sweater or jacket again. I was happy in my own company, chasing a wasp as he made his rounds in our garden or watching the tenacious ants dedicate an entire day to walking up the pillars of the house; I found fulfillment in the company of a party of birds as they drifted silently through the garden. All the toys I needed were there for the foraging. Ant lions in their little conical sand holes absorbed hours of my time. I dropped large red ants into the traps and watched their doomed, primal struggle for survival. I spent most of my time immersed in wonder, oblivious to a big sister in charge of my safety.

Mom would come home to have lunch with us before returning to work. She'd be home for good at teatime, when we'd do crafts together, play in the yard, or go swimming in the river.

Sitting outside their huts in the village, the staff members idled wherever there was shade, sucking on summer mangoes and making little pyramids out of lychee skins. Bron and I likewise spent our summer days with a sticky layer of fruit juice dried into goo across our faces. And when the sun got too hot to bear, we would run through the sprinkler in the garden before being banished to the cool, dark recesses of our room to sleep out the afternoon.

"Mom, it's too hot to sleep," complained Bron, twirling one finger in her hair and sucking another, as she always did when she was tired or grumpy.

"Just put a wet towel over yourself and be still" was Mom's answer.

I'd wake with what wisps of hair I had (I was practically bald as a child) plastered wetly to my head, in a horrible mood. Nothing could shake this ill humor from me until Mom picked me up and cradled me under her chin, giving me a chance to gather myself. Then I had my tea. Mom used to call it my "bad hour."

Despite the discomfort of the summer heat, I felt connected to the universe and I knew who I was in the warmth of the moment, worshipping a mango.

The bush in the summer literally fizzes with energy, the sound of bees, wasps, wood borer beetles, and cicadas embodying the frequency of life. In the afternoons Dad and Mom would take me and Bron out into the bush. Lulled by the rocking of the Land Rover, with the scents of the summer grasses and sages crushed under the wheels and the whirring of dung beetles as they cruised the summer air, I'd often fall asleep on the front seat. I'd wake up with my head on Mom's legs. Bron would be on Dad's lap, steering the Land Rover as he sang to her, the words of the songs drifting with our thoughts, each of us lost in our own worlds.

Sometimes we would stop at our favorite pan, or watering hole, next to a termite mound that had a sharp ridge for a top and two conical sections that gave it the look of a rhino. Dad would stop the Landi, have a good look around for predators, and then say, "Okay, go for it!" and off Bron and I would run to ride our rhino.

As the afternoon wore on, rays of religious light arched across the sky, and the world became washed in sepia tones of yellows and golds that deepened until the vibrancy of the colors seemed impossible. The day seemed to hang suspended for a long moment as the sun tiptoed along the ridge of the mountains and everything began to recede into a mood thick as treacle. Then, in a moment made more sudden by the preceding slowness, the sun dipped in a trail of blues, rippling out from the horizon into an eventual faint purple that was the transition from day into dusk.

A pair of frogs perched on the picture frames in the living room. They were like ornaments that moved around the house, as if by a poltergeist; Bron and I never knew where they might appear next. They croaked before it rained, like an early warning system. The flies that zipped in through the front door to escape the heat of the day would beat themselves against the windowpanes, pushing against an invisible barrier with all their frantic force, perhaps thinking that pure rage could make a whole wall move. An aura of moths rotated in a mist around what they thought was the moon, duped by an artificial porch lamp. The lizards roamed the courtyard like shrunken dinosaurs, pouncing on insects that had wounded themselves in the nightclub atmosphere under the porch lamps. The geckos likewise gorged at the lamps. I took the animals' stories as my stories. I believed I, too, could move walls with pure force, that the porch light was the truth of the moon.

Immersed in nature, I knew I was a part of God's creation. They say that spiritual experience creates the illusion that we're connected to everything. I've always felt that spiritual experience is dropping the illusion that we're not. Growing up at Londolozi nourished that sense in me from my earliest years.

Mom and Dad often had to visit with the guests in the *boma* in the evening, leaving me and Bron in Lucy's care. Sometimes we would go to the *boma* with Mom and Dad, and Bron and I would play in the river sand that made up the *boma* floor. When we began to tire, Mom would take us to a nest she'd devised of pool lounge chairs and blankets just outside the circle of firelight where the guests dined. She'd make a big show of tucking us in, and we would fall asleep with the scent of burning wood under a bowl of stars, knowing that Mom and Dad were close. It was a gentle time, and we were the beloved young ones of the village.

I was happiest, though, when Mom put me into my own bed herself and sang to me, soft and lilting: "The sun's gone away and the moon's not come/And the lambs and the kids they have all gone home./And the stars are twinkling up in the sky/And it's time for Boydie to go bye bye bye."

———

I had a sense of being loved but not terribly fussed over when I was a child. Worrying over small imperfections while living in the bush would be a recipe for madness. After all, Mom had two babies in diapers at a time when the house had no electricity. Sterilizing bottles and nappies was a huge job, requiring a great drum of hot water—what we called a donkey boiler. I always wore Bron's hand-me-downs—with two kids eighteen months apart, Mom wasn't going to waste anything, and she refused to get too technical about which baby wore what. She just plucked clothes from the pile, and if I ended up in a pink shirt now and again, no worries.

As Londolozi became more successful, Mom's wardrobe necessarily expanded. There were stylish dresses, even the occasional glamorous gown, for when she needed to travel abroad to conferences as our ambassador or play hostess to a gala in one of the camps. But she always seemed to prefer her standard uniform of a crisp white oxford shirt, practical khaki pants, and white takkies, or sneakers.

As no-nonsense as Mom was, she always knew when I needed her gentleness. If I smacked myself on something, Mom would give the injury a gentle rub, then reprimand the offending object: "You naughty chair! How dare you hurt my Boyd! You must go to the corner immediately." I'd be fascinated, the hurt forgotten. "Here, take a bit of sugar water," she'd say and rub my back, murmuring, "Oh dite, oh dite"— "All right, all right"—until I calmed.

She let me, an eternally shy little boy, stay pressed up against her legs until I felt safe enough to explore. I was always needing her to ground myself amid the new faces of ever-changing guests, reaching up to grasp her index finger, or molding myself against her when we were in the Land Rover. She'd lay a blanket down under the knobthorn tree in the front garden and take a rare moment of repose while Bron and I raced around. Every now and again I would press my forehead against hers, my touchstone. She'd let me snuggle into her shoulder and she'd rock me gently, one hand stroking or tickling my back. Her hands were always so cool and soft, redolent of Anaïs Anaïs powder. I can still remember how wonderful they felt when I was running a fever and she would stroke my forehead over and over, gently pushing back my curls. I knew that when she was around, I was safe.

They say that your home is a reflection of your life, an external representation of the inner workings of the house's inhabitants. As monumental an achievement as the creation of Londolozi has been, the construction of our family home is equally a reflection of my parents' spirit, its beauty the result of Mom's sheer grit. My father claims he baked every brick of our house here and constructed it according to the feel and design of a drawing he made in the sand all those years ago when he and Uncle John took their first fateful decision. Our home is set on the riverbank amid the foliage of the ebony trees, the porch overlooking a riverbed where the elephants stroll serenely, feeding off the wild date palms, and the nyalas and kudus peer in your windows. Our house lacks the veneer of money but holds all the warmth of a beloved work in progress. Like our safari business, it runs with a rhythm that creates its own soul comfort, with my mother as the engine that keeps it ticking along.

It moves a few inches left every year, the cracks appearing as if by magic in the muddy plaster—adding charm, or so we say as we stare up at them while drinking beer on the front porch, trying to placate my mother, who takes those cracks very personally. As bush people, we make light of the cracks just as we make light of other things that go wrong. We're primed to simply pop open another beer and say cheerily, "Oh, well now, it's just gone to shit." Pioneers find a philosophical nature in many heartbreaks and sweetness in an unexpected victory. That house is Mom's victory, and she means to maintain her preeminence over nature within it.

Bush houses require more maintenance than any city dwelling; they are always under attack. Home maintenance is a common source of friction between my parents, since my father comes from his own mother's tradition of "it's perfectly all right."

"Gran, there's mold in the jam."

"It's perfectly all right."

Once she knocked her glass of wine into her plate, bathing her entire dinner in a pool of Burgundy. "Gran, let's get you a new plate."

"Nonsense. It's perfectly all right."

Mom does not accept this. Something is either right or she is going to *make* it right. Dad gets to soar above it all like a bateleur eagle; it falls to Mom to mire herself in the mundane details of home repair. Whenever we have the occasional rat outbreak, our house looks as if a pack of Staffordshire terriers have been released. The rats have developed a taste for Mom's favorite sandalwood soap, which she's placed in every bathroom, so they periodically eat holes in the doors to get to it. The rats attract the snakes. My father would happily bathe with gnawed pieces of sandalwood soap and turn a blind eye to the snakes, but Mom will set so many traps that walking through the house is like strolling in a minefield.

At one stage our roof was leaking so badly that when it rained, we'd dash outside to sit under the knobthorn tree for shelter. Mom told Dad to fix the problem, but, as always, he was satisfied with the status quo. Mom was soon sighted dangling precariously from the roof, trying to drape a tarp. She finally delivered a loving ultimatum: Fix it or die. Dad fixed the roof.

Recently my mother had one of those weeks when it seemed as if the whole world was conspiring against her. She'd spent hours driving and walking around Londolozi, seeking out leopard orchids, each one secretly hidden in a separate grove. She'd roped herself up into each tree to extract them—a bit of a job in itself—and then painstakingly transplanted them into the crooks of trees around our house so that at certain times of year they would explode in fountains of yellow. She'd treated those orchids like family, making sure to speak to them each morning. "Grow! Grow! Grow!" she'd shout out the window. (This is standard operating procedure for Mom. There's a sausage tree in the courtyard near the safari lodge that got chewed down by an elephant. Every day as Mom passes it, she grasps the stump and utters a fervent "Love! Love! Love!" And damn if that tree isn't making a comeback!) There are half bottles of Super Bloom plant food all over the house, a testament to her nurturing nature. And then an elephant knocked down the fence and got into her garden and ate all her leopard orchids. God, those orchids had been her pets, and now they were all on a safari through the large intestine of an elephant.

This is typical of the onslaught Mom has had to deal with: carving out some time and fossicking all over the vast terrain to find the ultimate natural ornament for our home, only to have her curatorship undone by a plundering pachyderm. Everywhere I look in our home, in every public area, in every guest suite, Mom has placed the perfect painting, the most beautifully detailed fabrics, sculptures, flowers. Her inner beauty comes out in the spaces around her.

———

While they may have stumbled into their adventure together so very early in life, Mom and Dad have remained utterly, passionately committed to it for forty years. Mom has always been devoted to Dad, even though he irritates the bejesus out of her. And Dad has never, ever overlooked an opportunity to credit her. At every public event I've ever attended, Dad has praised Mom's efforts first and foremost.

"When you first meet someone," he told me, "you're jolted by those great electric sparks, but what you hope for is someone who will always give you that warm glow." This is what my parents have. They can't bear to be apart. Dad often tells Mom how much he loves her. When Mom comes back from town after a supply run, he kisses her as tenderly as if she'd shipped off for a year. The only time Dad ever sulks is when Mom flies off without him to some resort convention. My parents' marriage gave me an incredible model of love and stability—but more important, an idea of how important it was to be on a team together. Bron and I never thought of partnerships as separate from one's mission in life, because Mom and Dad shared theirs.

———

It hasn't been easy for Mom, living with two guys who refuse to plan or save. Any bit of money my father or uncle has ever made has been thrown right back at some grand project designed to save wild areas. Strong families aren't built around rock stars; they're built around rocks like my mother.

FOUR

FRIENDI IN THE STORM

"FRIENDI, COME HERE!" Bron cried out.

"I'm scared," I called back, crouching in terror behind my bed.
"Yes, I'm also scared. Come here!"

Perhaps you have never experienced an African thunderstorm. These nights of wind and drenching whiteness stand out in my memories of childhood like exclamation marks. The crashing thunder booms like ten thousand gongs and shakes your insides at a solid 9 on the Richter scale. The lightning comes down in sheets, not bolts, bleaching your retinas. You feel as if you're under attack by squadron after squadron of Stuka dive-bombers.

That night, the wind shot into all the tiny openings of the house so what was concrete and safe started to scream like a banshee.

The electricity had gone out. Bron, always my protector, braved the blasting darkness to save me. I heard her small voice above the thunder: "Friendi, I'm here." She led me, our sweaty palms pressed together, past curtains that flailed as if animated by ghosts, to my parents' room. The thunder rattled the doors and the lightning cracked a cowboy whip above my parents' bed, where Bron and I fled to the shelter of Mom's arms. Dad was away. The sideways rain lashed the house as demons moaned from the blackness outside. This was a real beast of a bushveld storm, the lightning striking all around, the smell of burned earth rising as granite rocks were cracked open by the energy in each bolt of pure channeled white-hot rage.

We searched for one another's faces in the brief moments of illumination when lightning flashes filled the room. "There, there." Mom tried in vain to convince us that the storm was merely "God moving his furniture." She stroked my hair, waiting for the storm to calm, my heart to slow. But I could feel her shaking next to me. She must have felt so alone.

Suddenly we heard the front door burst open, rattling like death on its hinge as the house inhaled a blast of wind. Mom went rigid next to me as we listened to footsteps approaching along the passage outside the bedroom.

"Shanny! Shan! Where are you?"

At two in the morning, in the vortex of a storm, Uncle John, knowing that Dad had gone to town, had walked from his house next door through the dark to check on us. I could smell the cotton of his soaked jersey, the crisp scent of the storm, the wildness of the wind sticking to him as he slumped into the chair at the end of the bed.

"We're okay, John," Mom said. "Hell of a storm, hey?" I could feel her body relax ever so slightly.

With Uncle John keeping vigil in the chair, visible in the strobing lightning, water dripping off the tip of his cap, I fell asleep, Bron's arm resting on mine.

———

Bronwyn had my mother's glossy dark brown hair and determined mouth. Mom's eyes are dark hazel, while Bron's are chocolate brown. Bron was the ultimate girly girl, insisting on keeping her hair long, always done up in fancy ponytails or plaits. While I wore the same dirt-colored camouflage as Dad and my uncle, Bron glowed in bright pinks, lime green, and spotted leopard tights against the dun colors around us. She often tied her doll to her back with a towel, like a Shangaan woman caring for her baby. She occasionally exchanged her favorite ballerina outfit—pink leotard, tutu, tights, and slippers—for a raid on the corner of Mom's closet that held a few glamorous party dresses for fancy dinners. Bron would safety-pin the gowns up the back, twirling the voluminous skirts as she choreographed dance routines to Whitney Houston, a glamour-puss among the rest of us with our frayed, tattered khaki.

Left to my own devices, I would never have abandoned my post in the yard, watching the ants or wasps. Bron pulled me out of myself with endless ideas for fun. I couldn't have asked for a more amazing playmate and companion than my sister. Our main preserve was the front garden, which in those days was fenced in by reeds. "Come on, friendi, let's play Cowboys and Indians!" Bron would call. We'd be at it for hours, making elaborate tents out of seven or eight chairs pushed together and covered with blankets, our cozy world inside. From there we rode out to capture the bad guys on our broomstick horses, their heads made from socks stuffed with cotton wool and button eyes, strings standing in for reins. Bron led the expeditions to eat the small, tart berries of the buffalo thorn trees that grew all over the village. She would spend hours standing at the base of a tree, carefully plucking the red treats from between the dense mat of thorns, her bright clothes glowing against the brown tree limbs.

When a plane crashed at Londoz and the wreck languished on the runway, awaiting repairs, it was Bron who announced, "Boyd, you gonna be the pilot; I'll be the air hostess." It was she who dubbed us Squeaky and Squawky and organized spying expeditions on the adults, hiding us under the dining room table to eavesdrop and report.

After every storm the fireflies burst out, magical orbs moving as randomly as electrons. "Friendi, let's see how many we can fit in a jar!" she'd call out. Bron appointed me her assistant fairy catcher, and we dashed around the front lawn grasping passionately at the mystical baubles of light. That image is framed in my mind's eye: nature teaching us to pluck flecks of light out of the darkness.

The next morning Bron would grab my hand and we would run naked to our bikes, a pair of secondhand BMX cycles that were usually hobbled by acacia thorns speared through the tires but were perfect for destroying puddles.

"Friendi, into the puddles!" Bron would scream. "Fast as you can go!"

There are few joys greater than being a naked child riding a bike into a puddle. That glorious mud seeped into our pores and baked hard onto our skin. *I am that land. It is in my body.*

————

Our photo albums make it clear who ruled whom in early childhood. As creative and fun-loving as she was, Bron had an inborn seriousness. Uncle John even called her "Mom" because she was forever telling him where to sit, what to eat, how to behave. My sister's benevolent-commander face was generally set in a concerned scowl as she led me somewhere, one protective five-year-old hand on my bald little Kojak head. Bronwyn absorbed endless worry so I could be the "free one," and I flourished in her shadow.

My sister carried the responsibility, made the plans, and did the grunt work, too. Each year she would meticulously organize a little Nativity play, to which we would subject all of our family and friends. Through-out her planning and rehearsals, I would clown around, strapping a tinsel-covered halo to my ear and pretending I was picking up radio signals from God.

"Boyd, stop messing around—you're ruining everything!" Bron implored. Later, when the show was in action, I would stroll onstage like a show pony, my carpenter Joseph upstaging even the baby Jesus. I was extremely shy in any new situation, but once I felt comfortable, I quite happily played the buffoon. Bron made it easier for me to come out of my shell by taking charge and ordering me about.

With her overdeveloped sense of responsibility, Bron seemed intent on becoming an adult as quickly as possible. At the time, I thought we were spying for the fun of it, but now it occurs to me that Bron was trying to glean instructions so she could grow up faster.

At the age of eight, Bron decided that she was going to be a hotelier. She forsook her pink leotard, fashioning her own uniform out of khakis and a white shirt, and declared herself a kind of assistant camp manager. "Hello, welcome to Londolozi," she would tell guests. "Please let us know if we can do anything for you. I'm going to the kitchen now." She hustled herself two rand a day—about twenty-five cents—and reported for duty to the general manager every morning. While I was poking sticks into termite mounds, she was working side by side with grown-ups on the kitchen shift, rolling balls of dough, baking bread, making chocolate truffles, chopping and prepping for all the meals. She helped set up drink stops so that guests driving through the bush would happen upon these magical oases. For daytime picnics she helped spread blankets, arrange beanbag chairs, and display snacks and games. For the evenings, she accompanied the camp manager to lay out starched white tablecloths and silver and hang lanterns from the leadwood trees, then set out giant cheese boards, fixings for gin and tonics, buckets of Champagne.

Our paths were clear. I was going to be a conservationist, like Dad and Uncle John. Bron, with Mom's natural gift for organizing to the finest detail and thinking up ways to delight guests, was going to rule the business world.

To me, Bron was always supremely competent and creative. It's always surprised me that she didn't see herself that way. She seemed polarized between extreme uncertainty and absolute clarity. This was especially true in the bush, since she didn't spend as much time there as I did, with Dad and Uncle John, and didn't have my physical confidence. She saw that things came easily to me, that I was more able to clown around and shrug things off, while she had to work harder to make her mark. But what I admire most about her is that she'll never, ever back off from a challenge.

Bron has always had a particular dislike of elephants. Perhaps it's because the occasional elephant would crash through the reed fence in our front yard—never while we were playing there—and then trample through the other side. People ask her if she ever had a bad experience. "A few," she'll say. "The first one was in a previous life when I was an Indian princess and an elephant sat on me." She dispenses this casually over dinner with such charm and grace that people seem to simply accept it.

One morning Bron and I were out driving in the bushveld with Uncle John, who'd brought us along on his daily morning ramble in search of something interesting to film. Days like this one could be dodgy. Uncle John would wake us at four in the morning, then have us sit for six or seven hours watching a leopard, waiting for it to hunt. We'd get tired and thirsty, but Uncle John would wave off any complaint. Hours of excruciating boredom might be rewarded with a few minutes of action if the leopard went for a kill.

On this day, Uncle John had deposited Bron behind the wheel of the open-topped Land Rover so he could focus on the job of filming, but he forgot she was ten and not a thirty-year-old rally driver. Bron was piloting us home when the tarpaulin-like ear of an elephant flapped in the bush ahead of us. Bron froze. She wasn't blindingly afraid, but she knew that elephants had been culled and shot at in nearby Kruger National Park not so long ago and it wasn't uncommon to run into one that was still a little pissed off with people. While hundreds of stories told of elephants walking peacefully by, she was well aware of the more headline-grabbing accounts of elephants maiming and killing. No doubt being in the open Land Rover added to her concern. Even if a roof offered little protection against an angry elephant, a false sense of security was better than nothing.

"Jonno, you come drive," she pleaded. She looked like a tiny doll behind the massive steering column.

"Nah, don't be a nafta," Uncle John said, dismissing her fears. "What you gonna do one day when you're by yourself and you see an elephant? Drive on." John waved one muscled arm toward the path, his sleeve even more torn than usual. Uncle John has a skewed finger, so when he points straight, it looks like he's aiming off to the left, which can make getting directions challenging. Bron's large brown eyes squinted briefly in the direction he was pointing, and then her beaded Alice headband started to bob as she shook her head no.

As if he'd overheard the conversation, the elephant, a large bull, burst out of the bush and set off toward the Land Rover at a brisk lope, his ears flapping with each step and his trunk rocking from side to side. I was crapping myself in the exposed backseat of the Land Rover. You see, I'm also scared of elephants. I just don't tell people, to keep up macho appearances.

"Jonno, please come drive. I *hate* this," Bron begged again.

But Uncle John saw this as the perfect opportunity to teach Bronwyn how to reverse a Land Rover, although she'd only just gotten a bead on how to drive one forward. "Now look here, Bonna," he told her professorially, putting her tiny hand on the gearshift. "Things work in opposites when you reverse, so you're going to want to—"

Bron let out a choked sob while I dove under the seat, screaming with frustration. The elephant was quickly closing the gap between us, and here was Uncle John, playing the role of the swashbuckling hero fumbling through a huge ring of keys to find the one that starts the ignition, while the bad guys are breathing down his neck.

"Bonna, slow down; think clearly," said Uncle John.

By now Bronwyn was crying and in complete mental lockdown.

"Think! What do you have to do first?" offered John.

"Get out of here!" screamed Bronwyn.

"Bonna! Calm down; read the situation. The elephant's not aggressive—watch his body language." Elephants have very expressive bodies and provide much information about their mood and distress level by the carriage of their head and the position of their trunk, tail, and ears. "See, his trunk is down, he's throwing sand over himself, his ears are flapping. You can tell he's relaxed," said Uncle John. "If he was interested in us, he'd lock his ears forward and be sniffing the air."

Bron was in no mood for a lecture on animal behavior. "Please, just drive!"

Two titanic wills had met and both of them had lost track of the elephant, which had picked up speed and was now a mere fifteen yards from the car. He looked as if he was going to charge after all, his large ears locked forward, his full attention on us. He paused briefly to lift his trunk like a trumpet to drink in our scent.

The elephant's moment of assessment was Bronwyn's call to action. She was no longer scared; she was *angry*. Ignoring Uncle John's instructions to reverse, she mashed down the gas pedal and charged the elephant.

Now it was my uncle's turn to scream: "Stop, Bonna, for God's sake, stop!" But once engaged, Bronwyn isn't big on backing off. She unleashed a snotty, teary snarl that, combined with the roar of the Land Rover, frightened the elephant so much that he turned tail and ran for the bush. John, realizing there was nothing left to do, simply gave himself over to the situation. Sporting his vampire-like grin, his canines sticking out beneath his top lip, he turned back to me and said, "Well, that's one way to do it!" Bronwyn started to giggle with relief through the tears, and soon we all completely lost it.

I see those same threads from that day now: Bron's reticence, her feeling of being underprepared for whatever the elephant of the day is. I see my sister as a vulnerable little girl in a pink tutu among the dust of the

African wild. She's afraid and unsure, and then, as if a channel has opened to the forces of the sky, comes a clarity that vanquishes all fear, the way light dispels dark. And I see someone who can summon courage, who stands so rooted when I get lost, who can charge when she must.

I always thought I was tough, but it was my sister who put aside her own fear in those blazing night storms to come get me first.

FIVE

NEVER PANIC IN THE BUSH

"FRIENDI, WE GONNA PLAY SHOP SHOP," Bron announced one day. We planned easily for a week: prices, goods, location, displays, tablecloths. I had to construct everything, from the shelves to the till. Bron was in charge of advertising, which meant that pretty much everybody at Londolozi had been mustered to attend and purchase our wares, mostly fruit and little bags of popcorn.

We were doing quite the booming business when Uncle John suddenly burst in, a bandit mask pulled over his face and a toy gun pointing at our gizzards. He promptly held us up, knocking over stalls and cleaning all the money out of the till. Bron was furious. "Uncle Jonno, stop it!" she screamed. Uncle John just laughed and continued kicking the place to pieces. "Guys setting up a business? You gotta think security!" he barked, then fled. Bron and I looked around in despair: overturned tables, stained tablecloths, fruit rolling everywhere—all our hard work ruined. Bron began to sob. We both felt horrifically embarrassed; effectively the entire camp had seen the debacle.

Uncle John sat us down later for a chat. I think he felt bad; he hadn't expected us to be so upset by what he'd thought would be a cute joke. Bron was still very cross. "Uncle Jonno, I don't think it was very nice of you," she huffed.

"No, Bonna, but just listen," Uncle John said. "You're growing up in Africa. Can't just be mono-focused. You've got to look at the whole situation. When stuff goes wrong, you don't cry about it; you pull yourself up and keep going." Uncle John never missed an opportunity to give us a true bush education. His methods could be harsh, and Mom had been very upset with him as Bron had sobbed, "Jonno robbed us!" but to be fair, his training worked.

Uncle John tried to prepare us for the harsh realities of African life. The Sand River at Londolozi has always been sacred to my family. Long before in-ground pools by manicured gardens made their appearance, the river was where Uncle John would lead me and Bronwyn on hot summer days. Hours could go by seemingly in minutes as we swam and played games of dropping twigs and branches into the current and running downstream to see whose won the race. Sometimes Uncle John would let us "shoot the rapids." We'd release ourselves into the wild current, and after a tumble downstream, he would capture us in his burly arms. Once my uncle missed me at the collection point at the end of the rapid and I washed downriver, choking and sputtering. When he finally pulled me out, I was shaking with fright. I got a brusque reprimand instead of the hoped-for comfort. Shaking me gently to be sure I was listening, Uncle John warned me, "In the bush you never panic. When you panic, your brain turns to sponge." This wasn't meanness; this was a crucial lesson in survival, and I never forgot it.

———

Bron and I were bush people; we grew up fast. "You're the man of the house," Dad told me when he had to leave on business. I was all of eight or nine. "Look after your mother and sister until I get back." Dad made sure I knew where the key to the gun safe was, the order of people to call in case of an emergency.

Whenever I came back from a walk in the bush with Dad, Mom would matter-of-factly strip me down, toss my clothes in the laundry, and put me in a Dettol bath to get rid of the ticks. She groomed me like a monkey, parting my hair and checking my armpits for the stubborn hangers-on. Her doctoring was necessarily pragmatic, given our lack of proximity to anything resembling a pharmacy. She had an unfailing belief in the same two solutions, no matter what the malady.

"Mom, I have a sore stomach."

"Well, rub some arnica oil on it."

"I did that."

"Okay, I'll bring the hot water bottle."

If her back was against the wall, Mom might bring out the Rescue Remedy. Her variations on this limited repertoire got us through many a cold, scratch, and fever. In fact, I'm fairly convinced that if one of us had lost an arm, she would have calmly administered arnica oil to the stump. Mom prescribed the pills she did have like a resident pharmaceutical artist, handing out random instructions with impressionistic flair: "Okay, it says take two three times a day . . . . So you know what? Take one twice a day and we will see how you do."

We never bothered to treat scratches, and as the family doctor said, "When I got a call from the Vartys, I would immediately book a surgery."

Mom and Dad enforced strict rules. We were banned from walking around barefoot because of the snakes and weren't allowed out unattended lest something try to eat us. When Bron and I played in the sand pit outside the kitchen, we had to be under constant surveillance in case a snake tried to slither into the area.

When one of us cried, my father would fix us with a withering stare and say, "Stop it—you'll attract the lions in." My mother would politely pour tea in the foreground while Simon the gardener calmly murdered a python in the background. Dad would dunk a biscuit as a child pulled an impala leg across the garden. We're basically an unflappable family, although when a deadly mamba dropped onto my sister's cot, Mom immediately promoted Simon from gardener to full-time guardian.

While other kids were getting yelled at or lectured by their parents for losing the TV remote or not putting away their video games, what stopped me and Bron in our tracks was my parents' low but insistent "danger voice," which meant we had to snap to attention without question.

Dad's cardinal law was: Get information before you act. Whenever I saw a dangerous animal, every fiber of me wanted to flee right away. I would feel Dad's arm come around my shoulders, the palm of his hand onto my chest. He would drop down onto one knee behind me so that his mouth was close to my ear. "Slowly, Boydie, assess," Dad would tell me. "Look at him. Does he notice you? Is he interested in you? Aggressive? Figure that out first." I would study the potential predator. "Okay, now that you have information, start to chart your retreat."

Because of the way my parents taught us about the world, it didn't feel dangerous. If you don't know how to cross the street in New York, it's hazardous, but once you learn, you manage the risk. It's the same in the bush. I saw my upbringing as undeniably idyllic. Who else had wildebeests, kudus, and vervet monkeys scampering through the garden, or a river right next to their house for swimming? When I was young I was under the impression that everyone raced the monkeys for chocolate during the Easter egg hunt. When most kids were getting their first bike, I was driving a Land Rover. My father bought my sister and me a short-wheelbase Landi when we were about ten or eleven. We named it "BB Jeep," for Bronwyn and Boyd's jeep; driving it, we were masters of our destinies. Getting a bicycle when you're young is pretty awesome, but I'd choose getting a Land Rover any day.

Dad taught me to drive with a methodical patience. We were parked on a dusty two-track in the trusty old Series 1 Land Rover. He had always let me steer the car, but on this occasion he simply cut the engine and got out and walked around to the passenger side, where I was seated.

"Move over" was all he said.

I slid over to the driver's seat, feeling dwarfed by the depth of the foot well and the size of the steering wheel.

"Put this under you," Dad said, handing his old bush jacket to me. Seated on the jacket, I could reach the pedals and look through the gaps in the center of the wheel to see the road.

"Okay, now just listen and do what I say. Clutch, brake, accelerator. Left leg drives clutch and nothing else, right leg drives gas and brake. Got it?"

"Got it," I repeated.

"Say it back to me," he said. I did. "Right, clutch in," he directed. By pulling against the steering wheel, I had just enough strength to compress the clutch.

"Okay . . . give it a little bit of gas." I jammed my right leg down. "Too much. Less, less . . . that's right. Now slowly let the clutch out." He gripped my left knee to control the speed at which I could release the clutch.

The car started to splutter forward. Dad pressed his other hand down really lightly on my right leg to hit the gas. The sound of the engine changed, and I felt the car begin to move honestly forward.

"There you go," he said. "Now let go of the clutch; if I catch you riding it, I'll flick your ear. You're driving." He smiled. "Clutch in, foot off the gas. . . . Second gear." He pulled the stick back, and the old Landi gave a little skip. "Right, you're in control."

Dad made a big show of leaning back in his seat and pretending to go to sleep. We chugged along, the swaths of thick brown grass brushing against the Landi's underside as impalas darted across the road. I was driving; it was no big deal. Dad had made the transition elegant and simple. And without saying a word, he had told me how much he trusted me. Driving was for adults, and with simple, calm instruction, in less than ten minutes, he had turned me into one. Dad had a way of making you feel more grown-up than you were. He never made the challenge too much of a big deal. He simply acted like it was normal, and you knew he wouldn't let you fail.

The front garden, where Bron and I played, was about as close to a literal Eden as I could ever imagine. The green grass—something my mother had struggled to create in the harsh, dry conditions—was an animal haven. Our lawn mower was a small group of warthogs that came in to graze, folding their hooves back so they could walk on their knees as they clipped the short grass into a golf-ready green. Woodland kingfishers nested in the big knobthorn tree, the central feature of the garden. Their arrival in summer was an occasion for celebration. Bron and I spent long hours watching them burst out of the holes in the thorn tree in a turquoise flurry of flapping, use their long, sharp red beaks to collect batches of insects, then return to their nests amid chirps of delight from within.

The nyalas, with their comical dashes of white war paint, and the sweet-faced bushbucks also liked to spend time with us in the garden; they enjoyed snacking on the trees Mom had so painstakingly planted. They became so friendly with us that we were able to walk closely by them with no more reaction than a brief pause from their chewing on some leafy shrub. To look into the eyes of the antelope is to truly see the gentle nature of the animals.

A blue-headed agama lizard lived in the nearby acacia tree. Every time anyone approached, he scrabbled up the trunk in a flash of beaded cerulean. Once up the tree, he bobbed his head slightly, as if waiting for our approval of his climbing skills.

The francolins strutted around like they owned the place. Mom called them her "fat friends," but Bronwyn complained that they woke her each morning with their raucous calls outside her window. The jewel-toned sunbirds locked onto the shibodi aloes, looking like green-and-red tracers of light as they darted from one nectar-laden bloom to the next.

Tortoises periodically made the epic crossing of the garden in search of a new flower bed to feast on. The vervet monkeys who lived in the nearby ebony trees occasionally jumped onto their backs for a shell ride.

We had plenty of other regular visitors, of course. The lions mated outside the room where we played poker. A certain hyena began making periodic appearances at the dinner buffet, hauling off great wedges of Gorgonzola in her massive jaws. We dubbed her Gorgy. "Bloody Gorgy!" huffed the head chef. "She's killing my budget!"

As I got older, my perspective shifted. Humans were supposedly here to watch the animals, but I couldn't shake the feeling that they were watching us.

Growing up amid this extraordinary open-air menagerie, Bron and I nevertheless longed for the touch of normalcy we read about in books and saw on television: a pet. Our parents refused, doubtless convinced that any such animal would be eaten instantly. So Bron and I treated every tortoise we came across in the bush as our pet. At one stage we turned the empty plastic pool in the garden into our secret terrarium and stashed every tortoise we found in there, only to discover that tortoises, despite their cumbersome appearance, are incredible escape artists. We once spotted one of our prisoners scaling a chicken-wire fence, placing each oval, horned foot into a circular segment of wire and then heaving himself up like an agile rock climber. We soon got bored to tears with our shelled companions; a tortoise as a pet is about as riveting as a salmon on ice.

Bron was forever trying to nurture the birds that flew into the glass windowpanes of our home and injured themselves. We tended to them with the intensity of world-class neurosurgeons, Bron's concerned, focused little face peering down at the patient between the curtains of her chocolate hair. All the birds died, despite our efforts to funnel gallons of sugar water down their throats. This mystified us, since our mother had inculcated in us a rabid belief in the placebo effect of sugar water to cure anything.

Eventually, after years of hectoring our parents, Bronwyn was finally allowed to keep an orphaned squirrel. Naturally enough, she called him Nuts. She fed him biscuits and fruit. She rubbed his stomach with a warm facecloth, the way his mother would have licked his tummy out in the wild to help his digestion. She made him a cozy bed in a laundry basket filled with soft rags. Ecstatic after all that time of not being able to have a pet, Bron channeled years of pent-up girlish love into that little squirrel, cuddling him like the bush's own version of Tiny Toons' Elmyra Duff: "I'm gonna hug you and kiss you and love you forever!" She followed him fretfully as he scampered around the living room, stopping only to investigate someone's ear as if it were a hole in a tree that he might like to sleep in. Nuts eventually met his final reward when he leapt out of his laundry basket and was mistaken for a rat by a Shangaan housekeeper, who thought she was being helpful when she malleted him with the back of her feather duster.

The depression that descended on the Varty household was thick and bleak. Dad attempted a lecture on the nature of life and death, but he stopped when Bron howled in a bloodcurdling voice, "He was so innocent . . . innnoooooceeeeeent!"

Finally my parents could deny Bron no more, and they agreed to break all the rules and get her a dog. "Dogs can be useful as an early warning system in the bush," Dad conceded. "But don't expect me to do any of the work; a pet is a big responsibility."

We selected Tatty—short for Taittinger, as in the French Champagne—out of a squirming litter of golden retriever puppies because a swirl of soft fur on her head made her look as if God had laid his finger on her.

Tatty certainly was a blessing. She was four fluffy, golden legs of love.

When she was happy, which was all the time, she wagged her whole body, not just her tail. It took all of us about thirty seconds to fall totally in love with her. Dad, naturally, fell the hardest.

Tatty was a terrible watchdog. Bron and I joked that we would know there were intruders because her tail wagged even more exuberantly than usual. In fact, we spent far more time watching over her than she did over us. When she went out after dark, we had to constantly protect her from any dangers that might be lurking about, like the leopards that wouldn't have thought twice about turning her into a late-night snack.

Tatty's only great success was guarding a pair of Dad's old gum boots on the front steps from Gorgy the hyena, who tried to teethe on them nightly. She would lie behind the screen door that led to the front porch all night, panting in the heat like a reliable generator. Then she'd let out her most deadly bark—a dainty "woof"—if Gorgy showed. This would send Dad leaping out of bed to investigate, clad only in his underpants.

Tatty adored me and Bron, but she reserved her greatest love for two things: my father and buffalo dung. She could find a steaming pile of dung anywhere. And when she did, she would wallow in it passionately, her glee indescribable. But her remorse was clear on her face when she padded back toward the house.

"Taaaaattyyyyyy?" Dad remonstrated, and Tatty's ears flopped low. "Taaaaaaaaaaaaaaattyyyyyy?" Her head dropped to inches above the ground. Then Dad lowered the boom: "Tatty, you're a naughty dog." He'd inevitably be the one to hose her down under the acacia tree. Her expression throughout the scrub-down bespoke both remorse and a defiant streak that suggested she'd do it again in a second. After she was cleaned up, she'd bestow her favorite token of apology on one of our laps: a sock she'd stolen from the wash. How could we not forgive her?

Tatty was a huge pet upgrade from our tortoises and squirrel. She took commands. The most we'd ever been able to hope for from Nuts was that he'd scamper toward a proffered cookie and take it from us. Tatty gave us all a sense that she loved us profoundly, a feeling one never gets from a pet tortoise. Living with Tatty was an experience in our own home that echoed what we were seeing in abundance around us. We didn't hold dominion over nature; we and the animals *were* nature. Our ability to survive and flourish depended on that understanding.

———

Bron and I grew up magnetized by two polarities: we were rooted to our own piece of earth, yet we knew that in Africa all manner of circumstance could snatch it from us in a moment.

Dad turned even a casual campout in the bush into an important life lesson about these uncertainties. "Tonight we're sleeping out," he'd tell us before heading off to work. Bron and I would spend the entire day collecting firewood, sleeping bags, mattresses. He'd get home at half past four and we'd head out deep into the bush, finding a patch of open ground so we would have a clear view all around. We'd make a huge production out of setting up camp and the beds, then starting a fire to cook our boerewors sausages and cornmeal pap, all slathered with "train wreck"—a tomato-and-onion gravy. Then Dad would make us take turns on watch. Bron and I would alternate sitting up by the fire with a flashlight, keeping an eye out for hyenas or other dangers.

When I was on watch, I felt I was the only person awake in the world. The darkness amplified each sound, but I needed to keep my wits about me. I didn't want to be the one to bother Dad for an embarrassing non-event like a scrub hare bounding toward me. If Bron or I did see a hyena prowling close, we'd wake up Dad to chase it away. Now and again, an elephant would break a branch, which would snap like a pistol shot through the cool night. The scops owls would unleash their "prrrr" every ten seconds, like a perfect nighttime metronome. Just outside the glow of the fire, I would watch the sparks return to their home amid the stars . . . or that's the story I would tell myself. I felt an overwhelming sense of place on the earth in what others might call isolation.

———

Like our ancestors before us, Bron and I subscribe to the belief that you die "when your number's up" or through some Newtonian physics unique to the bush: "He was pushing it, and you can push it in Africa for only so long." Our upbringing has given us a lifelong habit of being on the lookout for where things might go wrong. Even now we'll be at a pool party amid the merry tinkling of ice in glasses and the chatter of guests mingling, laughing, drinking—and we'll be prepping for the inevitable disaster, thinking, "Right. If this one gets too pissed and falls into the pool, we can do this, then this, then that." This is the nature of growing up in the safari business. There is such a thing as being *too* self-sufficient. It's hard to be lighthearted and in the moment when you're always making contingency plans.

Bron and I bathed in that culture of coping and getting on with it. By our standards, we weren't in danger. We were Africans.

SIX

UNCLE JOHN

"FASTER, FASTER! FUCK, NOT SO FAST! . . . Left . . . no, right! Right! . . . No, *left*!" I jerked the steering wheel left and right, trying to follow the confused instructions Uncle John barked from his unsteady stance in the rear of the old Land Cruiser. An accomplished wildlife documentarian, he was trying to get some good footage of a hyena feasting on a giraffe, using the heavy camera he'd set up on a tripod in the back of the truck. Once the hyena picked up the giraffe's leg and began to tear across the clearing, he ordered me to gun it in hot pursuit.

Branches smashed into the sides of the Cruiser, gouging deep scratches in the paint. With his usual torn clothing and his hat flaps whipping in the wind, Uncle John was part drill sergeant, part captain of a ramshackle pirate ship. "Faster, Boyd, faster! Jesus, right, right, *right*!" He was clearly enjoying himself; pursuit of animals across the wilderness is his passion.

Then the inevitable happened. He screamed "right!" and I turned left. His arms flailed as his calves caught the side of the pickup and he toppled backward, pulling the camera and tripod with him. I heard a crunch as he hit the ground. "Bloody Arab!" he shrieked at me, following up with more vicious insults as he chased me around the truck. Eventually he calmed down and wandered off to retrieve his handgun, which had fallen out of his holster in the melee. From that day on I wore a bangle on my right wrist so I would never again confuse left and right.

In my defense, I *was* only eight at the time. And even though I'd been fielding Uncle John's requests to be his filming assistant for years by then and, like many farm boys, I was quite good behind the wheel, it wasn't always easy to see over the dash, even with a jacket or cushion on the seat.

———

Uncle John became a filmmaker because he'd gotten tired of driving guests around—"Have to be too fucking nice to them all the time, buddy." While the rest of my family enjoyed interacting with the guests, he hated catering to their demands, and even more he hated always getting grass seeds in his eyes as the Landi patrolled the dusty paths. He'd taken to strapping on swimming goggles to protect himself, a bizarre look that failed to endear him to our visitors.

"I can't take another game drive," Uncle John moaned. "Eh, this is bullshit. I'm burnt out. If I see another guest, I'm gonna kill him. How do we get fewer visitors?"

Dad pondered this. "If you want fewer people, double the price."

"Okay, let's double the price. As of tomorrow, we're doubling it." John immediately called the reservationist. "Liz, if you get any more inquiries, tell them it's going to cost twice as much." With that single act, Dad and Uncle John doubled their revenues.

Uncle John still hated catering to guests, although he showed brief interest in a new direction. One Sunday, he strode up to Dad and shook the newspaper in his face. "Dave, I need to talk to you about something." He displayed a full-page ad for something called "sex safaris." Somebody had opened a lodge with the enticing tagline "Come on safari to our lodge. *All* your needs will be taken care of."

"You know, Dave," Uncle John cackled, "we need to know about all the competition in this game. I need to go down there and check out the product. I'll come back and tell you what it's like."

He never did, but that didn't stop him from inviting every female guest around the campfire to "Come to Room 13." The lodge had only twelve rooms. "Room 13, for the complete safari experience. Part of the package—you get me!"

Uncle John was fine being the occasional campfire troubadour, but he really was fed up with guiding. His heart lay in making nature documentaries, and Dad saw that as a great way to build the Londolozi brand. He and Mom were happy to take over guesting duties while John raced around in his torn clothing, chasing the next shot.

In this new role, Uncle John leaned heavily on Elmon. Elmon was the ultimate naturalist; he'd been born under a tree next to Londolozi and grew up literally hunting and gathering off the land before any stores opened in the area. Elmon and his brother Phineas had been raised by their uncle, Engen Mhlongo, a man with an ancient knowledge of the land. Elmon knew exactly how to find and film leopards and lions.

Largely because of Elmon and the time they spent together, Uncle John is one of the greatest naturalists you will ever meet. He has a deep understanding of the way nature works, and he has a greater connection to the energy of animals and their habitat than anyone I've ever known. He has dedicated his entire life to conservation efforts, especially by documenting animals in the wild, long before Steve Irwin made being close to dangerous animals cool. And when I say "dedicated his entire life," I mean it literally. When Uncle John—also known as JV—decided to befriend a female leopard at Londolozi, he and Elmon spent more than thirteen years with her and filmed all nineteen of her cubs, some from the day they were born until the day they died. He was with Manana, that leopard matriarch, until her death. When he befriended some Masai in Kenya's Masai Mara, it grew into a seventeen-year relationship, and the documentaries he shot there—*Savage Instinct, Troubled Water,* and *The Super Predators*—have won international attention for the plight of nearly extinct animals. His latest passion is for saving the severely endangered tigers of Asia. His *Living with Tigers* is bringing new hope to the cause.

As a boy, I absolutely idolized my uncle, ripping the sleeves off my own shirts in imitation of his ratty wardrobe—what friends took to calling "JV couture"—and begging my parents for a green peaked cap just like his, with a flap that protected his ears and neck from the sun and thrashed about in the wind. Beginning at age five I became his faithful assistant, and so my most defining years were spent tracking leopards and learning to swear—something my uncle did a great deal of when he missed a good shot. The day would begin at about four a.m.: he would wake me and I would stumble around my bedroom, pulling on my torn khaki outfit and hat. Next we would devote fifteen minutes to trying to get his film Landi started, my job being to press the accelerator down when he screamed "Now!" from under the hood. Then we would fetch Elmon and go out to shoot "high-action sequences." "Buddy, we need a high-action sequence," he'd tell me as we chased after a crash of rhinos or a herd of zebras. Much more often I'd hear, "Fuck fuck, fuck, we missed that action sequence!"

My uncle's temper is renowned in the district; his Shangaan name, Ntilo, means "Thunder." I learned when I was young that the best way to stay safe during an eruption was to join in with double the vigor he was pushing out. If he threw the beanbag the camera rested on, I stomped the beanbag; if he punched a tree, I ran headfirst into it. My displays of rage seemed to surprise him. In the face of my irrationality, he became philosophical, which is the truest part of his nature.

As I've learned to my peril, there's almost nothing Uncle John won't do to get, or at least set up, the perfect shot. Once I came across him far out in the bush. He was clad in only a pair of green shorts and sandals, his trusty .30-06 rifle over his shoulder. "Hey, buddy," he said, high-fiving me. "Is that a rhino down in that clearing? Okay, let's go stalk it. What's the rule?" I chimed the answer: "When we do the stalkie, no talkie." And off we headed, down into the clearing to stalk a rhino with a rifle that would be about as effective as a pop gun if the beast charged us.

Another time he decided in the middle of the night that he needed a better location for the documentary he was making, and that he would be better served driving twelve hours through total darkness to a spot in the middle of a different province. He was faced with one problem: his only transportation was a Land Rover with no cab, no front right fender, and virtually no ability to turn any direction but left. He wasn't deterred in the slightest. I watched him load the truck's bed with so much crap that it looked like the Beverly Hillbillies were having a garage sale.

Rain began to fall as he wired a broken side mirror from an old Opel Kadett onto the flip-up windshield and duct-taped an old license plate onto the grid on the front of the vehicle. By this time, the rain was pounding down. He ducked into his house, then emerged thirty minutes later wearing every item of clothing he owned, as well as a welding helmet he planned to use as a combination crash helmet and rain visor. The only problem was that what he gained in facial protection he lost in visual acuity, as the combination of the dark glass goggles and the Land Rover's faint headlights rendered him blind as a bat. He strapped a hyena-chewed tarp over the entire contents of the pickup but had only enough rope to tie one side down. He then boarded his craft looking like a portly, sodden Darth Vader and proceeded to power off down the muddy drive, engine roaring and tarp slapping and whumping. He got stuck about forty yards from his house. This sent him into a blind rage that ended with the right-hand tire taking the brunt of a savage beating. It also confirmed for me that one should never start a Land Rover journey if the only positive you can think of is "the gearbox heat will keep me warm."

Perhaps the greatest testament to Mom's unflappability was her trial by fire during Uncle John's most outlandish brainstorm, *Bush School.* He figured that the best way to educate kids about nature would be to create a TV series built around kids living the experience. At the time, Mom was running the small nursery school at Londolozi, which Bron and I attended with some older village kids. Her curriculum was the usual arts and crafts, storytime, and snacks appropriate for six-, seven-, and eight-year-olds, and because she was the local teacher, Uncle John naturally asked her to be the star of the show. What he failed to mention was that by extension she would have to anchor and present a twelve-part series with no previous TV experience.

The sketchily conceived show was typical of Uncle John's scattershot approach. With his trademark optimism, he figured he'd just gin it up, then get Dad to sell it to Disney. Just as they'd done with Londolozi, John would act as what Dad called "the tip of the spear"—he would throw himself at anything with überconfidence. Then Dad would put in the strategic business structure and, in many ways, make John's mad ideas possible. Mom, just as typically, would add structure and depth to a Varty brother's radical, off-the-cuff idea.

Mom rose to the challenge. Uncle John gave her only the most general guidelines. "Okay, today we're gonna do a show about camouflage. Say that, then say how a lot of animals camouflage themselves." He handed her a torn sheet of paper duct-taped to an old clipboard on which he'd scribbled a few suggestions: *Talk about how leopards' spots break up their outlines. Mention how insects use cryptic coloring.* "Okay, got it? Good. Now let's go." Then, right on the spot, with no script whatsoever, Mom had to fill up fifteen minutes.

Mom smiled broadly into the camera. "Now, children, today we're going to talk about camouflage. Who knows what camouflage is?"

My friend Simon Bannister raised his hand. "Well, sometimes it means, like, when an elephant walks past some eggs and it can't see them and stands on them."

Mom shot a worried glance off camera. It had just occurred to her that the kids were unscripted, too. "That's right, Simon. Camouflage is when something is in disguise and you can't see it."

Another kid piped up: "One time I saw, I saw an elephant, but then it went into the bush and I couldn't see it anymore."

"Yes, that's right," Mom said smoothly. "Did you know that an elephant's gray skin gives it ideal camouflage in the bush?" She glanced at the notes Uncle John had handed her. "Does anybody know what the word 'cryptic' means?"

A brief puzzled silence; then a girl offered, "One time we were watching TV with my gran and it was a show about a detective and the detective had to go all around and he had to solve a lot of clues and some of the clues were cryptic."

Mom took a deep breath, no doubt screaming inside her head. "Well, yes, Size, that's right. Some clues can be cryptic, but the cryptic I want to talk about is cryptic coloring, which is not really a clue, but clues can be cryptic, especially to detectives, who have to decrypt them"—Mom was in the weeds now—"but I'm not talking about detectives. I'm talking about cryptic coloring, which is when an animal blends in with the bushes and the leaves around it because its colors are similar."

Just at that moment one of the kids had a coughing fit, then nudged his buddy. "When we get home, should we play He-Man?"

"Cut!" Uncle John yelled, and we had to restart the tape so the sound would sync up.

Uncle John didn't trouble himself by explaining the how-tos of film-making to us kids, so we were baffled most of the time. We'd be told to "look as though you've seen an elephant"—the shot would be edited in later—but we never quite caught on. For one scene I had to flap around in a spider monkey outfit while Bron, having donned a hot, cumbersome gray crocodile costume, clambered along on her stomach—a tough assignment for someone with visions of Barbie and the Rockers. The days were long; we'd wake up at five a.m. and get hungry and tired as the shooting dragged on. I hated being told what to do. It made no sense to me that we'd be in the bush, the ultimate free-form paradise, and have to follow some kind of direction. I managed to screw up the whole of *Bush School* by falling down the stairs and scraping my nose. Uncle John wasn't shooting the episodes in any particular order, figuring it could all be edited later for continuity, but I foiled the plan, my face alternately clear and clotted by enormous scabs in the same scene.

Uncle John made the show in his cannonball way. Mom was surprisingly good in the series, pulling from her extensive knowledge of both the bush and child wrangling. Dad, with his almost charmed good luck, managed to sell it to Walt Disney Television. Much to everyone's astonishment—except Uncle John and Dad's—the Disney executives absolutely adored the idea and Mom. There was just one catch: they didn't want twelve parts; they wanted fifty-two. Mom gamely went back and shot forty new fifteen-minute episodes in three weeks. *Bush School* originally ran in 1993 and was seen by more than fifty million people.

———

When Uncle John wasn't filming, I watched him from the sidelines as he and Dad dominated the epic battles of Gazankulu district league soccer. Gazankulu was an endless tract of dry bush designated as a homeland for the villagers by the apartheid government. In Gazankulu League, you didn't choose which direction you'd like to play during the coin toss; you chose whether you'd like to play uphill or downhill.

The crowd, a motley crew of villagers, sat on the hoods of ramshackle cars and Land Rovers or under the branches of acacia trees and screamed and howled at the changing fortunes of the game.

"Coke, Coke, cross it, you Arab!" screamed Uncle John at Alfred Mathebula, the barman, a.k.a. Coke.

Uncle John was the center forward by declaration: "Buddy, center forward, that's the position for us! Gotta be where the action is!" His soccer cleats had seen so much play on the stony fields that the studs were worn flat; they were as slick as ice skates on the gravel pitch.

Dad had a reputation for shoulder charging and spoiling. He would scream up the right lane in a pair of Adidas sneakers with a hole at the toe. The ultimate wingman, he was supposed to make a great cross to where John waited at the goal mouth. "Pass! Pass! Pass!" John would scream. He was so desperate to score that he wasn't above using his fist or elbow, squelching the opponents' appeals to the referee—Dad doing double duty—with a "Bugger off, it's a goal." This inevitably provoked a game stoppage as the other team sat down in protest, which only incited another shouting match—and then a staff walkout the next day if John had been particularly obnoxious.

Occasionally the rangers from the nearby MalaMala Game Reserve would come to play. Once when MalaMala prevailed, Uncle John was so angry that he canceled their transportation home, saying, "You guys can walk." The guests on the afternoon wildlife-viewing drives that day encountered a fifteen-man squad with socks sagging around their ankles, heading east through the bush. If, God forbid, a guest joined the game and played against John, all bets were off. Even if the guest was a most valued customer, the owner of the Taj Mahal, and had flown halfway across the world, Uncle John would trample or punch him in his quest to get a sack of tanned leather into the goal.

I loved watching Dad hit his great looping crosses, which Uncle John would pounce on for goals. The brothers had a natural cohesion that produced results. If there was a penalty shot to be taken, Uncle John would sub a player out and put a six- or seven-year-old Boyd Varty on the field.

"Okay, buddy, just like we practiced," he'd say, setting the ball on the penalty spot. In the garden, we'd rehearsed a move called "double dummy," which was him running over and pretending to take the shot and me following and actually hitting the ball in. He trusted me, he put me on the line, and he let me go for it. It worked. When Uncle John called me onto the field from the backseat of the Land Rover, parked askew under a tree, I would see myself as a man, forgetting for a moment that I was so young, the way some small dogs have no sense of their size.

———

Around Dad and Uncle John, anything seemed possible. Once, in Johannesburg, our family car, a Mercedes, was stolen. Most people in South Africa in the early nineties would have simply accepted this as a reality of living in a country whose metropolitan areas had a high crime rate. Not Dad and Uncle John. A week later, Dad got a phone call from an unknown woman. "I'm not going to tell you what my name is, but I know you Vartys from the films you make, and I want to let you know that your car is in a house next door to me where some bad people live." She'd looked at the registration and tracked Dad down.

Dad phoned Uncle John. "Hey, John, listen, the car's been stolen. Can you get to this address?" John clapped a .44 Magnum onto his hip. That .44 Magnum is the central feature of Uncle John's life and, indeed, a symbol for his maverick character. Next he commandeered a tow truck. "You're hired," he told the driver. "Follow me." John arranged for the head of security at Londolozi to meet him at the address. Meanwhile, Dad phoned a friend who flew a medevac helicopter: "Fly to this place and see if you can locate the Mercedes." "Ya, I can see it." "Well, hold in your position." Dad started feeding directions to John, who arrived on the scene like Dirty Harry with a tow truck. With the helicopter hovering overhead, John hooked our car up to the tow truck and sped away.

———

Uncle John made me grow up fast. He would decide that he needed footage of an incredibly dangerous situation—say, a wounded hippo. "Buddy,

I'm gonna go in there and try and get the shot," he'd say, passing me the rifle. "If something happens to me, I'm relying on you." When I was ten, he handed me a panga as we prepared to barrel through a crowded town with our Landi laden with expensive camera equipment. "Buddy, anyone tries to grab anything, you just bash 'em with this."

Bron has the best description of Uncle John: "He'd get you involved in a war, then be the only person who could get you out." There was no doubt that he absolutely adored me and Bron. He didn't have kids of his own until he was in his forties, so he happily took us on many of his adventures.

As should be abundantly clear by now, nothing is impossible if Uncle John sets his mind to it. When he decided he wanted to make a movie about raising two leopard cubs, Little Boy and Little Girl, he ended up starring in it himself, with Brooke Shields. I can't say that *Running Wild* was the perfect showcase for Uncle John's dramatic skills, but it did feature some amazing footage of baby leopards, not to mention a splendid scene of John throwing himself into the Mara River and trying in vain to rescue the male cub from the jaws of a crocodile, all the time wailing, "Come back, my beautiful boy, come back!"

Uncle John's showmanship and maverick flair may put him in the limelight, but that's not where his heart is. His heart is, and will always be, with the animals. In his forties, he met Gillian van Houten, a prominent news broadcaster, who became his life partner. He picked me and Bron up and took us on his first date with her, at a burger joint in Johannesburg. Shortly thereafter, Gillian moved to the bush and they started living together. Not a year later, he found a lion cub whose mother had abandoned it just hours after the cub's birth. He named her Shingalana, which is Shangaan for "little lion." John's love and devotion to Shingalana were instantaneous and total. After only the briefest consultation, he and Gillian decided to raise her, knowing that with this one spontaneous act, they'd made a many-years-long commitment.

Lions are pride animals and bond very strongly with the people who raise them. Shingi grew deeply fond of Uncle John, Gillian, and all of us who played with her. By the time she was fully grown, it was not uncommon for this four-hundred-pound lioness to doze on you lovingly, just as she'd do in the wild with her pride.

Shingi was hugely mischievous. One night, I was walking from the kitchen tent to the fireside with a bowl of popcorn. Out of nowhere, Shingi, who I thought was in her sleeping enclosure, hit me like a ton of bricks. She was then about 120 pounds; at ten or eleven, I was only about 90. As I sprayed popcorn in mid-collapse, I remember thinking, "Please, God, let this be Shingi" and not a wild lion that had decided he liked his people seasoned with a fine layer of popcorn salt.

When Shingi got bigger, Uncle John and Gillian relocated her into the bush in the remote Luangwa Valley, in Zambia, to give her more space. As Shingi started to catch her own game, she presented a serious hygiene issue, as she liked to drag her carcasses into the tent and feed on the comfort of the bedspread. Maybe your house cat likes to bring chipmunks in for you, which is problem enough, but having a 170-pound puku sprawled across your pillow can be a little challenging. It never seemed to faze Uncle John.

Uncle John's relationship with the leopard cubs certainly changed his scientific view of nature into something with softer lines, but feeling himself a part of Shingi's pride truly solidified the idea of the deep kinship between people and animals. His time with Shingi marked a shift in direction for him and, as well, for the philosophy that would become a huge part of Londolozi.

Although Dad and Uncle John had schooled me in the idea of being an outside observer of nature, the concept hadn't had time to gain any traction before I found myself running down a dry riverbed with a poodle-sized Shingi in pursuit. It was proof of what I'd always known deep down: that some members of my family weren't human.

Uncle John was a dreamer, often a reckless one, and in his own wacky way, when you least expected it, he was incredibly generous and big-hearted. I was in his car once when he stopped by the side of the road so he could buy the entire sad load of wilted flowers from a vendor. "Sometimes you just gotta help a guy out," he told me.

My fondest memories of my early days with Uncle John are of the two of us singing songs together as we returned from a successful morning of filming. Uncle John would be at the wheel, his hat blowing in the breeze, chucking sections of sour naartjie fruit into his mouth as we belted out Elton John and Tim Rice's "Circle of Life," from *The Lion King*. My job was to join in on the chorus to provide the song with more oomph to combat the rushing wind of the open Land Rover. After years of doing this, I became conditioned to the routine that once the work out in the bush is done, one has a good sing as one heads for camp. This has meant some strange moments when I've absentmindedly belted out a tune on the way back from a game drive, only to turn around and see the shocked faces of guests never before treated to the Wheatus version of "A Little Respect."

Uncle John can play any song with the four guitar chords he knows. Most of the love songs he's written have been about the cats he's worked with. When he got malaria and was forced to leave Zambia for a while, Shingi swam alongside the boat that transported him across the river to where a Land Rover was waiting. She then trotted along-side the Landi just like a dog for as long as she could. Maybe you could say my uncle was the love of her life. Each evening Shingi would walk out onto the sand at the edge of the water and watch the far bank as the sky turned to powdery watercolors. She was waiting for his return.

One day while he was walking her, Uncle John and Shingi were at-tacked by four lionesses intent on killing them both. When one of the lionesses made a fierce charge at Uncle John, Shingi ran out in front of him to take the brunt of the attack and ended up in a brutal fight. Uncle

John tried to break it up with his whip. Shingi saved Uncle John by meeting the lioness's charge, and my uncle saved her by going in with the whip. Sadly, later there was a second attack, and Shingi died of her wounds. Shingi was his great love. There is no doubt in my mind that a part of my uncle died with her.

SEVEN

THE FLYING LIFE

THE BEECHCRAFT BARON, a twin-engine plane, is a trusty six-seater, but Mom's best friend, Anthea, was a nervous flier, so Mom was doing her best to keep up a distracting stream of chatter during the brief flight from Mkuze, in the Natal Province, in eastern South Africa, to Richards Bay, ninety miles away, a typically African puddle jump. Dad was riding up front with the charter pilot. Mom was in one of the backward-facing seats behind him, facing Anthea, who was sitting in the back row, facing forward. In a blink they were on "long finals," perhaps eight or ten miles away from the final approach to the runway. Suddenly there was a great explosion—BHAA!—and Anthea was covered with guts and feathers and a bit of wing, which clung to her head like an awkward hat, as though someone had lobbed a blenderful of bird over her. Mom, confused—why was her neck wet? what was that howling sound?—turned around. Wind was now roaring through a huge hole in the cockpit window. The pilot was conked out in his seat, his lap full of shattered glass, his temple impaled by the beak of a woolly-necked stork, its severed head and neck plastered limply to the side of his face.

Woolly-necked storks are huge birds, standing about three feet high, with skinny pipestem legs, huge black bodies, and thickly feathered, long white necks. When they collide with a plane in midflight, there's a lot of wealth to spread around. It was a bloodbath straight out of *Pulp Fiction*.

"We're gonna die!" Anthea screamed, clutching Mom's thigh in a death grip. "We're gonna die!" Mom gave her the patented Mom slap. "Shut up! We're not gonna die! I won't let us!"

Dad, who was also completely strewn with bird parts, seized the controls. Mom calmly reached into her bag and pulled out, of all things, a flying checklist—typical Shan. She twisted around to give it to Dad. When the pilot came to, he pulled the beak out of his temple and groggily retook the controls as Dad meticulously went through the list. "Rate of descent?" Check. "Throttle?" Check. "Fifteen degrees flap." Check. "Call the tower for a priority emergency landing." Check.

They got the plane in, climbed out shakily, and wordlessly made their way to the washrooms to tidy up. All in a day's flight with the Varty family.

Flying had entered our lives once Bron turned six and had to go to "big school." Up to that time, Mom had homeschooled her at the Londolozi nursery school; now Bron would need to begin a more formal education in Johannesburg. Mom and Dad had a grand vision of puddle jumping between Joburg and Londoz. If they learned to fly, an hour and forty minutes in the air and they'd be back in the bush. Besides, Grandpa Boyd, who'd been a member of the South African Air Force, believed that flying was one of those things that defined a life.

So off Mom and Dad went, to get their own flight training. (Uncle John also took up flying, but he gave up when he forgot the clipboard with the checklist on the dash one day and it flew through the back window as he began to lift off.)

Mom and Dad's grand vision of the Vartys in flight went off more or less as planned, with "less" perhaps being the operative word. Their philosophy continued to be "Ready. Fire. Aim!" The fact that my parents were barely competent behind the controls and had chosen to put us at what the posh northern suburbs called "undue risk" seemed to have escaped them. On Friday afternoons they would pick us up from our primary school, where I'd joined Bron. During the week, we'd stay in town in Johannesburg, sometimes with Mom, sometimes with Dad, sometimes with our grandparents. Reunited with both our parents for the half-hour drive out to the airport, we'd be allowed a brief greeting before being banished to the realms of silence—or, as my parents called it, "Flying Mode." Bron and I were bursting to talk about our school week, but our parents enforced silence, mentally buckling down for the flight, no doubt wrapped in the terror of it all and murmuring the prayer of all pilots without many flight hours under their belts: "Please, God, let it fly." Any attempt to redirect their attention—"Mom, I'm hungry, could I have a sandwich?"—would earn us a warning glare. "*Quiet!* We're in Flying Mode!" It was a crime to speak, and in doing so we were likely to be the sole cause of all danger associated with this situation. In fact, our parents seemed rather happy to lay the likely cause of a calamity squarely at the door of their two young children for a few words from the backseat rather than on their own highly dodgy ability to fly.

At the airport, we'd board our four-seater Cessna 182, nicknamed Rio for her call sign: Romeo India Oscar. Rio smelled like petrol in the back because Mom or Dad would test the fuel in the gas tank before takeoff, then toss the gauge back between our seats; the pungent odor almost made us vomit. Once we were airborne, Flying Mode was even more strictly enforced as our parents took turns consulting the maps and reading off the flight checklist to each other. The puddle hops went off largely without incident, except for the time a lone impala broke out of the woodlands and bounded across the runway just as we were coming home to Londoz. We narrowly missed hitting it head-on, which could have been disastrous, but we heard a loud thunk as it connected with the wheel skid. By the time Rio stopped, Uncle John, who'd driven out to greet us, was already loading it onto the back of his Land Rover for dinner.

Rio's longer exploits weren't always so fortunate.

We were coming home from a family vacation at Lake Kariba, in Zimbabwe. The week had seemed promising at the beginning. We'd be taking motorboats out onto the lake and fishing for tigerfish, orange-finned, dark-striped monsters with great long teeth and an outsized reputation for fighting. The reality was a bit disappointing. The five exciting minutes of powering out in the motorboat to the middle of the lake were followed by ten boring hours listening to the grown-ups talk and drink. Bron and I were forced to wear big puffy orange life vests the entire time. The vests reeked of mildew, it was stinking hot, and we couldn't swim because of the crocs.

I was relieved when it was time to climb into Rio and head for home. We stopped in Harare to refuel. About a half hour later, somewhere around Masvingo, we heard an ominous sputter, and the engine started to run rough. I didn't understand it at the time, but this was a seriously bad scene—it meant the engine could cut out at any moment.

"Put your life jackets on!" Mom shouted at us.

Bron looked out the window. As far as we could tell, the plane was flying in a perfectly normal way. Also, Zimbabwe is landlocked—red earth as far as the eye can see. "Why?" my sister asked. "What's going on?"

Big mistake. We'd made the critical error of not reacting immediately to the Flying Voice. When you're in Flying Mode, you just do what you're told and shut up. Mom's arm came around like a serpent, striking indiscriminately at whatever it could reach. This is the best description of my family I can find: we go down slapping. "You kids just put your life jackets on!"

Bron and I began struggling with the straps and buckles. Mom felt around behind her seat and snatched up the blue-and-white checkered cheesecloth pillows our grandmother had embroidered—"Bron" in blue and "Boyd" in red—which we always took along while flying, for naps. Mom jammed them onto our laps. "PUT YOUR HEADS DOWN!"

"What?"

"PUT YOUR HEADS ON YOUR PILLOWS! BRACE POSI-
TION!"

This was Mom and Dad's first major air crisis, and they were going
to handle it. They'd have to call in an emergency landing to Zimbabwe
air traffic control. Dad positioned Rio to "trim for glide," which meant
putting her nose down so that the plane would start to descend, allowing
us to gain speed and get lift so that we would keep flying even as we
steadily lost altitude. They prepared for a forced landing. That meant
picking a spot where they thought they could get the plane in without
hitting a tree or rocks or water—and manage to arrive just as the plane
was running out of speed. Too high, and they'd miss it. Too low, and
we'd be in the trees. Or they could "dead-stick" it—that is, hope to glide
without power—to the nearest runway. Those were the choices.

Bron and I could tell that things in the cockpit were starting to heat
up. Mom had the map out and was attempting to work out their route
with her protractor—two degrees wrong, and we'd be miles off course.
Dad was looking around, trying to figure out if we could make it to a
runway in Masvingo.

"Hold on to your false teeth!" Mom called back to us. To this day, I
have no idea where that came from.

Somehow they got Rio down, on a sad little grass airstrip in Masvingo
where the windsock hung completely limp. There wasn't even an air
traffic controller. We all sat silently, staring at each other. Then Mom
herded us out of Rio and under the wing of the plane, the only shade
available. Dad disappeared and somehow managed to find a mechanic to
look at the plane. Somewhat anticlimactically, once the mechanic had
fixed the problem, we got back in and headed home.

Whenever you're in a situation that's going wrong, you can't help
thinking how silly you were to get involved with it in the first place. I
wonder what went through Mom and Dad's minds while Rio's engine
was running rough. Did they ever think, "Why are we flying our precious children around Africa in a biscuit tin?" At the time, they seemed

so supremely confident that it never dawned on me that they'd put us in danger. My parents had a pioneering spirit, and like all pioneers, they measured risk against the vision of the life they wanted for all of us. Given a choice between playing it safe and fulfilling that vision, they chose the latter.

My parents finally upgraded us, from Rio to MTV (Mike Tango Victor), a Cessna 210—a faster plane with six seats. MTV had a singular quirk: a tiny bit of the throttle stayed on after you cut it just as you touched ground, so there was still a little bleed of power. The plane would slow but would not stop completely unless you gave it another hard yank. This slipped Mom's mind once as we hit the airstrip at Londoz. She was standing on the brake with all her might, the stick pulled back, the throttle off—and *the plane wouldn't stop*. We were quickly running out of runway. Dad sat beside her, screaming, "Brakes! Brakes! Brakes!" Mom made a split-second decision and steered MTV into a marula tree, crumpling the front and wing—and stopping the plane.

Why hadn't my dad simply yanked on the throttle or told Mom to do it? Because he wasn't "pilot in command." From the moment you've buckled yourself into the cockpit, it needs to be crystal clear who's in charge. The pilot in command makes all the decisions, and in an emergency, you need one person to get the plane on the ground. Mom and Dad had learned this lesson early on and were absolute sticklers about it. Whenever they'd hand over the controls, they'd confirm, "You have control." "Pilot in command" is also an operating theme in their marriage. There's conflict when one strays into the other's area of command. If Dad starts telling Mom how to host lodge guests, or if Mom starts to tell Dad what time he should go on a game drive with them, you can rest assured that a storm will be brewing.

Twenty years later, Mom still relishes Dad's retelling of the forced lob into Masvingo, but any mention from him of the marula tree crash can fire up a punch-up of unspeakable proportions. "You were pilot in command!" Dad protests. "I fully understand that," Mom responds frostily, "but seconds before we hit the tree, you might have pulled on the throttle." "Well, you were pilot in command!" "But we hit the tree!" Two decades hasn't washed away the reproach.

———

Having grown up with all these near misses, I'm a very nervous passenger. Ironically, I'm even more afraid in commercial planes, as I feel more out of control; at least in a small plane, I could fumble with the controls on the way to death. I'm a wreck around takeoff and landing. If the engine changes pitch, I'll vault out of a sleeping pill–induced nap to full red alert. You'd think that I'd be used to it, but when you've hit an impala, a marula tree, and a vulture in a small aircraft—once, on the way back from Joburg to Londoz, we looked up and there was a pair of vulture legs sticking out like two-taloned turkey drumsticks from the front curve of the wing—you start to get a bit jittery.

The other thing that makes me a nervous passenger, particularly on large African airlines, is the fact that I've been in a number of African repair shops. I know how "cannaking"—mechanical repair—works in Africa. A certain rhythm must be followed at all times. Everyone must stand around the broken mechanism, staring at it for a very long time. This action must be accompanied by a lot of head scratching and tire kicking. Next a guy called Velhaphi—and there is always an outback mechanic called Velhaphi in any bush workshop—will suggest that "it is impossible to fix this situation." This pronouncement will be followed by some debate. Then, after another ten minutes of deliberation, it will suddenly be hit upon that, in fact, the entire problem can be solved using strawberry jam and a beer can—but just for "temp." African people are incredibly resourceful; someone will always come up with some left-field plan. I've seen this little drama play out with all manner of African mechanical creatures, from water pumps to tractors. I would be very surprised if a similar situation isn't playing out in a Congolese airline's repair shop as we speak. It's a testament to Africans' unsurpassable hope and ingenuity, and the reality that things are usually falling apart.

Time has made my parents more circumspect about living literally on the fly. My mother, in particular, no longer seems to want the stress of trying to work it out as you go along. Nowadays she would rather just drive herself somewhere than get involved in some Varty aviation scheme. My father . . . well, he knows a lot more, knows the dangers better, and still gets in the plane and trusts himself. I don't think his spirit will allow him anything else. The word "irrepressible" comes to mind, even if something in his eyes now speaks of a little doubt. Mom still flies with him, though truly and justifiably scared. For them, now as ever, dying together beats living apart.

EIGHT

MADIBA

"A VERY GREAT MAN WILL be visiting us," Dad told me. "Some-one who's going to change our country." A major figure in the African National Congress was coming to Londolozi. I expected some-one dressed in a sharp suit, his eyes hidden behind designer sunglasses. Yet when I walked into Nelson Mandela's bedroom with the breakfast tray, I found no stiff head of state but a warm, unaffected man.

Mandela sat up, and I put the tray next to him. He thanked me gra-ciously and began chatting about the previous night's game drive: "Oh, last night we had an amazing time. We saw a leopard. We saw it jump onto the back of a buck."

The man we all called Madiba (his family tribal name) radiated hu-mility, walking the grounds in a beat-up boxer's T-shirt, old tracksuit pants, and scuffed slippers. He was still trying to adjust to his immense stature after being released from twenty-seven years of isolation, most of it in a cramped coffin of a ten-by-ten cell on Robben Island. His inno-cence had been utterly destroyed by forces of which I was then blissfully ignorant, yet somehow during that unjust imprisonment, he had restored his own soul.

It was 1990. Mandela had become one of the most famous and inspiring people in the world, yet parts of him were still deeply imbedded in his years of prison life. People close to him within the ANC realized that he needed a period of adjustment and recovery. Enos Mabuza, an activist who had been close with my family for years, believed that Londoz, where apartheid's tentacles had never reached, would be the perfect place for Mandela to relax. Most important, if the people wanted to put themselves in his path, they'd risk getting eaten—an unusually compelling deterrent.

Three months after his release from prison, Mandela paid the first of many visits to our reserve. At first he stayed in one of the guest chalets, but once he became more comfortable with the place, he preferred the quiet of our family cottage, where the accommodations were far more modest: a bed and a bookshelf. He liked the simplicity and being away from the hustle and bustle of the camp. He fell into a nice routine each morning: he would sleep in and then have a late breakfast with my uncle. Having already returned from an early morning's filming, Uncle John would sit at the head of a large stinkwood table, pour his muesli, and cut a very ripe banana into it. In true JV style, Uncle John treated Mandela exactly the same as he treated everyone else: as an equal and a friend. I have no doubt that if Mandela had been out in the bush during an amazing action sequence, Uncle John would have made him a camera assistant. Nelson would sit to John's left with a plate of fruit, and they would discuss recent events on the reserve, including the highlights of the morning's footage and the animal sightings from Mandela's latest game drive, which never failed to enchant him. I joined them often, although I can't say that, at age seven, I fully appreciated what momentous occasions these were.

A few weeks into this routine, Mandela invited Uncle John to join him for a more official lunch at the camp with some ANC members who had come to the reserve to see him. Once again, I expected sharp suits, but these men were dressed in typical strugglewear: jeans and black leather jackets, more like union leaders than politicians. From the time they arrived on the front deck of the camp, it was clear that this was an event beyond the casual breakfast-in-slippers routine. When it came time to be seated, Uncle John, in a rare moment of tact, headed for a side seat at the table. Nelson stopped the proceedings. "No, John," he said in his gracious way. "I would never take your place at the head. Please come and sit here."

Whenever I went into the village with Mandela, it was clear just how important he was. People flocked around him, not in a mobbing way but at a respectful remove. Everyone just wanted to drink in his peaceful presence. Years later, when Oprah Winfrey asked him to be on her show, he agreed, then asked, "What will it be about?" He didn't seem to comprehend that viewers would be on the edge of their seats, waiting to hear the story of a man unjustly imprisoned for twenty-seven years, who upon being freed immediately reconciled with his jailers and guided a reunited country toward freedom.

Madiba was at Londolozi at the start of the CODESA talks between the ANC and the National Party, of which F. W. de Klerk was the president. The country was fragile, and tensions were high; the talks between these deeply opposed parties were meant to be about how to communicate on equal footing in the future. Almost immediately, the right wing of the National Party drove an armored vehicle into the latest summits and took them over, waving their old South African flags, as inflammatory a gesture as raising a Confederate flag in post–Civil War America. Mandela asked Dad, Mom, and Uncle John to charter a helicopter to fly him to the scene immediately.

"We won't do it," they said. "If you land at the scene, they'll shoot you."

Mandela didn't care. "I must be with my people. Charter me a helicopter."

The argument grew quite heated. "*We* are your people," Dad told him, "and it doesn't help us if you fly off and get shot. We'll charter you an airplane and fly you to a nearby airport and you can get a report before you go in." Mandela stormed off. Shortly afterward, he returned and agreed with my parents and uncle. As it happened, by the time he flew in for the summit, the revolution was over and everyone was out having a barbecue.

This wasn't the only time we saw Mandela assert himself on behalf of his people. One Saturday night, reports came in that ten people had been murdered in Alexandra Township, a poor black slum—more casualties of the Third Force, a group dedicated to the breakdown of negotiations between the ANC and the National Party. The Third Force was essentially made up of terrorists who committed atrocious acts and blamed them on one party or the other to try to blow apart the fragile peace.

We had an ancient TV in the family room with bunny ears antennae. The next morning as Dad and Mandela watched the news, they saw only a snowy transmission of this tragedy. Our phone lines were down for scheduled maintenance. In classic Londolozi style, Dad came to a last-minute rescue with a jerry-rigged radiophone.

"De Klerk!" Mandela screamed into the line, trying to get his point across through heavy static. "I'm warning you! If the Third Force doesn't stop, I'll pull out of the negotiations!" The connection was so terrible that the future president of the ANC and the current president of South Africa couldn't hear each other. Dad was frantic: the whole future of our country rested on a fuzzy phone line. Luckily, Dad was able to get the phone working and persuade Mandela to speak into the transmitter instead of holding it to his ear, and he and de Klerk came to a resolution. In late 1993, Mandela and de Klerk shared the Nobel Peace Prize for their work in negotiating a peaceful transition against the backdrop of imminent civil war. And in 1994, Nelson Mandela became the first democratically elected president of South Africa.

Mandela's visits coincided with one of the worst droughts we'd had in a long time. The Sand River had almost run dry because of a dam up-river controlled by the Gazankulu districts, a big reservation system. The Nationalist government at the time offered no protection for the water-ways. Some farmers set up their farms right on the river, siphoning water for their land, building dams wherever they pleased, with no legislation to protect other people who likewise needed this vital resource. There was corruption and tribal infighting, a general disconnect between government policy and what people needed. Dad flew to Gazankulu to plead our case.

"You've got to open the water for the people downstream," Dad said.

"No, our people need the water," the local puppets of the government replied.

Dad flew back and told Mandela about the dilemma. "When I'm in power, let's talk and solve this problem," Mandela promised. That very night there was a great downpour. All the staff members met in the village; everyone stood in a circle and offered thanks for the rain. Mandela gave a speech, saying that Londolozi was in line with his vision for the future of South Africa, a society of racial harmony.

Mandela proved true to his word; when he became president, he involved Dad in the drafting of the National Water Act, which mandated a more democratic handling of rivers. People could no longer deny others an essential resource by blocking it upstream.

It was Mom's dream for Madiba to do the foreword for the book she'd been working on, *I Speak of Africa: The Story of Londolozi Game Reserve*. This book was deeply important to her. Filled with lush photographs from the reserve, it not only told the story of the lodge's beginnings but described our family's philosophy on conservation. Originally, not wanting to cash in on their relationship, she sent her request through his foundation, the Nelson Mandela Children's Fund. Weeks dragged by as her message got bogged down in bureaucracy. Finally, my mother decided to throw caution to the wind. She phoned the security desk at the Union Buildings and cheerfully talked someone into giving her Madiba's home number. Such was life in the new democracy. She called his house directly. "I'd like to speak to Madiba, please."

The clearly flummoxed person on the other end of the line told her to hold on. Moments later Mandela came on. "Madiba, it's Shanny from Londolozi speaking."

"How wonderful to hear from you. How are you?"

"Oh, just fine. I wanted to ask you something."

"Do you mind? I'm just in the middle of watching the news. Could I ask you to ring me back in ten minutes?"

When Mandela picked up the phone ten minutes later, it was with a warm "Now, my dear, how can I help you?"

"Oh, Madiba, this is a long shot, I'm sure you get asked to do this a million times, but would you consider writing the foreword for my book?"

"Yes, it would be my pleasure."

Within twenty-four hours Mom and Dad had driven to Pretoria, to the office of the president. Madiba had put his thoughts down, and his letter was given the official seal from the president's office. It appears as the foreword to *I Speak of Africa,* opposite a gorgeous rendering of Madiba with Dave, Shan, and John Varty. I was particularly moved by the final paragraphs:

> During my long walk to freedom, I had the rare privilege to visit Londolozi. There I saw people of all races living in harmony amidst the beauty that Mother Nature offers. There I saw a living lion in the wild.
>
> Londolozi represents a model of the dream I cherish for the future of nature preservation in our country.

After Mandela became president, Mom was staying at the Balalaika Hotel in Johannesburg when Mandela suddenly walked into the foyer surrounded by press and security. Spotting her, he broke from the crowd and walked across the lobby to greet her, holding her hand for an extended period of time in a typically African way as they chatted. My mother was blown away. Years later, when I was captaining a cricket team, she would remind me of Madiba's example: "It's the little things, Boyd, the little things that make the great leaders."

Twenty years after the morning I met Madiba, in the room that is now mine, I realized all over again how extraordinary he was, and is. He'd woken up exactly as I am doing now, just a few pounds of bones and blood and gristle and tired muscle. He had to generate within himself the energy to extend the restoration of his country beyond that small human body. I couldn't imagine how he must have felt, emerging from the terrible isolation of prison immediately into cheering crowds, a whole nation desperately in need of what he represented.

Mandela is revered by all for the way he catalyzed change in our country. His birthday will always be a major holiday at Londolozi, filled with singing, dancing, and eating. I join in the wild games of soccer played on a field where lions have been known to sit and watch. In the heat of competition, race becomes irrelevant, with players and fans of all colors cheering and embracing; cooks and bottle washers clink glasses with wealthy First World guests. A flood of children snitch dollops of icing from the cake that says, "Happy Birthday, Madiba!" The Londolozi Ladies Choir, made up of cooks, housekeepers, and other staffers, provides a rousing soundtrack.

Nelson Mandela is proof that one individual can change the world.

NINE

ELEPHANTS ALL AROUND

I WAS WITH PHINEAS, ELMON'S older brother, out in the bush. He was tall and very thin, in his fifties, with a roguish smile and smart sideburns. At age ten, I was too young to go out in the bush by myself, so if Dad or Elmon couldn't take me, Phineas would be my guide.

The coarse sand of the dry riverbed crunched under my bare feet. It was hot, even as dusk started to arrive, and bushbucks on the slopes of the ravine were making their way to the floodplain on the riverbank above our camp. Phineas and I had laid down a tarp to sleep on and made a small fire beside it on which to cook a francolin. I'd spent the first three hours in this campsite stalking through the shady river glens, trying to bag a fowl with my .22. I felt very grown-up being out for the first time without my father or uncle, preparing to sleep on the ground overnight with someone else, just the two of us. It was very exciting for a young boy. But when I eventually shot the francolin, I didn't feel the thrill; I just felt a little cold. Phineas showed me how to pluck the chicken-sized bird and place it in the coals of the fire. As if on cue, there was a rumble of far-off thunder.

Then something answered the thunder. Out of the reeds a giant bull elephant lumbered straight toward where we were sitting, his trunk cocked to drink in the smell of smoke and sweat, his ears tuned to the sound of our breathing. I could hear every footfall as his feet scuffed and compressed the sand. Not a cricket or a bird made a sound; it was as if the court had fallen silent for the king.

My heart started to race. I slid closer to Phineas, watching him for a reaction, but he stayed calm.

Although the elephant was only a faint outline in the dark, I could see his white tusks rise when he lifted his head. I flushed with excitement as the giant creature came closer and closer. Phineas's hand fluttered, a signal that meant "Stay seated." The elephant approached the edge of our tarp. I felt as if a mountain had come to say hello.

Phineas shifted onto his haunches in case he needed to stand up quickly and create a ruckus to scare the elephant away. He had no gun. The elephant was so close that his breath blew dust from the sandy riverbed onto me. He was so still, his skin twitching, his ears like satellites aimed forward. I saw that he wanted to proceed down the river but was uncertain if he could pass between us and the steep bank. He stood there, considering, for what felt like hours, although it was perhaps only four or five minutes. With a final swish of his head, he strode past us.

Phineas chuckled quietly. I was shaking, but for some reason I didn't feel afraid—or if I did, I have no memory of it. I felt nervous about facing the rest of the night—it was now nearly dark—but I was also thrilled and proud that I'd be able to tell the story when I got home. We'd had an encounter—and bushveld adventures were all about encounters.

For the rest of my life I would return often in my mind to that ten-year-old boy who had been visited by a mountain.

———

Elephants walk through the spirit as much as they do across the earth: they are the ambassadors of peace, the universal prayer, the *om* in motion. The footsteps of the great matriarchal herds bind the earth together like the stitches on quilts sewn by our grandmothers' grandmothers. Elephants are ancestor spirits while they are still alive.

It seemed fitting to me, then, that my own grandfather's encounter with an elephant was a pivotal point in the history of Londolozi, a fusion of the patriarchs with the matriarchs. A bull elephant charged him, and he shot it six times with an underpowered rifle. It was within ten paces when he managed to turn it back. I've often thought how different the story of Londolozi would be if that elephant, and not a heart attack, had killed my grandfather. Would my father and uncle's reverence for the great pachyderms be any different? Would they have fought so hard to keep the farm they loved if it had been the place where my grandfather had died, trampled back into the earth by an elephant? I'm always amazed by how the fate of generations can pivot on single moments.

––––––

When Dad and Uncle John began working on Londolozi in the seventies, almost all the elephants had been fenced into Kruger National Park. The fence closed off the natural migratory path of elephants and wildebeests. It had been erected as a "veterinary fence," but essentially it turned Kruger National Park into the perfect military buffer between apartheid South Africa and the advance of communism in Mozambique, ninety miles to the east of Londolozi. To my parents and uncle, that fence was a powerful symbol of man's destructive influence on the land.

Next door to Londolozi, Kruger was culling elephants. Meanwhile, Londolozi had only five elephant bulls in the whole area. Dad and JV needed more; Ken Tinley had told them that elephants are natural deforesters—by feeding on scrub bushes and pushing down large trees to eat the leaves, they promote grassland. In accordance with Tinley's advice, workers at Londolozi had used heavy machinery to clear out some of the scrub, and the land had been responding wonderfully. As the grassland returned, the wildebeest and zebra numbers were beginning to improve. The elephants would accelerate the restoration of the land to its original state.

Since Kenya had a thriving elephant population, Dave and Uncle John traveled there on dubiously obtained Paraguayan passports; South Africans weren't welcome in Kenya, or much of anywhere else, because of sanctions against apartheid. Dad and Uncle John had devised an ingenious plan to get elephants onto Londolozi's land; they'd bought themselves a tiny percentage in the "Dundee Crocodile Farm" near Iguaçu falls in Paraguay. By Paraguayan law, this made them landowners and therefore eligible for Paraguayan passports. They managed to get through Kenyan border control by flashing this questionable paperwork and saying "Sí, señor" to every question a border patrol officer asked them.

There they met with naturalists who confirmed Tinley's claim that elephants could translate woodland and scrubland to grassland. They came back bounding with enthusiasm to stock the park with elephants and set up a mission to raise money for the effort. They managed to talk their way into a meeting with a Kruger Park official. These two long-haired twenty-somethings with droopy mustaches—who, incidentally, had just been baton-charged by the police because they'd protested apartheid at Wits University—sat across the table from the old-guard official and laid out their plan: "Listen, we want to catch elephants in Kruger."

"You'll never pull it off, but if you get a permit, I will help you," he told them. They got the permit, and the Kruger game rangers, to their credit, were on board. "This is fantastic! This'll be brilliant," they said. Next the brothers needed to line up a helicopter from which they could dart the elephants with sedatives. This would be the first live moving of elephants ever undertaken, and it was fraught with problems. How much sedative to shoot into an elephant? How big an elephant should they choose? If it was too small, would it survive? How would you transport it? There were no guidelines.

After they successfully darted the first elephant, they tugged to get her into her box—twenty-five Shangaans on one end, with a vet on the other end jabbing antidote into her bum to rouse her just enough so she might walk. The operation went perfectly until the elephant took a deep breath and the box just disintegrated around her. There she stood, completely awake, with no box, surrounded by twenty-five Shangaans. They scattered in every direction. The elephant ran around, trumpeting, then finally took off into the bush.

The next day, the brothers and their workers reinforced the crates, caught smaller elephants, and successfully transported eight of them in large crated trucks. Some survived, but unfortunately some were too small. And the project was out of money.

Eight elephants weren't enough. They would need more money and went to New York to get it. The brothers were fans of ABC's *Wide World of Sports*'s two-hour weekly special, which sometimes sent celebrities on adventures in the wild. They heard that the program had done a story on a famous elephant, so they wrangled a meeting with producer John Wilcox.

"Listen," Dad told him, "we're gonna catch elephants in the Kruger and relocate them to Londolozi. Would you like the film rights?"

Wilcox barely looked up from the phone conversation he was involved in. "I've done elephants. We don't need elephants. Africa's too far. No, we're not interested." He punched a second button on the phone and addressed himself to another caller. "Yeah, yeah, what do you want?"

John said, "We're going to dart helicopters from elephants." In the heat of the moment, John garbled his words.

"What?" Wilcox covered the receiver.

"I mean, we will dart the elephants from a helicopter and hang them from the helicopter so we can relocate them."

Wilcox hung up the receiver. He was a filmmaker; they could see him thinking in pictures. "If you can do that," Wilcox said, "I'll do the show."

Dad looked at John. "What the fuck are you saying?" he whispered angrily. "No one's ever hung an elephant under a helicopter."

John smiled and whispered back, "Don't worry, don't worry."

In short order, Wilcox sent a crew of eighteen men to cover the transport of ten elephants. The plan was to have Cheryl Tiegs, then the highest-paid model in the world, and Ben Abruzzo, an adventurer who'd flown across the Atlantic in a hot-air balloon, dart the elephants from a balloon.

Dad was having trouble convincing helicopter pilots to go along with the next part of the plan. "Listen, you guys, you have to catch an elephant and sling it under the helicopter."

The pilots wanted none of it. "That's the biggest bullshit—you don't have to use a helicopter. You can just transport them in trucks."

Dad and JV were not deterred. They were determined to get those elephants to Londolozi. They eventually convinced the pilots to do the darting and help them muscle the elephants into the trucks. Out came Wilcox and his crew. "You've never seen a goat rodeo like this in your entire life," Dad told me later. "We had two still photographers and a second helicopter. A hundred people showed up, including Cheryl and Ben and hangers-on and hangers-on to the hangers-on. We had trucks and low-beds and proper crates and two helicopters and film crews and groupies and cousins, uncles, and aunts—and Johnny Wilcox." Wilcox set up the camera and hooked a fellow on a harness dangling from the helicopter to film the whole operation. Then the veterinarian who'd flown 250 miles to do the darting opened up his box of tricks to discover that he'd left the sedatives back home. The whole day collapsed. Wilcox went ballistic.

The next day, the drugs arrived, the elephants were darted from the helicopter for transport by truck to Londolozi, and Wilcox got magnificent footage. That night, everyone celebrated into the evening around a campfire. Cheryl Tiegs had brought Peter Beard, her future husband, who was Kenya's voice of conservation and a maverick like Ken Tinley, who'd also joined the festivities. They began to fire each other up. Somehow, in the alcohol-fueled haze and smoke, Peter announced, "Cheryl, we're going to have a party at Studio 54. We'll invite Mick Fleetwood to perform. We'll get Steve Rubell"—one of Studio 54's co-owners—"to donate all the gate money to a trust for elephants." Johnny Wilcox would donate the day's footage so it could be projected on the disco's walls.

Dad and Uncle John were ecstatic and threw themselves into preparations for the fund-raiser. The party cost $67,000. They ultimately raised $69,000, netting them a scant $2,000—and earning Dad the eternal resentment of Mom, who'd had to miss Mick's performance at the hottest disco of the day because Dad had left her back home at Londolozi to "mind the shop," feeding the film crews and repairing Ben Abruzzo's balloons, which had gotten ripped by thorn trees during the elephant transport.

From the middle of apartheid-infected nowhere, Dad and Uncle John had created international attention. Most important, they'd managed to move twenty-five elephants to Londolozi. Kruger National Park began to rethink its elephant-relocation policies. By April 1983, there were forty-two elephants in Londolozi. A year later, the first elephant calf was born to an elephant relocated to the reserve. Today there are more than a thousand elephants on this land.

———

My grandfather survived that charging bull the way Jonah survived his whale, so that Dad and Uncle John could one day relocate the first elephants into Londolozi. After their shaky reintroduction, they now roam freely between Londolozi and Kruger National Park, leaving an invisible trail of peace.

In the late eighties, when Uncle John wrote an article for *The Star,* an influential South African newspaper, protesting the fence, he was viciously attacked by the leaders of the national parks board. Yet he was right. For years the Vartys lobbied to take it down, and in 1994 they prevailed. A piece of that fence sits with my mom's most prized senti-mental possessions on top of a yellowwood cabinet in our house. This rusted length of barbed wire quietly broadcasts the magic that comes from laying down our barriers and letting nature heal the divide.

––––––

Try as I might, I could never transfer my love of elephants to Bron. She continued to admire them in theory but not actually like them. Uncle John was perhaps somewhat to blame for that.

When I was eleven, Uncle John became a father; he and Gillian had a lovely daughter named Savannah. She was born in Johannesburg but spent her infancy in tented camps way out in the bush wherever John happened to be filming. JV loved Savannah upon arrival and quickly became putty in her tiny hands. Bron and I were godparents to this golden angel who bathed in buckets in the tent camps. Savannah quickly became a favorite part of our visits with our uncle in the bush.

When Savannah was still very small, perhaps two or three years old, Uncle John took her, along with me and Bron, for a picnic at a beautiful place called Tatowa Dam. After the large dam had been dug, the earth wall had never sealed, creating a small circle of clear water in a deep hol-low. We'd found a gorgeous area behind the dam, a grove shaded by the faded red and green leaves of the tamboti trees a stone's throw away from the pond. Uncle John laid out his usual spread: a couple of the tart citrus fruits called naartjies, some nuts, and a rotten banana. (Uncle John is never without duct tape, which he believes will mend anything, and rot-ten bananas, his all-purpose source of nutrition.) We were just about to leave when three bull elephants came ambling down to the water's edge to drink.

The documentarian in Uncle John leapt into action. He jumped into his Land Rover, which he'd converted into a mobile filming unit by tear-ing out the rear seats and replacing them with foam-filled black boxes to house his cameras. Then he reached into one of the compartments and pulled out his gigantic Arriflex. I knew what came next: my job would be to carry lenses and batteries while Uncle John rolled film. He barked out his usual bullet-point briefing as we shouldered our equipment:

"Buddy.

"You and me.

"Gonna.

"Sneak in close.

"Bonna." He looked over at Bron, who was already narrowing her eyes in suspicion.

"You stay with Savannah."

He swerved back to me.

"Buddy.

"If they look like they might iron us.

"Hit the water."

Meaning: if we get charged, dive into the dam and swim underwater to escape. John's number one lesson was: Always have an escape route.

We set off, leaving Bronwyn silently fuming that we'd entangled her once again with elephants, her nemesis.

Uncle John was in his element. We soon set up on top of a large, grassy termite mound, and his eye was pressed to the lens while he captured the three bulls refreshing themselves. Finally the elephants finished drinking and began to head around the side of the dam, toward us. We were directly in their way, which could be a problem if we surprised them. If we were going to move, I thought, we should have done so long ago. Now our only option was to be very still and hope they wouldn't notice us, which was unlikely, given elephants' keen sense of smell. Uncle John, I feared, was completely oblivious, his eye still jammed against the camera. He was simply zooming the lens out as they drew closer, intent on his footage, all sense of depth perception lost. I was horridly aware of their proximity, but a good bearer never questions or runs without his cameraman.

The elephants were practically alongside us when Uncle John lifted his head from the eyepiece. "Jesus!" he said. There wasn't a lot Jesus could do right then. "Slip down the back," he whispered. We were crouching behind the termite mound when the lead elephant froze eight yards away and cocked his trunk. Slowly the trunk rose over the top of the mound, like a periscope. My heart was racing; we'd been found. John, however, had a goofy grin on his face. This is what he lives for. He pointed at a warthog hole in the mound. I knew what he was telling me: *If the elephants charge, crawl into the hole.* Thanks to my hunting days with Elmon, I'd seen warthogs up close, with their razor-sharp incisors and fetid breath. There was no danger of me ever going into that hole.

Astonishingly, the elephants walked right by us. Unfortunately, they were heading straight toward where Bron had been left with the responsibility of her little cousin. There was no way for us to get back to her. Bron was on her own.

At the sight of the herd, Bron's first thought was *"Damn Uncle John and his elephants!"* Then she calmly swooped Savannah up into her arms, walked over to the Land Rover, and ripped a child-sized wad of foam padding out of one of the camera cases.

"Time to play hide-and-seek!" she told Savannah, who looked mildly puzzled as Bron tucked her inside the duct-tape-strewn camera box. "Now, don't come out until I say!" She then folded herself into the foot well of the passenger seat and pulled the picnic blanket over her head.

The elephants sidled up to the Land Rover. One expertly forked up a discarded naartjie peel and snacked on it. Then they moved on.

Fuming, Bronwyn crawled out from the foot well and released a none-the-wiser Savannah from the camera case—"Surprise, sweetheart, I found you!"—and Uncle John sighed with satisfaction, having had exactly the kind of picnic he likes best.

Bron caught my eye and gave me the "this guy is a freak" look she saved especially for Uncle John, but we both knew that as much as we hated his exploits, we loved them, too.

Looking back on my various encounters with elephants, I'm struck by the way concern for my physical safety sullied my ability to absorb the immense sweetness of their spirits. I want to go back to every elephant I've met, feared, avoided, run from—and this time stand my ground. Let them sit on me, like Bronwyn's nemesis in her Indian lifetime. Let them toss me into the trees or impale me on their tusks, run me down like the bull that didn't quite reach my grandfather—anything, if it comes with that bottomless calm only elephants possess.

———

Even though my parents have spent years in the bush, they will go out each afternoon to get their elephant fix for the day. I tag along as often as I can. "This makes my heart sing," says my dad from behind the wheel of the Land Rover, with my mom in her Panama hat sitting next to him. "This is what we always wanted." A love for nature deepens with age. Perhaps as we become less attached to our own vitality, we're able to draw in more of the energy and depth of love that the natural world can give to the human spirit.

The return of the elephants to Londolozi was an act of great healing, a reclamation of something wild. Our wellness is tied to this healing. In 1854, Chief Seattle said, "If all the beasts were gone, man would die from a great loneliness of spirit." I still hear people quote this as if that danger lies in the future. Perhaps this is because they have never known the company of animals. They don't realize that the great loneliness is upon us already.

Wherever you are, with whatever means you have, if you reclaim a piece of land for nature, your world will grow kinder, more benevolent. Create havens—for animals, for other people, for yourself—and let this reflect into the world. Fight for space in your own backyard, in an acre or a flowerpot or simply an embrace of the longing for company that lingers in your wilting heart. If you take this one step toward them, no matter where you are, the elephants will come to you.

TEN

THE CRASH

D AD WAS THE ONE who picked up the ringing phone that Saturday. It was early morning. Immediately, we got nervous. Calls at
that time in the safari business rarely meant good news.

"Ah, Jesus . . . where?"

His whole demeanor changed in an instant. My mother walked
briskly toward him from across the room.

"Shit. . . . Do you know how high they were? . . . So you're not sure if
they're alive? . . . Some are? . . . Okay, give me an hour."

Dad hung up and let out a big sigh. He had a determined look on his
face, the look that said he was about to spring into action.

"Your uncle has been in a chopper crash in Zambia. From what we
know, he and the rest of the crew are alive but badly hurt. Some might
be paralyzed. They're still in the wreck."

A Saturday in South Africa means very little is going on, while in
Zambia, a diamond-in-the-rough nation a thousand miles to the north,
it means nothing is going on. My uncle had managed to crash in one of

the most remote places in the world, deep in Zambia's Luangwa Valley. Dad knew that time was of the essence. He needed to pull off a miracle if Uncle John and his camera crew were to survive.

Since the death of their father, Dave and John had always looked out for each other. Dad couldn't fail the brother who'd been willing to punch out pilots and commandeer Christiaan Barnard when his own life had been in danger.

Mr. Logistics swung into action. Dad instantly turned our home into a major base of operations. Mom's job was to track down the right phone numbers—at one point she was tracing the number for the president of Zambia—while Dad made nonstop calls, running four phone lines at a time. Within hours, he'd managed to charter a plane—large enough for the EMTs and all the injured crew—and staff it with paramedics. Uncle John had a friend in Lusaka, Yusef Patel, who seemed to know everybody who was anybody in Zambia. Dad got on the phone with him.

"Listen, Yusef, I don't care what you have to do, we have to get the paramedics from Mfuwe Airport into the valley. There are scouts there who know where the wreck is."

Yusef went to work. We were all on a knife's edge. At age twelve, I wasn't religious, but I slipped off to my room and began to pray for the return of my iconic uncle.

Deep in the Luangwa Valley, Uncle John and most of his crew—Elmon Mhlongo, Willi Sibuye, and Karen Slater—were lying in and around a crumpled tangle of metal. On Friday, they'd been filming aerial shots when the tail rotor had snapped, the helicopter had lost all directional control, and they'd begun to spin madly, then fall out of the sky. By some miracle, Rob Parson, the pilot, had managed to crash the copter down on its struts, which no doubt saved all their lives, as the struts absorbed a huge amount of the impact. Rob was stuck in the chopper, while the rest, in the back, had been thrown to the ground. They lay there in the fading light, watching the sun drop lower in the sky, knowing no one would find them.

A deeply spiritual person, Karen had been practicing meditation for years. When the chopper had lost control, she'd begun to meditate and her body had become completely relaxed, which likely contributed to her incredible ability to rally after the accident. After some time, she'd pulled herself to her feet and begun a solo five-mile trek through the bush to try to get to John's tented camp so she could radio for help. She had to wade across the Luangwa River, renowned as having one of the densest populations of crocodiles in the world. Astonishingly, she made it back to base camp, where she discovered Loyd Gumede.

Loyd is a parenthesis of a man with a gentle, moon-shaped face. He was from a small village north of Londolozi and had a reputation among the villagers of being a few jets short of a squadron. My uncle had hired him to give him a bit of a leg up, figuring that the job of lighting man for a film crew was fairly self-explanatory: see an animal, shine a light on the animal. Despite this, within the first few months Loyd had distinguished himself by forgetting his simple tasks at crucial moments. My uncle was constantly exploding with rage over Loyd's forgetfulness: "We were here, the leopard was there, and I knew that the kill would happen right in front of us. . . . Then fucking Loyd forgot to turn the lights on!"

At times during filming, Loyd and Uncle John would have only each other for company for months on end. Loyd was the designated cook, so each night he would prepare the only thing he could make: sadza porridge, which Uncle John would eat without complaint until he felt as if cornmeal might come out his ears. Loyd was truly Zen in his simplicity; Uncle John said that he wanted to make a movie about him called *Still Life*.

My uncle had once entrusted Loyd with a critical task. He was to drive to the distant town of Mfuwe, easily a six-hour trip in the wet season, because Uncle John desperately needed some documents signed in order to prevent the impounding of his only vehicle, an old Hilux pickup he loved. Loyd set off on the epic journey through mud, rain, mad elephants, and bandits. He returned five days later. I witnessed the following conversation.

"Loyd, you made it?"

"Yes."

"All the way to customs?"

"Yes."

"Did the drive go okay?"

"Yes."

"You met the customs officer?"

"Yes."

And then a hopeful: "So did they sign the papers?"

"No."

"Why not?"

And then Loyd uttered the words that have immortalized him in our family for the rest of time: "*Eziko lu* ballpoint." Despite nearly five days on the road, Loyd had failed at his mission because there was no pen at the customs office. Uncle John's truck was duly impounded, and we did a great deal of walking after that.

Loyd had gone with Uncle John to Zambia as a member of his film team, remaining at base camp while the others took off in the helicopter. On the day of the crash, he behaved in a way that would allow him to be forgiven for all past and future failings. After hearing about the accident from Karen, Loyd waded across a waist-deep, crocodile-infested section of the Luangwa River in the black of night to tell the park scouts the position of the crash. He then crossed the river again—near the spot where Karen had initially crossed it—to lead the scouts and eventually paramedics to the scene. Armed with blankets, he stationed himself there and defended and cared for the wounded crew throughout the night as they lay helpless in the bush. My uncle is certain that along with Karen and basic first aid, Loyd, with his provision of blankets, was a major reason why they survived that night. Loyd had steel in him, and I admire him for this.

Back home, Dad was ecstatic. "When you're in a tight spot, you definitely want a Shangaan with you."

Meanwhile, through various nefarious channels, Yusef had arranged for a Zambian military helicopter to ferry paramedics to and from the scene of the crash. Mr. Logistics had pulled off an incredible feat, aided by Karen's resiliency and Loyd's inspiring loyalty.

I waited at the Milpark Hospital, in Johannesburg, for my uncle to arrive in an ambulance from Zambia. It had been twenty hours since we'd received the news that he'd crashed. John looked appalling, but he gave me his signature high five as he rolled by me on the gurney, saying, "Good to see you, buddy." There was blood spattered on the beaded bangle given to him long ago by the Masai as a symbol of their friendship and acceptance—a bangle he never took off. If anyone was going to come back strong, it would be Uncle John. In a strange way, seeing him lying there, bloodied, heavily medicated, with tubes and drips everywhere, didn't break my awe of his invincibility; instead, it ratified it.

The vertebrae in Uncle John's lower spine had been completely compressed by the impact of the crash, but the paralysis would slowly recede and he would walk again. The other members of the crew would likewise recover over time, except for Rob Parson, the tenacious pilot, whose split-second maneuvering of the helicopter had no doubt saved everyone else's lives. Sadly, Rob died a year later of complications from his injuries.

Over the next few months, while his back healed, my mother visited Uncle John regularly. She fed him and tried to stifle her annoyance as he issued monosyllabic instructions, the only way he could exert control over his helplessness.

"Peas," Uncle John ordered. He lay flat on his back in his hospital bed with his mouth open like a baby bird's.

"Chicken."

"Broccoli."

Finally Mom had had enough. "You will get what I give you," she snapped.

Once they started arguing, I knew things would shortly be back to normal.

Loyd shows up at Londolozi from time to time. He'll sit calmly on the steps to my uncle's house, waiting for him to return from the bush so they can catch up and share a meal. He is as quiet and unassuming as ever, a true still life, yet he reminds me that most true acts of heroism—reflections of one's deepest nature—remain unknown to the hero.

ELEVEN

THE GREAT MIGRATION

DECIDED TO LAUNCH A massive conservation effort, rivaled in scale only by the efforts to save three gray whales trapped in Arctic pack ice I'd read about a few years before. As the dry season approached, the edges of the pond near our house began to recede; small pools of catfish could be seen flailing around in the muddy water. I knew that in a few short weeks, if the rain didn't come, the puddles would dry up completely and those big old catfish would become a part of the food chain. Already a fish eagle had begun to sit expectantly on a dead tree nearby, in anticipation of the feast to come. My catfish might not be as sexy a species as whales, but I believed they were just as important.

The plan looked like this: walk down to the edge of the puddle, which was about the size of my bedroom, wade in, catch a fish, put it into a large trash can filled with water, then take it to the river, where it might continue to live in peace and harmony for the rest of time. Repeat until the several dozen were rescued. I had put aside about half an hour for the whole operation.

At ten, my enthusiasm overrode my logic, and I naïvely thought I could catch terrified catfish in murky water. Without a net, I flailed around trying to grab them, like a blind man chasing a piece of wet soap across a polished floor. I achieved nothing, and my mood swung from jubilant determination to utter dejection, a common state I'd noticed in conservationists like Dad and Uncle John. It was at just this moment that Jerry Hambana drove up to the pond in a beat-up old tractor.

Jeremiah Hambana was a Shangaan man with the most gentle, soft features and the broadest smile. He'd been working at Londolozi for many years. He waved but said nothing, just grinned at me. After taking in the scene for the better part of ten minutes with a quizzical look on his face, Jerry unhooked a sharpened panga that had been secured to the side of the tractor with an old piece of tire tube and ambled off into the bush. He returned a few minutes later, dragging a large piece of buffalo thorn behind him.

Jerry reached the edge of the pool and nonchalantly dropped the thorny snarl into the water, holding on to one end of the branch as if he were casting a net. Slowly he pulled it out of the pool, allowing it to drag along the bottom, trapping about ten fish in the tangle of thorny branches. Jerry picked up two of them, presumably for his supper, and, laughing to himself, walked off. Example is often the most powerful teacher. Using Jerry's technique, I had the rest of the fish in the trash can and headed to safety in no time.

———

My Shangaan elders' approach to learning was an intuitive one that invited me into nature. In contrast, "big school" in Johannesburg, which I attended with Bron as soon as I was six years old, was all about sitting still, being told what to do, what I must learn every minute, and reading instead of experiencing things firsthand. I couldn't see the point of it. I lived for the weekends, when our parents would fly us back home so I could resume my real education.

Unbeknownst to me, however, when I was ten, my bush education was to come to an abrupt end.

———

Against all odds, my parents and uncle had made Londolozi into a business that ticked along. Their next big vision was to replicate the Londolozi model all over Africa by restoring the land and creating sustainable lodges. Dad and Mom founded Conservation Corporation Africa, or CC Africa, in 1992 to make conservation commercially viable while Uncle John continued to shoot wildlife documentaries. This was ecotourism, an idea well before its time. Dad and other members of the team would find investors and shareholders who would help establish self-sustaining lodges and camps throughout Africa and, in so doing, preserve the land. CC Africa would eventually open twenty-three lodges across the continent, including sites in Kenya, Tanzania, Zimbabwe, and Zanzibar.

In the northeast of South Africa, near the Indian Ocean, lies a region known as KwaZulu-Natal. It's crowned by a remote area called Maputaland, which, while rich in unspoiled wetlands and marine reserves, nevertheless was home to some of South Africa's poorest residents. Some of the land had been destroyed through poor farming techniques. Mom and Dad set their sights first on some derelict pineapple farms. They wanted to bring the land there back to life; they called it Phinda, or "the Return."

Nothing fires my parents up like the next great adventure, and they threw themselves into this one. The plan was to create a reserve of sixty square miles in the midst of Maputaland's direst poverty. Dad wanted to reconnect the surrounding rural communities with the land. He believed Maputaland's beauty was worth saving, although his sales pitch acknowledged some small bumps in the road.

"Hi, I'm Dave Varty, here in your posh bankers' offices to raise money to start a game reserve in Maputaland. Yes, all the farms there are bankrupt, but that's a good thing, because it means we can buy them cheap. Yes, it floods twice a year, but that's only an issue if you're in farming, and we're gonna be in tourism. Yes, malaria is rife in that area and the Zulus are a warlike people who consider it part of their kingdom—and there's a very real chance that they'll start a civil war with the Xhosa-speaking ANC, but obviously that's subject to getting rid of the apartheid government, which the rest of the world has, thankfully, put sanctions on. Anyway, I think you should give me your money, because even though you can't see it now, I believe this will be a great project for restoration! One day Phinda will be a better investment than gold!"

Dad delivered this pitch for madmen with pure vigor and absolute passion. He eventually secured the funding, most particularly from Mark Getty, a grandson of J. Paul Getty, who managed to get the rest of his family on board.

Mom and Dad began working insane hours. Dad traveled to Phinda so often that we barely saw him. He'd be dashing about, overseeing great crews removing fencing, debris, and old rusty farm equipment; working the phones to secure funding; reintroducing elephants; fixing the ecology of the land; driving into the community to calm down a tribal chief before the enraged Zulus could protest. Even when Bron and I were with them on weekends, Mom and Dad were totally consumed by CC Africa business, and Dad often had to leave to oversee the recapture of escaped elephants, handle a construction snafu, and so on. Mom took to calling Phinda "the gorilla." "Got to go wrestle the gorilla," Dad would tell us as he disappeared once again.

Eventually, from a run-down collection of farms with old windmills, barbed-wire fences, rusting equipment, and virtually no animals, Dad and CC Africa would create a gorgeous reserve that was home to the Big Five, more than four hundred species of birds, and the highest populations of white rhinos in southern Africa.

In the meantime, though, there was no time to shuttle us kids back and forth to school. Ironically, my parents' vision of creating more reserves where people could experience nature in a new, profound way meant yanking me and Bron out of our own idyllic environment.

"You'll be going to a new environmental school," Mom told me and

Bron, describing the school near Phinda where she had enrolled us. "You'll be riding horses on a farm! You'll board during the week, and then Dad and I will fly in and pick you up every weekend. It'll be an amazing education!"

Whatever its aspirations, at that time the school was a place of last resort for troubled kids whose parents lived far away in broken homes. Despite its marketing, it seemed more like a reform school in disguise, the messianic redeemer of wayward children. The idea of getting little Johnny out of the mall, off crack, and into the wild must have been a great relief for the parents of these renegade children. Bron and I, by contrast, were in the small minority whose parents were still together. We were flung into a world where you got up at six to make your bed and slept locked in a room with thirty-four other kids. Everyone wore identical uniforms. Conformity was the operating principle.

For the first two weeks, we weren't allowed any contact with our parents—the longest we'd been without them. I was gentle and under-sized, a sensitive ten-year-old child of nature thrown in with these loud, troubled urban kids. I might as well have stuck a target on my chest. I was badly bullied from the beginning. A kid named Rory seemed to take special pleasure in beating me up. He was big for his age, with thick wrists and arms like a gorilla. The first time he hit me, solidly across the face, was one of the most shocking moments of my life. The mixture of rage and shame I felt was so unfamiliar. As my own blood dripped onto the porcelain bathroom basin, I wanted to run and hide.

Bron was foundering too, completely out of step with all the other girls and what they were doing, wearing, talking about. She was battling to fit in while all I tried to do was disappear into the crowd. But we knew we needed to be strong. From the time we'd been born, we had been told that our work was to protect nature and the animals. As young as we were, we understood what our parents were trying to do and felt an ob-ligation to play our part in it by keeping a stiff upper lip at boarding school. So Bron and I drew on the resources we'd learned growing up in the bush and attempted to adapt and survive.

The administration didn't seem to know what to do with us. Bron and I were constantly being tested. A bewildering sequence of verdicts was handed in: "These are the two most incredibly smart children in the world; they must go to the gifted classes." "These kids are retarded; they have to go to the special ed class." Eventually we were diagnosed as dyslexic. I was garlanded with other labels too: ADHD, hyperactive, a "problem child." With each label, I felt dumber.

Occasionally I'd sneak out of school and climb a hill, curl up on a large, flat rock, and cry in privacy. The instinct to be alone in nature led me away from everyone; if I could just spend some time out in the wild by myself, I could regenerate. Soon Bron figured out my hiding spot and snuck up to give me pep talks. "Boydie, we gonna be fine," she said, hugging me. "We gonna get through this. We've got the two of us."

Perhaps the pep talk was for both of us.

One of the embarrassing side effects of having a sister who models herself on a lioness was her tendency to get into my fights. In the middle of beating me up, my assailant would sometimes mysteriously go down, attacked from behind by my loving and violent sister. I knew that the bullying would only get worse with Bron facing down my torturers, so I tried to stick it out, becoming more unhappy by the day.

Our visits with our parents were far more restricted than Mom and Dad had anticipated. As "termly boarders," we could go home only four times during the school year. The first time back at Londolozi, Bron and I joined our parents at a dinner party. One of the guests, who had himself been sent off to boarding school at my age, asked me, "How's it going?" I confessed to being bullied by Rory.

He had a solution for me: "What you do is, you get your cricket bat. You hide in your cupboard. When that guy comes past, with no one else around, you jump out of your cupboard, and you hit him hard one time with the bat. Make sure you get him real good. He won't touch you again."

Back at school, Bron and I planned the mission together. I waited for the right moment with my hunter's instinct, then executed it to the last note. I came out of the cupboard in Rory's room in a classic leopard ambush; he was close and unsuspecting. The first he knew of me was when my cricket bat slammed into his shin. Rory went down instantly, with a thick bump on the front of his leg. I followed up my opening assault with a flat bat to the upper leg. My heart was pumping; this was not me, but it was what I felt this place required of me.

Rory never hit me again. After that, everyone saw me in a new light. I was respected and started to amass a posse. Much to my astonishment, girls started to like me. Sports, at which I excelled, brought me approval from teachers and peers.

Bron, meanwhile, took on a mothering role. There were lots of broken wings for her to mend. The school offered a window into a harsh world, and we saw students who had walked quite a journey. Bron and I spent our three years there as psychologists, advising the other kids on how to handle their parents' fights, divorces, and custody battles.

Some good did come out of our experience at the school. Growing up at Londolozi, we'd thought the whole world was perfect, that everyone was married and happy. Learning that this wasn't so made us more compassionate. We also realized that we'd been a bit spoiled. We'd never made our own beds, cooked our own meals, or washed a dish. At boarding school, we made our beds with perfect hospital corners; we kept our cupboards inspection-ready and our uniforms immaculate.

Bron soon emerged as a strong leader and was voted prefect by the students and teachers. She also became an expert rule breaker who knew how to smuggle in food, ignore lights-out, and shimmy across the narrow space between the top of the dorm wall and the ceiling to get to the room with the party.

In our second year, after being the goats at boarding school, we were running the place. By year three, Bron and I had more than reconciled ourselves to our fate; we'd been forced to create our own subculture, and now we were living with it. We'd learned to curse extravagantly— everyone at boarding school swore like soldiers. We'd developed an anti-authority "fuck the man" attitude, although we weren't quite clear on who the man was, or why we ought to fuck him. We wanted to hang out with our friends, whose small-town opinions we prized over the huge dreams of our parents.

Mom and Dad were losing us, and they knew it. One evening in Tanzania, they stood on the rim of Ngorongoro Crater, a sunken caldera that acted as a bowl for some breathtaking wildlife, ranging from flocks of flamingos in the salt lake to old elephant bulls ambling peacefully in the fever tree forests. They watched the sun set as this huge vista of Africa's majesty spread beneath them. Dad turned to Mom. "I can't believe our kids are missing this." Mom said, "Let's sort this out." They'd made their decision before the sun had dipped below the horizon.

———

Bron and I were waiting at the school gate when Mom and Dad stepped out of the car. I could see by the look on their faces that this wasn't going to be an ordinary Parents' Weekend visit. Then an unfamiliar young woman emerged from the backseat. She was pretty, blond, and looked kind. Now I knew something was up.

"Kids," Mom said, "we'd like you to meet our friend Kate Groch." The pretty blond woman smiled. Bron and I shot sideways glances at each other.

We drove out the school gates and headed for a restaurant. After we ordered, Dad, in his usual extroverted way, jumped right in: "So. We're taking you out of school. You're going to travel with me and Mom. Kate is your new teacher."

I couldn't believe my bad luck. I was in love with a girl called Tessa, who had recently kissed me with her tongue. I was convinced that she was my true love.

I slunk down in my chair and glared.

"Do we have to?" Bron huffed.

Kate looked slightly shocked to find herself in the middle of an awkward family barney.

Sensing our pointed lack of enthusiasm, Mom went into overdrive:

"You'll love it! You're going to be learning how to fix Land Rovers and see gorillas, and best of all, you're going to learn how to do thatching!" Why she chose this odd example I will never know.

Thatching was the last straw. Bron stood up and, with a flair for the dramatic, stalked off. "Whatever," she tossed over her shoulder.

Mom turned to me. "Yes, we think it's going to be for the best. We're traveling so much, putting up the camps, that otherwise we'd never see you."

Bron arrived back at the table at the same time as her mushroom soup. She sat down and started to cry the uniquely bitter tears of a fourteen-year-old girl.

"Do you want to be alone, maybe talk it over for a while?" Kate asked gently. I wanted to hate her, but she looked like everything that is good in the world. We didn't know it then, but she was already on our team. "You guys are really getting this dropped on you," she told me and Bron. We weren't being asked about it; we were being told about it. Kate understood how we must feel.

"No, not at all, we're fine," said Dad, giving a "we're one big happy family" grin.

The lunch eroded into a lot of snot and trauma, but despite our reactions, the plan was set. Bron and I would be heading off into Africa with our new teacher.

When Kate came to teach us, she was twenty-three, but she looked more like nineteen. She'd grown up in a perfect Pretoria family, gone to a good girls' school, come out of the University of Cape Town, and done her master's at the University of Pretoria. She was constantly at rallies, fighting against apartheid. Her activist streak turned out to provide her with the perfect temperament to deal with two teens dedicated to sulking.

The plan was for us to study with Kate for a week in Johannesburg, spend a week in East Africa, where Mom and Dad were building lodges, then a final week at Londolozi. Uncle John had come along to look at the land being earmarked for reserves in Tanzania to scout its potential for filming. I spent that first week glaring holes into the back of Kate's head when we drove anywhere. When it was time to fly to Arusha, Tanzania, Bron and I glumly packed our school bags. Kate tried to bribe us with Jelly Tots, a premium snack for the trip, but we weren't having any of it.

We spent the first night in Arusha, perched on the eastern ridge of the Great Rift Valley, in an old plantation house that had been converted into a guesthouse on the slopes of Mount Meru. It was hot, and Bron and I were cranky.

"Come on, you two," Kate told me and Bron, "we're going for a swim." This was the first time Bron, Kate, and I were alone together. I can't remember what we spoke about, but when we got out of the pool, we were bonded. There is no way to describe the moment when someone becomes your friend; it just arrives, as Plato said, "as an act of ancient recognition."

This was lucky, as Dad decided to change the plan. Again. "Your uncle John is going to be making a documentary," he informed us. "You, Bron, and Kate are going to be the sound crew."

"It'll be educational!" Mom informed us. We could hear the note of insane confidence in her voice. At least it wasn't thatching. Our week-long trip to East Africa was about to become a six-week extravaganza of "high action," Uncle John–style.

⸱

———

"Hold tight, hold tight, we're going down into the ravine!" screamed Moses, Uncle John's Masai friend, out the front window of the Land Cruiser he was driving.

"Don't worry about me, I'm solid!" I shouted from my perch atop the vehicle.

"Okay, just making sure!" called Moses.

Uncle John, below me, wasn't so sympathetic. "Buddy, stay on the tires or you'll dent the roof." I shifted my grip on the pile of spare tires

Uncle John had haphazardly strapped to the roof with ropes and pieces of shredded inner tube.

Thousands of wildebeests disappeared over the lip of a ravine. We tore after them.

Bron, Kate, and I were crossing the Serengeti with about two million wildebeests as they made their annual migration in pursuit of the rains. Each fall this mass of herbivores, accompanied by hundreds of thousands of gazelles and zebras, travels twelve hundred miles, from the hills of the Serengeti in Tanzania across the Mara River and onto the lush plains of the Masai Mara reserve in Kenya. There they will feed on the nutrient-rich grasses for the next four months before returning to the Serengeti. Along the way, nearly 250,000 of these bovines will lose their lives to exhaustion and dehydration. Lions, leopards, cheetahs, and other hunters rove behind the herds, hoping to pick off the stragglers. Those that survive the march will still have to make the onerous crossing of the Mara River, heavily patrolled by crocodiles. The great migration is one of the last remaining examples of the majesty of an open system in play.

Uncle John was the leader of the safari. Our two Land Cruisers looked like they might have been built by Noah himself. The one I was perched on had a broken speedometer and a door held in place with frayed wire. Various instruments were taped to the dashboards of both vehicles.

"So, what's the plan?" asked Kate.

Uncle John tossed a snaggletoothed grin over his shoulder as he manhandled the steering wheel. "Couldn't tell ya."

An avid environmentalist and educator, Kate had seen every one of Uncle John's documentaries. When he'd first leaned over and introduced himself—"Hi, I'm JV," a line from virtually every movie he'd ever made—she'd felt as if she herself were in a documentary. Initially Kate had seemed a bit shocked at being plunged so deeply into Varty World, but she'd given herself over to the spirit of things quickly. "Oh well, I guess 'make it up as we go along' is going to be the order of the day," she told us now. Still, sometimes she couldn't believe the madness of this family, even though she always liked Uncle John and got on with him. "Everything is stuck together with duct tape!" she'd remarked earlier. "And that uncle of yours, he's loony!"

From Arusha we headed to Ngorongoro Crater. I understood why my parents hadn't wanted us to miss this sight. The flamingos on the lakeshore looked like colorful garnishes on the rim of a cocktail glass. At Ngorongoro, every scene is set against the rising rim of the crater, which dances from grassland into misty jungle as the altitude pulls you toward the clouds. It's God's mixing bowl. Beyond the crater, we traveled through fields of yellow flowers, down into Olduvai Gorge—the "cradle of mankind," where early hominids had stamped their tracks in mud that had long since solidified, leaving a rocky trail of clues that had helped the Leakey family trace our evolution.

The Masai who had journeyed with us had no bags of any sort with them. Tall and regal, dressed in their traditional red shukas, or blankets, and beaded and tasseled necklaces, they looked like Roman legionnaires without armor. They were the ultimate nomads, able to sustain themselves in an almost magical way. They knew which tree's branches could be chewed into a fibrous toothbrush and so had no need for a toiletry bag. They did, however, make up for what they lacked in luggage by carrying weighty traditional weaponry, from machetes to long lion-hunting spears. "One of these days we going to leave Masai land and be in Wakuria country," said Moses.

The Wakuria are the sworn enemies of the Masai. The tribes have been attacking each other for years in the hopes of rustling the other's cattle, particularly on clear nights, when moonlight can help a running retreat. Recently the Wakuria did away with their traditional weapons and started carrying Russian-made Kalashnikovs: hence the reason we were armed to the teeth. As we drove out of Masai tribeland for a day in Wakuria territory, our carefree, relaxed Masai friends stiffened, adopting a frosty vigilance characterized by stony silence.

"What will happen if we do see Wakuria?" I asked Moses.

From his position behind the wheel, he gave me a sideways glance. "Blood," he said, maybe for effect.

Somewhat anticlimactically, the Wakuria never appeared.

———

It had become unbearably hot in the cab of the Land Cruiser. All of us had salty sweat stains raking tie-dye patterns over our clothing. The dust sucked in through the window had settled onto Kate's face; mixed with sweat, it made her look Polynesian. Bron was listening to a first-generation Walkman that was about the size of a household stereo. She'd become so bored with the sight of wildebeests streaming around us hour after hour after hour that she'd stopped looking out the window and was reading a book while singing along to Mariah Carey.

Meanwhile, Kate—we'd dubbed her "Teach"—was snapping pictures as the vehicle bounced along. She had a passion for photography; the click of her camera punctuated my mental snapshots with remarkable accuracy. "I'm getting some amazing shots," she bubbled. "I've never seen so many herbivores! Let's face it: wildebeests don't look that smart. Certainly not as pretty as zebras. Do you know why zebras have stripes? It's to dazzle predators as they run away from them—they can't tell where one zebra ends and another begins. That's why the collective noun is a 'dazzle of zebras.' This whole grassland is so fertile thanks to a thick layer of volcanic ash from thousands of years ago." Kate was trying to be educational, but it seemed more a case of safari babble.

A swarm of tsetse flies had infiltrated the Land Rover. A loving family member could swat you at any moment.

Smack!

"What was that for?" I snarled, glaring at Bron.

"You had a tsetse on you—would you rather I leave it?" she shot back.

Tsetse flies are famed for spreading sleeping sickness, but it's really their painful bite I feared. I didn't like getting bitten or slapped, so that's when I headed for the perch on the roof through the hatch Uncle John had cut for game-viewing purposes.

The advantage of the roof was that the tsetse flies were scattered by the wind before they could inflict their torturous bites on my skin. I could also hook my feet under the roof rack and suddenly lower my head and torso onto the windshield, like a splattered bug, nearly causing Moses a heart attack.

From this position I felt like I was at the bow of a boat in a fast-flowing river of wildebeests as they cantered around the Cruiser. Bearded, bovine, and black as anthracite, the wildebeests weaved with the organized chaos of a tightly packed flock of birds. We drove amid the herd as it issued its characteristic call of "gnu, gnu, gnu" with a powerful, endless drone. The herd split around the vehicle, individuals coming so close that I felt like I could reach out and touch one before it seemingly found another gear and sped away. Among the wildebeests were zebras, flashing black-and-white apparitions in the great clouds of dust. The earth was a giant drum resonating to the beat of six million hooves. Hovering above the wildebeests were swarms of flies. Down on the ground, the dung beetles, following the herd's trail of digested grass, rolled perfect balls of manure in which to lay their eggs. Within the migration were other life cycles, acts of death and renewal, ecosystems beyond what could be seen at first glance. Life perpetuated by death, death perpetuated by life. When I closed my mouth I could feel the fine crunch of African dust between my teeth.

That day in a sea of wildebeests, grassland, sun, and endless sky, I felt myself truly merging with the perfect intelligence of the natural system, God's own seemingly chaotic symphony. I was migrating with these ancient beasts on a journey motivated by a grassland that protects itself in partnership with the cycles of drought and rain. The rain greened everything in its path, and the wildebeests followed. I was entwined with an open system whose intricacies we cannot begin to perceive. I was humbled and inspired. To be in a migration is to be made small as a body and infinite as God's love, truly in the flow. Maybe Mom and Dad were right: this was the education I really needed.

I spent ten days on the roof as we flowed through the migration and the migration flowed around us. It was always amazing to watch Uncle John stop and film in the bush. Camera crews from the BBC, the Discovery Channel, National Geographic, and other networks were fighting for the best position at various crossing points so they could capture the tumult of thousands of wildebeests massing to plunge into croc-infested waters. Uncle John was nowhere to be seen. On the advice of some Masai friends, he'd be asleep under his frayed bush hat, half a mile from where the action was about to take place. Sure enough, at the last moment, a single wildebeest would break rank, run the half mile down to where Uncle John was parked, and leap into the river, causing an avalanche of pounding hooves to follow suit.

"Buddy, never follow the rules," he'd tell me. "Stick with the local knowledge and build relationships—that's how you get the shots." Then he'd offer up his trademark vampire smirk, having just canned the best high-action sequence of the day. After the first wildebeest jumped, thousands of others likewise took the plunge, and they churned through the water, swimming nose to tail, battling the current. Crocodiles began slipping off the banks in pursuit. The water boiled, foaming white as the crocodiles' powerful tails thrashed back and forth. Their jaws mashed down on wildebeests, pulling them beneath the surface. The air shrilled with wildebeests' alarm calls as they disappeared from sight. The ones who made it to the other side, heaving with exhaustion, found lions in wait. After so many hours of sitting around, I found the scene unbelievably thrilling.

After weeks spent crossing the grasslands, we finally arrived at a police outpost on the border of Kenya and Tanzania. It wasn't an official border crossing, but for the right amount of money, you could make it one. Uncle John went off to get negotiations under way while I left the dust-covered Land Cruiser and wandered over to a small tuckshop set up against the side of the building.

The shop was so short of stock that it was more of an anti-shop, a place you could go to gaze at what you couldn't buy. The Masai woman behind the counter wore a faded polo shirt over a traditional *shuka,* and Masai beadwork along with Western sunglasses. Having lost anything to keep, she had in a way ceased to have a purpose. Like many African store owners, she ran hers with a laid-back quality, moving as slowly as the heat puddled around us. This owner probably saw no more than two or three customers a day. When one showed up, she behaved like it was more of a nuisance than an opportunity. While she seemed completely depleted and without purpose, in fact she had all the power in this nego-tiation, as hers was the only store for miles.

Goats with squinty eyes and chickens with mangy plumage strutted and straggled around her. It was like an odd runt congress for the worst collection of domestic animals I'd ever seen.

Amazingly, amid all this torpor I spotted my quarry. In the back of the shop, stacked in cases that reached to the roof, were dusty crates of Coca-Cola, the true colonizer of Africa.

"Could I buy a Coke, please?" I asked the shopkeeper.

"Bottle," she mumbled, holding out her hand.

This confused me; surely I should hold out *my* hand and receive the goods—or was this small shop set in a parallel universe where every-thing happened topsy-turvy?

"Yes, a bottle will be fine," I tried, ignoring her outstretched hand.

"No, you must give me an empty bottle before I give you a full one," she explained.

"But how do I get an empty one?" I asked.

"First you must buy a fresh one," she said. Wasn't this obvious?

"That's what I'm trying to do!" I shot back. "So can I buy one?"

"No, not if you don't have an empty."

"What if I buy one and drink it here?"

I could see this was an option that hadn't crossed her mind.

"Okay," she said after a long pause, but she watched me suspiciously from the moment my fingers wrapped around the bottle. The soda was warm and as thick as molasses. She continued to monitor my every sip, as if at any moment I might make a break for it with one of her precious bottles.

This was Africa: eccentric to the core and addictive for the way its quirks became the things you missed the most when you left.

By this time, Uncle John had managed to cajole his way through the police post on the border, another example of how in Africa, "illegal" is just a place to start the debate. We made our way to his camp some hundred miles distant to spend time among the Masai.

Over the course of several years, Uncle John became very close with a group of Masai who lived in the Mara. He hunted buffaloes and lion with the herdsmen, and drove several of them to the hospital after a lion attacked them during a hunt. They allowed him to put up a tented camp on the banks of the Mara River on the fringe of the Masai Mara National Reserve. He also bought a rather nice herd of Nguni cows, which he co-owned with the Masai.

Uncle John had decided to make a movie called *Brothers in Arms,* a documentary about the tribe to which he had become so close. The film would place him inside the lives of the Masai and their *manyattas,* or homesteads, amid dwellings made of cow dung, sticks, mud, and human urine. And it would witness the fading light of one of Africa's most traditional tribes. Their lifestyle, which had been in tune with the great plains and its animals, was changing. The Kenyan government was trying to persuade the Masai to become wheat farmers because there was a robust market for this coveted grain. Some Masai leaders were encouraging the shift. Money had entered their life, and wheat was a way to get it. Bron, Kate, and I were thrown into that fading *manyatta* life as the sound crew for Uncle John's documentary.

The Masai's faces are sharp and eaglelike, but despite their ferocious appearance—something that has unnerved many a foreigner—they are, in fact, like most tribal people: focused on family life and extremely gentle. They don't walk; they glide across vast distances on the savannah.

The Masai are passionate about two things: their cows and their children, in that order. The greatest honor they can bestow on you is to offer you a drink of cow's blood and milk. A cow is pulled out of the herd and held down as it bellows for the safety of its companions. Then a warrior expertly shoots an arrow into its neck. A plume of perfect lipstick-red blood shoots into the air and is captured in a gourd. The cow quickly stops bleeding and is returned to the herd. Meanwhile, milk is added to the gourd, turning the concoction into a beautifully viscous teeth-staining red syrup. This is then handed to you with a loving smile. You drink it while making a big show of receiving the honor: lots of holding the gourd high up in the air, smacking your lips, and saying, "Mmm-mmm" and "What an honor!," all the time trying not to vomit up your spleen.

———

Bron, Kate, and I lived on the Mara River for six weeks in a tented camp that nestled in a cool grove of trees. The camp was complete with a mess tent, editing tent, and bucket shower. Kate had already figured out that, say, teaching a unit on carnivorous plants in Kenya made no sense, so she taught us everything she knew about the land and Masai culture and history. Mostly, she stepped aside and encouraged Bron and me to be adopted into the daily routines of the tribe.

I spent my days lying under a tree with the men, occasionally getting up to practice throwing a spear. During the middle of the day, when the sun blazed down, creating what Laurens van der Post called "Africa's real witching hour," stillness would descend on the camp. From up the hill, we could hear the tinkling of cowbells. Down at the river, elephants would be showering water over their wrinkled bodies. Under the trees the Masai, with scarlet blankets wrapped over their heads, would wait out the heat, sleeping soundly in the tall grass. I developed serious hero worship for these warriors. They had spears and knives and clubs; what boy wouldn't have been fascinated? The only time I ever heard of the Masai being afraid was when Uncle John took them to the sea and a wave tried to "steal their shoes." I slept side by side with them, hoping that my dreams would merge with theirs and in that other place I would be a warrior, too.

Bronwyn, on the other hand, had to fetch water from the river, carry firewood on her head, wash the cows' udders, and assist in milking. Each evening when we weren't filming, she would return to camp looking like she'd just spent the day on a chain gang, while I, still full of energy, practiced my stick fighting with Gordilla, a big, fierce Masai who was head of security.

"Hey, Bron, what an awesome day! I shot a bow and arrow!" I'd tell her.

She'd stand up and storm away, saying, "Go wash some cow udders, you idiot!"

Kate was able to avoid water-carrying duty because she was a teacher. Education is a mystical and sought-after attribute in many parts of Africa. Among the Masai, however, Kate had to navigate an unstable path. As a woman, her status was low, but as a teacher, it was high. Many viewed her as all-knowing. She fielded constant questions from the camp staff on topics ranging from math to culture. Much to her amazement, she was also consulted on various medical issues. There was always someone who had been hit, stabbed, clubbed, or speared. She handled these crises as best she could, but one day a Masai came to her with a lung punctured by a *rungu*, or club, and blood frothing out of his mouth. "Sorry, I'm a bit out of my depth on this one," she told him and dispatched him to the hospital. Sometimes I think the Masai invented injuries to have a peek at our well-stocked first aid kit. One Masai couldn't tear himself away from the hand mirror, turning it this way and that.

I was asked if I wanted to participate in a ritual that all young men go through to prove their courage. This involves placing a glowing-hot ember from the fire on any part of the body and just letting it burn there as you absorb the pain—a sign of manly prowess. Luckily, I was able to avoid this, as I had been through the ritual before and had the scars to prove it, although my glowing ember had actually been a cigarette lighter and I'd been heavily medicated on vodka at the time, courtesy of one of the guys in my dorm at boarding school. It's nice to know that young men in all cultures are linked by a mutual love of the game called "Let's see how badly we can hurt each other." The crew of young *morani,* the young warriors in the tribe, could tell I'd been through it and were impressed by the smiley face my ember scars had left, so they let me sit the game out.

The Masai allowed Uncle John to capture shots of daily life as it played out around us, almost all of the goings-on in the village. But from time to time he was forced into the dangerous and, fortunately, rare world of re-creations. These situations occurred only when Uncle John had personally witnessed something but hadn't been able to film it. He was one of the few outsiders who had been on a lion hunt with the Masai. One particular hunt had been initiated after an unusual event in which a lion had stupidly attacked a Masai cow—something most lions have wisely learned to avoid. The Masai had gone after the lion with spears and clubs. After a long pursuit, a massive fight had ensued, with the lion bursting out of the bush and mauling members of the hunting party as they fought it at close quarters.

Uncle John had witnessed the whole thing, saw how powerfully it reflected the values of the tribe, and decided to re-create this scene, complete with all the action and tension. He issued a rapid-fire report to Gordilla and another young Masai, Laveres.

"Okay, Gordilla, run into that bush and pull Laveres out. Everyone else, pretend like you're stabbing at the lion." Uncle John issued his instructions in his very sharp, very clear director's voice. This was then translated into Masai for the benefit of the group of men standing around balanced on single legs, leaning on their spears. They looked very confused; why should they pretend to hunt an imaginary lion?

"Okay, action!" screamed Uncle John.

Gordilla walked over to the bush and calmly pulled Laveres out. The other tribesmen stood around, more confused than ever.

"No, no! Do it like you're pulling him from the jaws of a lion! I'll shoot it tight for effect," shouted Uncle John. "And you guys scream like you're screaming at a lion." He turned to me. "Buddy, roll sound. Energy! Energy, people! Let's go again. Action!"

Again the energy was as flat as a pancake, since the Masai had no concept of acting and saw no point in walking around aimlessly, throwing out the odd stabbing motion with a spear.

"No, for fuck's sake, like *this*!" Uncle John screamed, yanking Laveres at high speed through the bush while the poor man complained loudly in Masai. "Pull him! Pull him! Buddy, roll sound! Roll sound!" Uncle John then dropped a shocked-looking Laveres and, still screaming at full volume, shoved the closest warrior. "Get in there! Get in there!"

The warrior, who didn't like being shoved, tried to hit Uncle John with his club. Uncle John, an accomplished boxer, backed up while expelling a blasphemous blast of "Jesus Christ"s. For a moment, I worried that I would be forced to defend him with the sound mike. Then Gordilla drew his knife to defend his cattle partner. Everyone was now screaming in Masai. Just then Uncle John turned to me. "Keep the sound rolling, buddy!"

The Masai had now squared up to each other. Uncle John picked up his camera, wielding it as a great weapon even as he captured shots of the men trying to club and stab each other. "Bonna, tomato sauce! Tomato sauce!" he shouted to Bron so she would shoot a stream of Heinz into the action for bloody special effects.

Just as we were about to become victims of a mass homicide, Uncle John screamed "Cut!," put down the camera, strolled into the middle of the fight, and started shaking hands with everyone. "Tell them that they

ABOVE: In 1926, just getting to Londolozi was an adventure in itself.

LEFT: An early hunting party heading into the bush on buckboard.

My grandfather Boyd Varty and his tracker after a kill. Hunting lions brought us to the bush, but hunting would later give way to a deep desire to conserve.

The early Londolozi start-up crew, young and unafraid, launched themselves into the safari business. My father is seated on the ground at center, with Uncle John second from the right and Shan behind Dad's right shoulder.

ABOVE LEFT: Dave and Shan during the decade-long wait for Dave's marriage proposal. ABOVE RIGHT: Uncle John reluctantly driving some reform school boys—the only guests they could get—across the Sand River.

Dave, Shan, and John with Madie Varty, the matriarch of Londolozi. She supported her sons' crazy idea for a safari business without hesitation.

Uncle John, in typical "JV couture," and Elmon Mhlongo tracking Manana, the Mother Leopard.

Uncle John and Shingalana, in many ways the love of his life. His relationship with Shingi converted John to the belief that animals are our kin.

Dad in his bath. Early ablutions did not fall into the category of luxury.

With his passion for flying, Dad is chief pilot of the White Knuckle Charter Company.

A wild male leopard jumps up to investigate Uncle John. Where other photographers would flee, Uncle John is always up for the "high-action sequence."

Winnis Mathebula, naturalist extraordinaire, was a second father to Dave and John. He had been gored by a buffalo and bitten by a black mamba, but his only weakness was telling stories in which he was the valiant hero.

Elmon Mhlongo, John's best friend and chief cameraman, filmed cheetahs in the Mara and leopards at Londolozi, and starred alongside Brooke Shields in a feature film. *(Photo: John Varty)*

At age eight, I was already piloting the Land Rover so Uncle John could get his "high-action shots, buddy."

School with Kate Groch, a.k.a. "Teach," included Ngorongoro Crater as one of its classrooms.

Teacher Kate rolls sound for *Brothers in Arms,* Uncle John's documentary about the Masai. A few minutes after this photo, a massive argument broke out among the heavily armed and reluctant warrior stars, which almost resulted in bloodshed.

Teacher Kate, Bron, our cousin Savannah, and me among our Masai friends after a day of filming. Later Bron returned to fetching water while I practiced my spear throwing.

Elmon helps me track a lion. My entire life is now guided by the principles of finding the right track.

Nelson Mandela at Londolozi. Everywhere he went, elated crowds would gather. Madiba's birthday remains a day of celebration at Londolozi.

In Luangwa Valley, this road is considered a good one.

Two lionesses take their freshly baked cubs on a stroll. Once hunted, lions are now protected and prolific at Londolozi. *(Photo: Rich Laburn)*

Because of the legacy of the Mother Leopard, Londolozi has become a place for amazing sightings of these wild cats. *(Photo: Rich Laburn)*

Martha Beck taught me how to follow my inner tracks. *(Photo: Rich Laburn)*

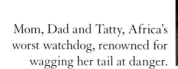

Mom, Dad and Tatty, Africa's worst watchdog, renowned for wagging her tail at danger.

The wire tusks at the Intention Circle, made from the fence that used to keep wildlife out of Londolozi, bring the hope of restoring a passage to the mountains for elephants. *(Photo: Rich Laburn)*

Riding around in the battered but beautiful BB Jeep, which survives to this day.

Stuck in the mud but inventing yet another escape: Bron's and my childhood in a nutshell.
(Photo: Elsa Young)

Friendi and me. Still best friends, still at Londolozi.
(Photo: Elsa Young)

The Sand River is a current of life that cuts through Londolozi. My father has spent literally decades protecting it for the hippos, crocs, and elephants that depend on it. *(Photo: Adam Bannister)*

The famous wildebeest crossing of the Mara River. It was here that Uncle John captured his best footage for his documentary *Troubled Waters*. (*Photo: Rich Laburn*)

When these peaceful creatures returned to Londolozi, it was a great act of restoration. *(Photo: Rich Laburn)*

Jamu was a young leopard with a gentle, affectionate nature. Unlike many leopards, she loved to sit close and put a paw on you while you prayed she kept her claws in. *(Photo: John Varty)*

were all brilliant!" he shouted to the translator. The fight immediately subsided and laughter broke out.

When a very famous leopard called Half Tail was shot by a poacher in the Mara area, Uncle John, a staunch anti-poaching crusader, decided to re-create the crucial moment when a Masai warrior ran into camp to inform him. The translator taught the warrior the exact English words he was to say. Then he was to answer a series of yes or no questions that would set up the next scene, in which Half Tail would be darted with a tranquilizer gun and her life saved. (Half Tail would go on to live many years, although Uncle John heard that she was eventually killed by another poacher.) The tribesman had been practicing his English lines all afternoon, but at the critical moment, things started to fall apart.

"Half Tail has been shot by han harrow!" said the breathless warrior as he jogged up to Uncle John.

"Is she dead?" asked Uncle John on cue.

"Yes," replied the warrior.

"Cut!" shouted Uncle John. "You're supposed to say no; otherwise the whole darting scene to remove the arrow dies. Okay, let's go again."

The Masai warrior dutifully jogged back into position, then replayed his grand entrance. "Half Tail has been shot by han harrow!"

"Can we save her?" asked Uncle John, who had no ability to stick to a script.

"No."

"Cut!" shrieked Uncle John, as Bron, Kate, and I collapsed in hysterics behind the sound mike.

Uncle John was also keen to capture a time-honored Masai ritual, the circumcision of the adolescent boys. This is typically done without anesthesia; it's considered dishonorable for the young boy to display any sign of pain. Afterward, he will wear a black cloth for months as the wound heals. The Masai wouldn't let Uncle John film the actual event, but they permitted a re-creation. They didn't know what they were getting themselves into when it came to Uncle John's exacting standards. Tensions were already running high on day four, after Grumu, a young Masai boy, had rebelled against having water thrown over him for the tenth time in the simulated circumcision scene.

"Buddy, get up on that roof there," Uncle John ordered, pointing to the cow-dung roof of the nearby *manyatta*. "We need some high-angle shots down into the village."

"JV, it looks quite flimsy," I said. Uncle John fixed me with the look a lion gives an annoying hyena. Needless to say, I wrestled the weighty old Arriflex camera onto my shoulder, clambered onto the roof, and gingerly started to position my feet as well as the legs of the tripod. Nothing but two inches of cow dung separated me from a giant fall. Then the inevitable happened: the roof collapsed beneath my feet. I was swallowed by the house and landed in a crumpled heap in the section where the young goats sleep. Just as my head was starting to clear, a woman who looked about three hundred years old appeared and in a rage over the state of her roof started to beat me to a pulp with a dried wildebeest tail while screaming something in Masai. It's amazing how reprimands are understandable in all languages.

But mostly the Masai didn't mind being filmed and were proud to showcase their traditions. I don't think it would have been that way if Uncle John hadn't built up such a good relationship with them over the years. And for all his madness, Uncle John was an amazing teacher. He taught me about filmmaking and how to think in pictures and, perhaps most important, instilled in me a deep passion to tell stories. I realized that if you really want to make an impact as a conservationist, it's not enough to do the work. You have to be able to communicate a message.

Things are changing in the Mara. The traditional scarlet-hued *shuka* is giving way to Western hand-me-downs; in these clothes the Masai, for the first time, look poor. Money and wheat schemes are disrupting the balance and harmony that has existed for so long between the Masai and their home on the great plains. Bron, Kate, and I may have had a last genuine glimpse of this tribe of warriors who live so close to the earth.

TWELVE

A LONDOLOZI OF LEOPARDS

L EOPARDS ARE ANIMATED BY MYSTERY. Their silhouettes house more than sinew and organs; they are the slippery boundaries between ourselves and everything wild we have ever wondered about. If you get a chance to be around a leopard, you'll discover that elements of this mystery will seep into your own spirit, making you a person who loves the unknown and is comfortable in your own secret nature. I'm not surprised that Uncle John and I have had a lifetime obsession with leopards.

In many ancient cultures, it is the secretive, solitary leopard that is the totem animal of the shaman. Uncle John set out to capture images of leopards and see if he could connect with these sacred felines. He declared himself the first emissary representing the people. Maybe it was the fact that my uncle has shamanic energy, too, or maybe it was a coincidence, but an emissary from the other side appeared. She took the form of a smallish female leopard with a broken canine.

Uncle John and Elmon Mhlongo were walking in an area of thick brush where, as a hunter, Uncle John had shot a male leopard fifteen years before. Suddenly a female leopard appeared. Unlike other leopards, she didn't immediately run away but allowed the two men to watch her from a distance for a good five or six minutes. Such a viewing is unremarkable by today's standards at Londolozi, but then it was highly unusual behavior for a wild leopard. Uncle John wrote of this first encounter, "I was transfixed by her beauty, her grace, the suppleness of her body and her haunting eyes. For me it was a defining moment, a life-changing event."

The leopard started to show glimpses of herself fleetingly, appearing to Uncle John and Elmon at a great distance. Sometimes they would go for days without seeing her. Then, just as they were becoming heavy-hearted, she would appear again, only to vanish like a great magician, giving them just enough hope that they would eventually connect with her, testing to see if she could trust them.

Over time, the relationship deepened. The leopard allowed herself to be seen with more and more regularity. The Shangaan called her Manana, or "the Mother." Uncle John called her "the Mother Leopard." The Mother Leopard was a talisman for how things were changing at Londolozi. The animals were starting to respond to the restoration of the land, becoming more trusting—and this, in turn, changed the people watching them. In Manana, Uncle John had encountered the animal to whom he would dedicate the rest of his life, through observing, documenting, and conserving.

My uncle spent hundreds of hours in Manana's presence. He watched her mate and have cubs. He gave her space when she was moody, her tail whipping in annoyance and a snarl on her lips. She went on to have nine litters of cubs—nineteen in total, all of whom grew up with their mother's trust of people.

Most of my memories of being in the bush with my uncle involve tracking or observing Manana. As she got older, the years of hunting, raising cubs, and simply surviving began to take their toll on her small frame. She began to rely more on her cunning as a hunter than on raw speed. Her fur began to loosen and soften over her wiry frame.

We were with her the night she was savagely attacked by lions, who encircled her, viciously charging from all angles. She was a ball of fury in their midst, but one of the lions bit her badly through her hindquarters as another struck at her from the front. The volume and ferocity of her growling made it sound as if she had a chain saw in her belly. Despite her wounds, she was able to escape, running wildly through the bush on her wounded legs. We gunned the Land Rover in pursuit, hoping that she would be able to make it into a tree. Lighter and smaller than lions, leopards can readily climb up trunks lions would have great trouble scaling. Leopards are also much more agile once in a tree, able to jump from branch to branch, whereas a lion's weight would prevent it from following. Ahead of us we could hear the savage growls as the lions worked as a pride to tear strips off her. My uncle, hard as he tried, could not remain an impartial observer; he crashed the Landi over rough terrain and saplings, screaming abuse at the lions. Eventually Manana made it into the trees. The entire event lasted only a few minutes, but it was a brutal few minutes.

The lion attack was the beginning of the end for Manana. Over the weeks that followed, she weakened, unable to hunt. Uncle John took a mattress out into the bush, laid it on the hood of his Landi, and slept day and night with her. He brought her an impala to feed on. One of these lonely days, when it was just the two of them out in the wild, he placed a bowl of water near her and she drank from it; this was an immense act of acceptance from a wild leopard. Over the course of three months, Uncle John spent as much time as he could watching over her, following her when she moved around the bush.

The Mother Leopard lived to the ripe old age of fourteen, very advanced for a leopard in the wild. Uncle John was devastated when she died. Their relationship lasted more than a decade, and he bestowed the honorific of "Manana" on her granddaughter.

The Mother Leopard's passing marked the end of an era, yet it spawned a legacy. So much of the success of Londolozi has been as a result of the amazing leopard viewing. In fact, we've decided that the proper collective noun is a "Londolozi of leopards."

———

Uncle John invited me and Bronwyn to be his assistants for a few months. He wanted us to help him raise a young female leopard cub deep in the heart of the Luangwa Valley, in Zambia. Having watched Manana raise several litters of cubs, he now felt up to the task himself. He'd taken custody of the young lady after some game scouts had found her mother killed by a poacher's snare. She was still very much a kitten, only a few weeks old. Uncle John decided that she would be the perfect subject for his latest documentary. He thought Bron and I would benefit from seeing the cub grow.

Kate agreed. After our first adventure together during the great migration, she'd understood that being out of school could give me and Bron life experiences we would never get in a classroom. Raising a leopard cub seemed like a great opportunity to push those boundaries. She would come along as our tutor. At age fourteen, I was excited at the thought of living in such a remote part of Africa, and I knew from past experience with Uncle John that our stay would be full of adventure. This also scared me slightly.

What I didn't know was that the thrill of being in a remote part of Africa meant that Uncle John would operate full throttle in what he called "Africa mode." Africa mode involved an odd mixture of John Rambo–like ruggedness, derring-do, and the occasional diplomatic feint. This could be simultaneously terrifying and reckless, as Uncle John has been known to throw the unexpected punch one moment and then become the great philosopher the next. Sometimes Africa mode was simply downright baffling, as when John negotiated for some three-month-old dried fish "to support the local economy"—that is, if you really believed the local market was supported by the barter of a pair of strops. Uncle John had of course invited Elmon Mhlongo along as well, but Elmon had demurred. "I'm never going back to Zambia," he told Uncle John. "Because the Coke is warm, and when you buy crisps, there are only five or six in the whole packet." This was a very typical nonconfrontational Shangaan way of expressing his concerns; a more straightforward statement might have been "The last time we went to Zambia, we nearly got killed in a helicopter crash!"

And so it was that Mom and Dad ferried me, Bron, and Kate out to Lanseria Airport, a relatively small airstrip on the outskirts of Johannesburg, where a single-engine Cessna Caravan aircraft was being loaded. No Varty has ever been realistic about what can fit into a car or plane. This tradition harkens back to when my grandfather, prior to a hunting trip to the bush, would load up the family Plymouth with more firepower than the Allied forces at Normandy and then ask the rest of the family to squeeze in around the edges. My gran would then try to fit a few cake tins containing food into the car. A fight over the proper priorities would ensue, usually resulting in a cake being flung out the window in the predawn departure light.

Uncle John fully subscribes to the "more is more" school of cargo loading. Thanks to him, we now know that small aircraft can't fly with fridges strapped to the wings.

The latest cargo battle was playing out on the tarmac, much to the pilot's consternation. The plane was already sitting at a grotesque angle, bulging like a pregnant guppy as my uncle tried to force what looked like either a diesel generator or a Land Rover gearbox into the aisle, flicking boxes of papayas over his shoulder and out the cargo door over the wailing protests of Gillian, who believed in the value of fresh produce. Meanwhile, I was unnerved by the six-foot fiberglass crocodile that was sunning itself on the tarmac, waiting to be loaded in. (Uncle John was always commissioning lifelike props he could use to get himself closer to the wildlife he was filming. He's spent hundreds, if not thousands, of hours plunked among herds of wildebeests and zebras, crammed sausagelike into fiberglass crocs, or inside the torso of a model ostrich with just his legs sticking out, the camera whirring.)

Eventually I was able to wedge myself into the plane between the crocodile and a box of Ensure nutrition shakes, as long as I kept my head cocked at a thirty-degree angle. As Bron, Kate, Uncle John, Gillian, and my cousin Savannah, then four or five, loaded themselves into the plane, Mom began to protest; she knew we couldn't get safely airborne. My father's reply was typical of what had aged her: "It's still cool; she should hop." Kate's eyes immediately widened. "I'm sorry, what did you just say?" Dad, realizing that Kate wasn't the calmest flier, pretended not to hear her. And so we went porpoising down the runway, my mother and father waving from the terminal lawn. As the pilot lifted the plane's nose for a shaky takeoff, I realized that our Zambia expedition with Uncle John was airborne . . . just.

The trip took us from Joburg to Londolozi to load some eight-man tents, then 200 miles to Polokwane to clear South African customs, then 500 miles to Harare, Zimbabwe, for fuel, then 460 more miles to Lilongwe, Malawi, for more fuel, then a final 150 miles to Mfuwe, in the heart of Zambia. By the time we arrived, it was evening and the border official had treated himself to a few warm quarts of the local brew; seeing the guppy touch down with more impedimenta than a gypsy caravan must have been like watching Christmas roll in early. I could tell by the glint in his eye that he intended to take us for big ammo; bribery is a time-honored art and blood sport in Africa. Uncle John had briefed us on landing to claim that everything was a "sample" and to expound how we filmmakers had come to produce a documentary on the amazing country that is Zambia.

From the very first exchange, it was clear that the border official wasn't buying. We'd already tried the most popular gambit, in which you place fifteen hundred rand in your passport and ask if you can simply pay a "spot fine" rather than import duties. No sale. It was time to unleash my secret weapon. I produced a bottle of Rémy Martin VSOP brandy. The official's eyes locked onto it the way a lion's eyes snap onto a lost baby wildebeest. Suddenly I was in the power seat. "You're right," I said. "We should rather sit here till your superior arrives, and then we'll agree on the import duties." In a moment, we were through: cameras, fiberglass croc, and all.

Uncle John met us outside in a Land Cruiser he'd somehow manifested from behind a terminal building. I don't want to say he stole it, but he may have borrowed it without the owner knowing. What I can tell you is that it was hot-wired and we weren't allowed to turn it off in case we couldn't get it to start again. "Load up," Uncle John shouted to our assembled crew. All the luggage that had made the plane look like a dying whale now had to be piled in and on top of the Cruiser. We were joined by a Zambian chap called Ben, who had a scar that arched from his hand up to the point of his shoulder. In between the slamming and crashing of loading the cruiser, he described to me how an elephant had "victimized" and "taken advantage" of him.

After we got to our lodge, we had to take turns getting up in the middle of the night to go tip diesel into the Landi as it idled in the car park, lest it stop cold. We also met Savannah's pet baby warthog, Hela, which had been waiting for her at the lodge. Hela was a stout, hairy beast with little tusks just starting to bloom from her prodigious proboscis. Her acquisition was something of a mystery; she was just part of the scene.

The next morning we awoke early to drive into the heart of the park. Our journey was supposed to take six hours, but it was the rainy season in Zambia and the road looked like a mixture of the Nile River and gorilla snot. Uncle John was deeply excited by the challenge, wrestling the steering wheel back and forth, elbows flailing. He punctuated his revving of the engine with the requisite "fuck," "Jesus," "bloody Arab," and "shit." The clunking and revving sent us lurching all over the luggage, breathing life into the fiberglass croc as we careened toward its gaping jaws, and provoking Savannah's warthog into a snorting fit, during which she began to gore Ben. As the wheels spun, Bronwyn received a blast of mud to the face, transforming her into a Kikuyu warrior. Kate looked on, shocked speechless. Suddenly the Landi lurched into a gutter and would go no farther. We were stuck.

For a long time we didn't see so much as a single car. I began to prepare for a night of fitful sleep in the rain, cuddled up next to Hela the warthog, drinking Ensure mixed with mud for nutrition.

My uncle, however, was thrilled by the level to which we had become stuck and took it as a chance to muscle about in the mud, trying to single-handedly push the truck out. At one point he slid in under the truck's chassis. "If it rolls on top of me and traps me underwater, buddy," he instructed, "just put a piece of PVC pipe into my mouth, like a snorkel." We were there for about three hours. Hela ran away into the bush, much to Savannah's distress.

We were at last rescued by an armada of fishermen, who, with the freakish strength of people who grow up in Africa, were able to pick the Landi up and carry it to a drier spot, where we set off again, Uncle John doing his flailing turkey dance and my cousin crying over Hela's disappearance.

We eventually arrived at the access point to my uncle's base camp in a section of South Luangwa National Park known as Zebra Plains. From here all we had to do was take a small banana boat across the river and then hike about two miles with all the equipment to the camp. Attached to the back of this motorized canoe was an engine powerful enough for the average kitchen blender. Naturally, Uncle John over-loaded the vessel. Water threatened to cascade over the gunnels with the slightest movement. Need I add that along the banks of the river were literally hundreds of crocodiles? Most of them slipped into the water as we motored past. Occasionally we would hit a sandbank and I would be ordered out to push us off. I was not happy about getting out of the boat, and this annoyed my uncle, who reminded me, "Africa's not for sissies."

One time as I clambered out, I set foot on a catfish. Terrified that I'd stepped on a croc, I let out a girlish scream. The disdainful look on my uncle's face made me wilt inside.

The camp was nicely set out, with three large tents under a sausage tree (named for its bologna-sized pods). Its thick foliage provided great shade, though we faced the ever-present danger of being brained by a faux bratwurst. The camp also had a kitchen tent and a pit toilet. Herds of elegant pukus and zebras grazed nearby. We dug a well in the riverbed for fresh water. I loved Zambia for the same reasons my uncle loved it; it is one of the last true wildernesses left, saved by its inhospitableness and remoteness.

In an exception to our usual rule of naming leopards by their facial spot configurations, as the local scientists did, we named Uncle John's leopard cub Jamu, after the indigenous leopard orchid. Jamu had the most wonderful nature. She was playful and, unlike most leopards, seemed to genuinely enjoy the company of humans. All cats within a species have distinct personalities. Just as you might have one house cat who's a lap sitter and another who seems always to be planning its escape, some leopards are more outgoing than others. Jamu was a lover. We would spend hours out in the middle of Luangwa, walking with her, watching her teach herself about her environment by climbing trees, pouncing on insects, and sniffing mushrooms.

Living in close proximity to a leopard affords you the opportunity to observe fascinating aspects of its nature you don't get to see even when close up in a Land Rover: the delicate manner with which they step, the intricate calculations they make in the middle of a stalk, the way they learn through countless failures when to pounce. There are, however, downsides.

Raising a leopard is like raising a kitten that's eaten a three-year supply of horse steroids. Whereas a kitten might scratch the corner of your couch, a leopard will eat half of it, leaving a fluffy wad of upholstered carnage in its wake. A kitten might give you a few scratches; a leopard will make you look like you lost a fencing duel. Play fighting with a young leopard is a good way to get a sense of its raw power. I came to appreciate just how physically inadequate the human body is in the wilds of Africa whenever Jamu lovingly kicked the shit out of me. Bron and I had to guard a toddling Savannah from Jamu's natural curiosity; she might have been knocked flat by a playful pounce.

Jamu had a passion for toilet-paper rolls. She would steal ours out of the latrine and, in usual leopard fashion, hoist it into the branches of the sausage tree. (Leopards often drag their kill up into a tree, where they're protected from poaching lions and hyenas.) After a few hours of chewing on the roll and jumping from branch to branch, trailing long white garlands and sodden clumps of masticated paper, Jamu had the tree looking like a frat house after a hideous keg party. She was also passionate about soccer balls, running them down, trapping them between her great paws, and generally mauling and killing them. Jamu bounded around the camp during the day, but at night we put her in a sizable central cage with branches all around it, so she could sleep safely.

Kate, Bron, and I shared a tent in the camp. Upon arrival, Kate instantly took exception to our new digs.

"This tent smells like a kill—does this surprise us?" she noted sarcastically.

In fact, the mattress I was sleeping on had previously belonged to Shingi the lion, and it had indeed been her favorite place to eat her kills. She'd bitten huge hunks of foam out of the mattress, so I was constantly misplacing a foot, hand, or elbow in one of the holes.

Kate surveyed the general chaos of our tent and set about creating whatever order she could impose on it, as was her wont. She cadged a table from the mess tent and set it up at the front of our tent with chairs: an instant schoolroom overlooking the Zebra Plains. She hung up mosquito nets over each cot. She put a mosquito repellent coil in a corner. The box holding the coil featured a graphic of a mosquito with a red circle around it and a line slashed across it. Kate cut that out and taped it to the outside of our tent as a quirky warning to winged invaders.

As the weeks wore on, the smell of carcass became a regular theme.

"If it's not the mattress, then it's beastly Riggi," Kate complained. Riggi was a guinea fowl Uncle John had asked me to shoot in order to teach Jamu how to go about dealing with a bird carcass. Unfortunately, when Jamu was presented with the dead bird, she had no idea what to do with it, so we kept it with us and offered it to her periodically, hoping she might catch on. The dead bird became such a fixture that Kate decided we needed to name it.

"Let's call him Riggi," she proposed.

"Riggi? Why Riggi?" I asked.

"As in rigor mortis," she said. Over the last couple of days, the bird had solidified into a sculpture with one leg sticking out at an odd angle, its claw curled up tight.

"That thing is now disgusting. It's been dead for a week!" said Bron.

"It's not dead, it's just resting," said Kate.

"Ya, he's just sleeping," I chimed in. Kate and I were both big Monty Python fans, as well as connoisseurs of Gary Larson's *Far Side* comics.

"Look, he just moved!" said Kate, pushing the carcass with a stick.

"You guys are so not funny," huffed Bron.

"Oh dear, I think he's got a sore foot," said Kate. This understatement cracked me up because one of Riggi's feet had, in fact, been chewed off by Jamu.

"Yes, a little tweak in the toe," I said.

Bron just rolled her eyes in surrender.

The staff of the small camp, all local Zambians, were very dubious about the wisdom of living with a leopard. Bronwyn, on the other hand, was very excited. The only thing that annoyed her slightly was the fact that leopards, which are incredibly soft to pet, have a general disdain for any kind of cuddling that confines them.

Our shower was a bucket with holes poked in the bottom. The bucket dangled from the branch of a tree by a frayed piece of rope. A tug on the rope opened a valve to produce a feeble shower. The sight of the wobbling bucket was far too interesting for a young leopard to resist, and

Jamu would scamper up the tree, launch herself from a nearby branch onto the bucket, panic when she realized it was full of water, and bite through the rope, leaving you with a concussion and both a bucket and a leopard on your head. Despite her intelligence, Jamu repeated this maneuver regularly.

John's life in the bush followed simple routines. He'd take an early morning walk with Jamu to get her used to the wild, then rest through the middle of the day, lying on his camp bed in a faded orange sarong, working on scripts for his documentaries. In the late afternoon, as massive cumulus clouds started to build in the sky, we would all go out and walk Jamu again, kicking a soccer ball for her and rescuing her from trees she got stuck in, my uncle always filming, with Gillian by his side doing still photography.

"Buddy, get down on all fours and see if Jamu will stalk you," JV commanded.

"Buddy, grab those cameras, batteries, the lenses, the sound mike, the rifle, and a blanket, get my .44, and bring me a banana."

In the evenings we would eat around the fire or sit in the kitchen tent. Each night we went through the same routine, with Uncle John doing his usual pantomime as he removed lids from the pots with a chef's flourish. "Tonight for dinner we have . . . pap and dried fish." Which was what we had every night.

After our initial crossing on the banana boat, I anticipated a long, happy time on solid ground before we had to set foot in it again. I was wrong. Uncle John saw the canoe as a vessel for adventure, and whenever we weren't filming Jamu, we trawled the river in search of dead, decaying animals. Most people, when they happen upon a carcass, happily run the other way. Not Uncle John; a good rotting carcass was the perfect bait for crocs, a means to gathering great footage.

Whenever we found a hippo or croc carcass, we would tow it to the bank and then rope it to a root so that we could lie concealed and get good shots of crocs feeding. The photography was easy. Getting the carcass to the bank was the challenging part.

The day we found a rotting young elephant that had drowned was cause for great excitement. "Buddy, it's like a floating balloon—the crocs are right inside it!" Uncle John exulted. It took us about an hour to chase the crocs off and then rope the carrion to the canoe. Proud of ourselves, we began to power off, but we'd misjudged a few things. For one, we'd stupidly thought that our electric toothbrush–sized motor would be sufficient to pull an elephant upstream. Secondly, when we took full power, the boat hydroplaned, and we nearly flipped. "Climb up and anchor the nose!" my uncle screamed at me, in his excitement forgetting to take his hand off the throttle. After an hour of screaming engines, we'd gone about sixty yards. Then we ran out of petrol. Uncle John reluctantly abandoned the carcass. It took us the better part of three hours to hike home.

Trudging back to camp, I realized that I'd developed a typically African resignation to whatever misadventure Uncle John brought into my life. Setting out with him always prompted nerves, and I could be sure of only one thing: that I couldn't be sure of anything. I took to hoarding food in my pockets, knowing that a "short walk" could easily become an all-day hike. Not going along was never an option, however, because telling Uncle John that I wasn't game would have been unacceptable to both of us.

———

Eventually it was time for me, Bron, and Kate to head home to South Africa, leaving Jamu and Uncle John to spend their days stalking zebras on the clearing in front of the camp. I was deeply happy to be getting in that boat for the last time.

As she grew older, Jamu's hunting excursions beyond our camp stretched from an afternoon to a day to several days. This is typical of how young leopards start to leave their mothers. Eventually she struck out on her own. We were very excited that Jamu was well on the way to reintroduction and going completely wild. At the same time, we knew that she was entering a dangerous period. She was starting to become a mature leopard, which meant that she posed a threat to other female leopards in her territory.

Tragically, we believe Jamu was killed shortly thereafter by one such territorial female who'd tried to warn a potential rival off her land several times, mounting increasingly threatening attacks. Uncle John found Jamu's chewed-up radio collar, and we mourned her. Bron and I were already back at Londolozi when we heard the news. Though we were terribly upset, we understood that this was the biggest risk of trying to do this job. Working with wildlife is an emotional calling, but it does breed a certain philosophical nature. You have to do the best you can and hope to get lucky. Jamu didn't get lucky. But we were happy that she had starred in a film that would affect so many people around the world. We gave thanks for the gift of a leopard who had lived both with us and with her natural wildness, who had lain down with us in Eden, like the lion next to the lamb.

THIRTEEN

TRAVELS WITH KATE

THERE WAS NO HOPE for the villagers. Column after column of marauding invaders swarmed the area, herding their victims into a tight circle, relentlessly closing off all avenues of escape. Then the attack began. I couldn't believe the extraordinary strength of the invading hordes as they bore aloft, seemingly effortlessly, the spoils of war, their helpless enemies. As I watched them from my outpost hour after hour in utter fascination, I couldn't decide whether these soldiers reminded me more of highly disciplined Roman soldiers or pillaging Vikings.

"Don't get bitten, Boydie," Kate warned me. "They've got really powerful jaws, and you might not be able to pull them off." Like me, she was stationed with her bum in the air, eyes and ears down in the dirt, watching the Matabele ants execute their raid on the termite nest. The Matabeles, sometimes called army or driver ants, are named after a particularly vicious tribe of marauders that swept through southern Africa in the early nineteenth century. I watched those ants for five and a half of the most entertaining hours of my life. I was amazed to see the termites carried back to the ants' nest like slaves, to watch the soldier termites demolished by the attacking force.

Although Kate's nerdship encompassed everything from inorganic chemistry, the Fibonacci sequence, and Bernoulli's principle to Carl Sagan, space, and *Star Trek*, she had a special passion for insects, especially the way they were put together and how clever all their adaptations were. She would effuse, "I love bugs" in tones generally reserved for how most women adore shoes or the latest handbag. "Imagine this creature was as big as you are, Boydie. If a praying mantis were as big as an antelope, it would be a deadly predator. If an ant were the size of me, it could carry this house around."

Once, as part of Kate's Global Insect Initiative, she insisted we drive four hours through rugged terrain to a place where we might see glowworms. "It's an amazing chemical reaction," Kate enthused. "A reaction between two enzymes, luciferin and luciferase." When we finally arrived at our destination, it was black as night and the location had murder written all over it. "Here we are! Let's turn our lights off and enjoy the fireflies," Kate said. And so we killed the lights and were greeted by complete blackness: not a firefly in sight. There was silence in the car for about ten seconds. Then Bron cracked, "What a sight!" We all fell apart.

That was Kate's teaching in a nutshell. She encouraged my curiosity. She never made me leave the ants and come do math; she allowed me to pursue whatever caught my interest and then made me responsible for getting the rest of my schoolwork done.

Seeing how we thrived with Kate's teaching methods, Mom and Dad had persuaded her to stay on with us as our tutor so we could continue to be near them as they helped set up CC Africa lodges all over the continent.

Kate had been quick to set the tone for the relationship. "I'm not here to tell you what to do. I'm here to help you learn as much as you want," she told me and Bron. Her attitude toward education was hugely defining for me. In formal schooling, we'd been taught to obey. On more than one occasion I'd been forced to learn the hard way, at the end of a thick stick. I'd been stifled by the bells and drills and had lost touch with learning for the love of it; I'd simply fallen in step with the school's rhythm. Bron and I saw that life outside the school system often required more personal discipline. Kate challenged us to invest in our own learning.

Kate's methods took the best of the bush education I'd gotten from my old friend Jerry Hambana and crossed it with the finest tenets of traditional education. She set the syllabus, to a large degree, according to wherever we were. If there were interesting mountains, we'd go hike them before learning the theory of their formation. First we would feel them, then think them. "Look here, Boydie, see how the plates are compressed, and it's causing the mountain to rise." Kate would point out the changes in contour as we hiked more and more breathlessly up a slope. When we got back to the bottom, she'd spread out a contour map and we could see why the concentric circles got tighter and tighter as the mountain's elevation increased. She taught us how to read the life of a river: "What stage do you think it's in? Why do you think it's meandering? What made this oxbow form?"

Kate always encouraged this kind of wonder. She drew up a syllabus but never wholly relied on it. We once lost the bags with all our schoolwork en route to Tanzania, so for the three weeks we traveled around, Kate just created a new lesson plan. That wasn't a big deal for her. Presented with a challenge, the inveterate lover of Winnie-the-Pooh simply plied her trademark phrases: "I must ponder" and "I'll have a ponder on it." No prescribed curriculum would ever win out with her over teaching us how to teach ourselves. "You can learn more from life than you can in the four walls of a classroom," she told me. "Just get the piece of paper to keep everyone happy, but don't let it be the answer. . . . You find your own answers."

It's hard to remember how rough so much of Africa was back in the mid-1990s. The war in Mozambique was over, but we could see its effects on the faces of people; we could read in their eyes all that they'd been through. There weren't a lot of South Africans traveling around Africa back then, and some who'd gone to Zambia, Mozambique, Angola, and Namibia had done so for the express purpose of destabilizing those countries. So when Kate, Bron, and I first started traveling with my parents, we were mostly welcome, but it was still a very wild Africa. The economy hadn't woken up. When Dad and Mom first tried to build a lodge in Tanzania, they couldn't even get wooden roofing poles, supplies, or food to the site.

We saw the positive effect of education in Zimbabwe and Zambia, even though the places were falling apart. The postcolonial governments might have allowed the infrastructures to crumble, but the people nevertheless were well educated and able to speak English. We slept in tents in the Serengeti, waking at dawn to find a wildebeest giving birth in the morning light. We camped on the banks of the Zambezi, made friends all over Africa, and learned to live and interact with all kinds of people.

By the end of our first year out of school with Kate, Bron and I had done and seen more than some people will in a lifetime. We'd been educated in the mind but also in the spirit. Mom and Dad then decided that we'd been through so much of Africa, they'd throw in their remaining savings to give us some international exposure as well. We'd have stints where they'd be nearby, and times when only Kate would travel with us.

Anyone else would have said it was madness to put a twenty-four-year-old in charge of two teenagers and tramp them all over the world. But my parents recognized that they could trust Kate. Her age had nothing to do with it. What made two teenage boys ready to build Londolozi? How on earth did my father find the love of his life in fifteen-year-old Shan Watson? How did Uncle John know he could trust me at age eight to pilot his Landi or cover him while he stalked a hippo?

Besides, Kate had proved herself as much mama lioness as teacher.

She saw her duty as protecting us, her cubs, whenever we were in her care. This was never more evident than when she noticed young men prowling Bron's perimeter.

Once a group of students from London's prestigious Eton College came to stay at Londolozi with their parents. The boys were all members of the Etonian Shooting Club, a terribly proper extracurricular activity for a terribly proper bunch of boys.

The boys were demonstrating their prowess for me, Bron, and Kate at our makeshift rifle range, which was really just a strip of flat land with a huge deserted termite mound at one end. After firing off a few rounds, one of the boys turned to Kate and said from a mouth that seemed to have a hot potato stuck in it, "So, Kate, do you shoot?" I thought I detected a bit of a pompous challenge in his voice.

Kate held out an empty soda can. "Go put this Coke can up," she told him.

When the boy had balanced the Coke can on the termite mound, Kate stepped up to the line drawn in the sand and, without batting an eye, threw the rifle up to her shoulder and almost instantaneously pulled the trigger: a classic snapshot. The can exploded off the mound.

"Good God," said one of the lads next to her. "That was fast."

Another boy ran to retrieve the can. When he brought it back, there was a stunned silence. Kate had managed to drill a hole perfectly into the hyphen between the words "Coca" and "Cola."

Kate positioned herself protectively in front of Bron, whom the boys had been circling all afternoon. "Right, who's next?" she asked, quick as a flash.

For the rest of their visit, the boys maintained a respectful distance from my beautiful sister—which might not have entirely pleased her.

"It was a total fluke shot," Kate confided to me later. To this day, she remains a legend among the members of the Etonian Shooting Club.

Kate taught us the culture of every place we visited, assigning us books to read. We would settle in a particular place for two or three months at a time, absorbing as much of the atmosphere as possible. Kate also handled the budget. "Your job is to be security, Boydie," Dad told me—helping us avoid pickpockets and bad areas, keeping up a general level of awareness.

In Australia, we visited lodges leading the ecological revolution and studied Aboriginal Australian culture. Kate and Bron were obsessed with Uluru, or Ayers Rock, a sacred site located in the Northern Territory. Kate had been reading *Mutant Message Down Under* to us so we could understand the Aboriginal Australians' plea to save the planet. She had a postcard that showed Uluru at seven or eight times throughout the day, bathed in glowing yellows, ochers, reds, browns; her mission was to photograph each of those shades.

We could feel the energy of the great rock as soon as we approached; it was hauntingly beautiful. It was also horrifically commercialized, with knickknacks for sale, displays everywhere, and crowds of people pushing and shoving. Signs invited visitors to walk up a "sacred path"; we instinctively knew it wasn't our path to walk.

A guide's job at Londolozi was simply to facilitate and interpret what was already happening around people in nature—to listen for animals' alarm calls, for example, and other language of the bush. The guides in the cities we traveled to had a much harder job of trying to make something interesting happen. Guiding isn't about giving information; it's about creating experiences. The guides at Uluru were guiding by rote, pushing visitors from point to point.

Instead, we sought out someone with an authentic connection to the desert to hike with us around the rock's base. He was an Aboriginal Australian man with a broad, square face, a wrinkled brow, and a gangly gait. His skin, a rich, rusty brown, matched the color of the desert.

He taught us about traditional "tucker"—which medicinal roots to use, what foods to forage, how to track the land through its songlines, the earth singing its own story through the bones, sinew, and veins of its hills and valleys. "Our culture is based on the relationship between the people and the plants, animals, and physical features on the land," our guide said. He described the Dream-Song, the universe's vibrations. "Your destiny sings to you," he told us. I wanted my destiny to sing to me too. He explained how all Aboriginal Australian art, often done entirely in dots, springs from the Dream-Time, the sacred, liminal space we all visit while we're asleep, where we can fetch the wisdom to guide our days and the medicine for healing.

In our two months in Australia, we often encountered racism against the Aboriginal Australian people. The man who ran our hotel in Alice Springs leaned across the counter and told us, "Be careful walking around at night. These Abos get drunk, and then no one knows what they'll do." Kate explained the "stolen generation" phenomenon to us, how Aboriginal Australian children were taken from their parents and trained to be domestic workers. We learned how alcoholism had pervaded the Aboriginal Australian culture as these people were herded onto marginal land, just like Native Americans. We saw Aboriginal Australian people outside the bottle stores, looking down and out.

We flew out of the area in a helicopter. As we gazed down, we saw that the entire landscape was composed of the same dots we'd seen in the artists' paintings. "Spiritually, they had to have flown to make them," Bron said.

I loved the Aboriginal Ausralians' concept of Dream-Time, the people's amazing capacity for storytelling, and their ability to live in tune with the wild desert. It was crushing to see how the culture had been smashed. As with the Masai, Western culture had come in and wiped out the ways of an ancient people. We of the Western world have lost our connection to the last people who could teach us those ways.

The rest of Australia seemed a bit prosaic after that. Kate helped Bron over her first major disappointment in life: her encounter with a platypus in the Melbourne Zoo. My sister had forced me and Kate there to see yet more koala bears. Bron loved their squashed faces and cuddly tufted ears. She loved the way eucalyptus leaves appeared to stone them out. She kept a running total in her journal: "Number of koalas seen to date: 32." We'd been to every park in Australia that had a koala. The Melbourne Zoo also advertised an aquatic terrarium with a platypus, and Bron was breathless to see this oddity. She was gutted to discover that the duck-billed peculiarity was perhaps fifteen inches long. "It's like a swimming rat with a duck's face glued on," she said, sulking. (Bron's second major life disappointment was when Kate took us to Paris to see the *Mona Lisa*. Both the platypus and Leonardo's masterpiece were supposed to be grand and amazing sights. Both were about the size of my foot.)

———

When the three of us set out for India, Mom and Dad's sole concession to civility—and probably safety—was to hire a car and driver for us. As a result, we saw much of the country from the backseat of a vehicle that looked as if it had driven in with the first British colonists. It was in fact closer to a go-cart than a car. Our driver, a stern mustached Indian named Rajesh, was a wonderful man, but as a driver he left a great deal to be desired. He drove using India's unwritten rule that the bigger car has the right of way. He liked to accelerate into oncoming traffic, swerving around other cars while shouting, "Chello, chello. Let's go!"

"Oh my soul," said Kate, clapping her hands in front of her eyes. "This is too much for me."

We traveled to Jaipur, the capital of Rajasthan—also known as the Pink City because the palace and most of the buildings were built of pink sandstone. The roads were congested with old taxis, rickshaws, cows, camels, and the odd elephant. Every single person had a stall of some kind, it seemed. Vendors would aggressively try to get our attention, in sharp contrast to African shopkeepers. "Yes, just have a look at this," one said, handing me a small sandalwood chessboard. "Fifty rupees." "No thank you, I don't want it," I told him, trying to hand it back. The seller quickly hid his hands behind his back. "Fifty rupees," he insisted. Finally, I simply had to put the set down and walk away. Another tried to fix my shoes while I was still walking in them, trying to charge me for the glue he'd used.

Rich, poor, beautiful, ugly. People with no legs. People living in mansions next to people living in cardboard boxes. I was completely dazzled in Rajasthan. When you have smashed into so many different lifestyles, you can no longer claim that yours is the only right one. It was a good lesson for a sixteen-year-old.

Outside the Pink Palace, Kate decided she wanted a picture with a snake charmer, a gentleman with exactly one tooth and a crafty-looking mustache.

"How much for a photo?" she asked.

"You give ten rupee," said the snake charmer, while tapping his sleepy cobra on the head until it reared up, strengthening his negotiating position.

"Okay, deal," said Kate.

No sooner had Bron snapped the photo of Kate crouching near the snake than the charmer, in a very uncharming manner, began the hustle.

"Now you pay me my twenty rupee!" he shouted.

"No, you said ten." Kate stood her ground.

"No no no no, you steal from me! Snake was sleeping, I had to wake him, so twenty rupee!" screamed the evil charmer.

"You're only getting ten," Kate said, resolved not to be taken advantage of. By now Bron and I had moved in close behind her; we weren't sure whether we wanted to back her up or hide behind her. The charmer started to brandish his cobra as a weapon, holding it up to Kate's face and advancing while bellowing, "Twenty! Twenty! Twenty!" in a deep Rajasthani accent.

Kate drew a twenty-rupee bill out of her wallet and threw it at the madman. "Let's get out of here!" she said, hurrying me and Bron away.

At a safe distance, she stopped, panting. "Bloody snake charmer just ripped me off! He took us! He actually *took* us!" Kate, with her natural inclination to see the good in people, was shocked.

"He hustled us for ten rupees," said Bron.

"I know! A whole extra ten! Poor snake, to have to live with a man like that." It was just like Kate to throw in her lot with the reptile.

"Kate, you do realize ten rupees is, like, four cents," I chimed in.

With this, Bron started to laugh hysterically. "You got ripped off for four cents! Wow, you really got hustled!" she cackled.

Kate and I were soon doubled over with laughter, too. "In our first week in India, we've been had for four cents!" she hooted.

After our run-in with the snake charmer, we got back into our trusty go-cart and flew past an endless display of camels, goats, and elephants, all strolling along the road wrapped in beautiful fabrics. Against the desert, colors in Rajasthan stood out like great swaths of neon graffiti in a dull subway tunnel.

We became such a tight unit, Kate, Bron, and I. Kate was constantly pushing us. We called her "Koo-Koo," "Teach," and the "Toddler on Tartrazine"—for the food dye some believed made kids hyperactive— because she never seemed to sleep. Bron and I, on the other hand, were teenagers who sometimes wanted to loll. Kate would have none of it. "First we're going to go to the maritime museum," she'd announce. "Then . . . then . . . then . . ." And she'd lay out an exhausting itinerary that embraced every notable building and historical point of interest, and even a glancing intersection with the life of Gandhi, her personal hero.

"No, Koo-Koo, let's hang out in the hotel room," we'd beg, to no avail. Off we'd go.

We took off for a place in the desert called Pushkar, which was supposed to be a secret town with a holy lake. Kate and Bron were in the back of the car, and I was sitting next to Rajesh, so that I could force him to slow down.

Pushkar might have once been a holy city, but now it was a holy city–

cum—opium den for travelers. Everyone had that shipwrecked look that is the camouflage of the traveler to India: beards, dreadlocks, necklaces, and hash-stained fingers. On every menu there were two options: chai or "special" chai. I have never been able to shake the feeling that our waiter mixed up the batches, because for two days I was either asleep or laughing. To be honest, I think all chai in Pushkar was "special" chai. Mini-tripping in an Indian opium den is a life experience you don't get inside four classroom walls.

Kate loved photography and taught Bron a great deal about it. "This is how you collect experiences," she told us, experiences being the most valuable things in life as far as she was concerned. She encouraged me to explore Lomography, capturing the essence of a place by snapping an unframed shot from the hip while walking through a crowded street. I was never interested in monuments or official sights; I was always drawn to the secret energy of a place contained in its teahouses or on its streets, shorelines, and forests. I wanted to spend a whole day watching a man sell vegetables so I could know a bit of his life.

———

India clobbered my senses: the sight of women glowing in saffron-and-orange saris, their arms sleeved with gold bangles; the smells of cumin and ganja, sweat and shit; the sounds of the muezzins calling Muslims to prayer; the tinkle of bicycle bells and the honking klaxons of overladen buses; the hiss of gas burners boiling tea. And yet it was the most spiritual place I'd ever experienced. Around every corner was someone doing *puja* at a tiny shrine, lighting incense, gifting altars with marigolds and smears of ocher. Every encounter came with a graceful "Namaste." I'd seen isolated church groups in South Africa, but here religion was the engine of every person's life.

Maybe it was the sheer competition for survival that bred belief in a higher power. I couldn't get over the utter press of humanity, how closely we breathed one another's air. Even in the mountains and parks, there was no place that wasn't jammed with people, no open space anywhere. When we landed in Johannesburg, the simple little park outside the airport looked amazing to me.

——————

In between jaunts, we'd retreat to Joburg and catch up on our more formal schoolwork. Kate would take us to the Apartheid Museum and help us study Zulu, the close relative to the tongue spoken by the local Shangaan natives. When we were at Londolozi, we'd silently let the rhythm of the place wash over us as we bashed out the school curriculum on the front porch of the house, the elephants trumpeting below us in the riverbed. Kate followed the syllabus from a school in Joburg, but we could rip through a month's work in a week.

We never knew who might stroll into our classroom under the ebony trees. And Kate was always open to those people's arrival. One day Karen Slater, Uncle John's filmmaking assistant and a survivor of the helicopter crash, walked over to us. She was tall and long-haired, with a bit of India's unique style clinging to her; she wore gauzy scarves, tops embroidered with Shiva's eyes, and billowing pants, and she always smelled like lotuses. "I was going to make some chai. Would any of you like some?" she asked.

"Yes, we would, and we would also like to learn how to make it," said Kate, and so math was put aside as we all trooped off to the kitchen to brew up a batch of Indian tea.

Later Karen offered to teach us how to meditate—something I longed to do because I'd once read about the powers bestowed on yogis who mastered it: being resilient to extreme cold, able to walk across burning coals, and even, for the very advanced, reports of levitation. It was this extreme control of the body through ascetic practice that fascinated me. Each day when Karen finished filming with Uncle John, we would take a break from school to go down to her cottage for meditation lessons. "Meditation is what helped me stay calm when we crashed the helicopter with your uncle," she told me. We sat and chanted together: *"Amaram hum madhuram hum. I am immortal, I am blissful."* I did not—or could not—fly, but a semblance of calm settled over me.

———

At the end of our fantastic voyage together, Kate, Bron, and I made a photo album of all the amazing locations we'd called our classrooms. There we were at Olduvai Gorge in the Serengeti. Under a giant tree by a water hole on the floor of the Ngorongoro Crater, where yellow-billed kites swooped down on unsuspecting picnickers and snatched sandwiches right out of their hands. Next to the Grumeti River. Inside a tent in the Luangwa Valley in Zambia. Standing in front of Uluru. On the deck at Londolozi with an elephant plucking jackalberries from the branches above us. On the roof of a Pushkar hotel in the heart of the Rajasthan desert watching some Israeli hippies getting loaded on bhang lassis.

We had all grown up together. When Kate first joined the Varty family, she'd had a couple of bridges to cross. For a start, she hated flying in small planes; we loved flying in them and occasionally crashing them. Kate is also a very meticulous person, a real planner. The Varty family, on the other hand, tends to wake up one morning and decide to go to Zambia. Then on the way someone will say, "I actually think Zimbabwe could be a better option at this time of year," and we'd point the nose of the plane a different way.

"You Vartys are loony!" Kate would exclaim.

By the end of our time together, however, she'd just laugh and say, "I don't even care where we're going; tell me when we land."

Kate is pure gentleness, but she is not to be crossed. She once told me, "I'm like a lioness. Don't mess with my cubs." Once, when the three of us went to a rugby match, a massive drunk fan draped himself over Bronwyn and tried to kiss her. Before I had a chance to move, Kate had closed the space between herself and the giant of a man and punched him flat out in the head. The whole crowd who witnessed it went quiet. It was so incongruous, the gentlest-looking soul in the world flattening some rugger bugger. It was without a doubt one of the greatest things I have ever seen.

Kate gave me confidence in my own mind. Under her guidance, I started to realize that I had a tremendous capacity to think, even if I wasn't the greatest technical student. I couldn't spell, and I couldn't do math, but I could look at something and discover what was important about it. Kate was always open to wonder; she encouraged me to let my mind stay in that state. She helped me develop interests in the things you'd often drive past, like trapdoor spiders leaping out of their hidden burrows to grab a passing beetle, or how sore-eye lilies bloom after a fire. Kate opened my mind to thinking outside the box. When Bron and I struggled with not knowing what the model was, she helped us realize that most of the time, you have to make your own model. "Guys, we don't know how this is going to look," she'd tell us. "We have to be the architects for our own experience." We all felt our way along and had a great time doing it—which is a wonderful way to live life.

Mom and Dad's decision allowed me and Bron to get the last fading taste of the old Africa, before cellular towers and the Internet tried to jolt us off the earth. How could I ever thank them for that? And for bringing a new teacher into our lives who would change us so completely?

After two years, we went back to boarding school, but we would never get a better education than under the focused attention of Teach. I can't recall ever not knowing Kate. We remain bonded to this day.

"Please don't take this the wrong way, but you know how pigeons come back to the same fence pole to poop?" Kate remarked recently. "I think I'm your pooping post."

"Take that as a compliment," I told her.

FOURTEEN

SHAKE, RATTLE, AND ROLL

G ROWING UP IN THE BUSH means dealing with a lot of dangerous animals: lions, Cape buffaloes, rhinos, hippos. But the most
fearsome ones? Parasites. From the grass we might contract tick bite
fever, which can be debilitating but at least is easily curable. If we waded
into the still pools of the river, we had to be on the lookout for bilharzia-
sis, which could cause anything from swimmer's itch to infestations in
the liver, bladder, or intestines. When Bron and I were infants, putzi flies
would lay their eggs in the coarse material of our nappies as they dried
on the washing line. Mom had to press the diapers with an old-fashioned
iron heated with coals to kill the larvae, which could otherwise later bore
down into our skin, causing nasty wriggling lumps that needed to be
treated with medication. But the biggest danger of all was always malaria. Female mosquitoes' bites transmit the plasmodium, which travels
through the bloodstream to the liver, where it can then wreak havoc on
every organ. You can stave off malaria through prophylactic medication,
as tourists visiting the country for a few weeks do, but you can't take the
medicine year-round; it starts to affect your liver. Numerous foundations

have distributed mosquito nets all over Africa in an attempt to slow the disease, only to find them repurposed as fishing seines. Every year, a million people die from malaria, many of them children.

————

When I was fourteen, I was out in the bush with the rest of the family when a giant of a thunderstorm rolled in. We had to race back to the camp with torrents of water and lightning coming down all around us. The next morning, we thought my chills and achiness were probably nothing more than the aftereffects of being thoroughly soaked the night before. We were wrong. Malaria has an incubation period of about two weeks, after which one starts to feel a bit achy, with light flulike symptoms. Then comes the sudden crash. You're hit with an immovable, ice-pick-behind-the-eyes headache. In the heat of the day, you find yourself shivering uncontrollably, then the next second sweating so profusely you soak the sheets. A few hours later that morning, the signs were unmistakable: I had malaria.

My parents have come close to losing people to malaria. Chris Irwin was the reserve manager of Londolozi when I was growing up. He was a former French Foreign Legionnaire and one of the hardest men I have ever met. Malaria felled him as if he were a small boy. He ended up in an intensive care unit in Johannesburg, on life support. Chris's family was back in Canada, and he'd listed us as next of kin. An old doctor from the lowveld who had consulted on thousands of cases of malaria advised my dad and uncle that the best chance they had was to take Chris off life support and hope that his body kicked back in. My father made the tough decision to turn off the machines. We held prayer circles back at Londolozi in the hope that God would play ball on this one. Chris survived, but after seeing what the parasite could do, we became far more vigilant. In fact, after a few macho guides tried to muscle through their symptoms and almost died, my parents declared that ignoring malaria symptoms, however faint, was a fireable offense. So when they saw me go down, about two days after the symptoms began, they reacted quickly and managed to get me onto a charter flight to Johannesburg. In hindsight, this probably saved my life.

I was admitted to a hospital and put under the care of a bald, worn-out doctor who looked like he'd spent the last three years awake. He had a pet phrase he loved to use to deliver the most appalling news.

"So it's confirmed; you have malaria. You were in a malarial area, so . . . it's to be expected."

"Turns out your kidneys are failing. You've got malaria . . . it's to be expected."

"Turns out the intensive care unit is full. The hospital is badly run . . . it's to be expected."

I was immediately put on a quinine drip. This resulted in slight deafness and intense nausea, which . . . "was to be expected."

Everybody thought I would make a quick recovery. My mother kept saying "we caught it early," which is the most important thing with malaria. The parasite rapidly multiplies and invades the organs if not detected and treated quickly enough.

But all was not well. By the end of that first evening, I was unnerved to discover that I could not urinate. My mother set off to find the doctor.

"There is something wrong with my son. You need to come now!" she told him.

"Your son has malaria, he's in bad shape . . . it's to be expected."

"Listen, Doctor, you get to my son's room *right now* or I will do something to you that *you* never expected!"

Later we found out that a lack of oxygen due to a fluid buildup in my lungs was causing the problem. I now had malaria *and* pneumonia. The doctor's arrival at my ward room coincided with the arrival of Uncle John, dressed in full camouflage combat fatigues, with boots whose metal buckles clinked as he walked; he was also sporting his usual .44 Magnum on his hip and a temper to boot. He resembled Jean-Claude Van Damme dropped onto the set of a John Wayne western.

The doctor began his chorus: "The fluid buildup in his lungs . . . it's to be ex—"

"Now, that's enough," said Uncle John, watching as I gasped for breath. "I request that you admit my nephew into intensive care. Immediately." Uncle John had seen enough cases of malaria—and held the family record for infections, at least a dozen—to know that I was starting to slide. He patted the .44 in his holster and glared menacingly at the doctor to emphasize the nonvoluntary status of his "request." Suddenly we were on the set of *The Godfather*.

The doctor's eyes widened, and moments later I was rocketing toward intensive care on a gurney at hypersonic speed.

All I remember about the intensive care unit was the doctor sticking a huge needle into my back and sucking fluid out of my lungs, removing the large elephant that had been squeezing the air out of them. I was in the hospital for two weeks; at times the doctors were unsure if I would live. Mom and Dad were shattered. They sat outside the ICU with Uncle John, weeping. Through a haze of medication, I remember asking a young nurse if she would like to "jump into bed with me." What can I say? She looked tired. Mom was doing well until my eyes rolled back in my head and I went into convulsions. She flagged down the nearest doctor.

"Sorry, not my case."

"'Not my case'? Well, it is now."

The doctor looked at my mother's face and realized that this was a simple statement of fact.

Ten days later, including five in the ICU, I was out of danger. The next time my uncle came to visit, he took in the flowers and the other visitors and the crisply attired nursing staff and declared, with a trace of disgust, "This place looks like a hotel!" The last time he'd had malaria, he'd ended up in a Zambian hospital. He'd been woken in the middle of the night by what he thought was the person next to him expiring but was in fact a dog panting heavily under his bed.

I emerged from the hospital a few weeks later emaciated and well reminded that Africa is not for ants.

FIFTEEN

A ROYAL WELCOME

I HONESTLY BELIEVE THAT YOU can learn more about the human condition as a safari guide than as a psychologist. In my late teens, I started working at Londolozi. I never get over the thrill of taking people out into the bush. It blows my mind that a few hours ago they were in a cramped apartment in New York or London and now we're heading out for an adventure in my backyard. They go out wanting to see the high-profile animals, the lions and leopards and elephants, all of which are awesome, but I also love how, given a chance, they will become equally fascinated by all the small, intricate things: the golden Calder mobiles of the garden orb spider's web or the croak of the starlings breaking the silence of a warm afternoon as they congregate to shout abuse at a large black mamba.

I love seeing the place through guests' eyes; I get reinvigorated by the adventure as we head down the windy sand tracks to where a seasonally dry riverbed we call the Manyaleti, or "Place of Stars," cuts through the property. It's the perfect place to find elephants and buffaloes feeding on the thick foliage of the riverbank or simply be rocked by the grandeur of the towering ebony trees and the way the clarity of light highlights the textured bark of each leadwood tree so that it looks like the crinkled skin of the great elephants. I've also discovered that people have more phobias than you would ever imagine: buffaloes, worms, feathers, spiders, insects, loud noises, skulls, teeth, dung—any or all of which are very likely encountered on a game drive. There are few things as disconcerting as taking a person with a bird phobia on a game drive, with the air randomly punctuated by bloodcurdling screams as a hornbill casually floats past.

One guest's obsession was fairies. Every few yards she would scream as if she'd just seen a lion killing a buffalo. "Stop, stop! Wow, those ones are really beautiful! Gorgeous, don't you think?" I consider myself very open-minded and have no doubt that she was seeing fairies, but it was a struggle to manage the group dynamic on the Land Rover as the other guests became more and more annoyed.

Martin was a welcome challenge for me. He was a seventy-year-old man who'd arrived at Londolozi in full safari gear, complete with a khaki bush hat with a zebra-skin band. An avid photographer, he informed me that he'd been on many safaris and that this would be his last. I was determined to make it a grand send-off and farewell from Africa.

Late in the afternoon on the second day, we were out in a quiet section of the park when we came across some fairly fresh leopard tracks. Solly, my tracker, and I decided that we would leave Martin by himself in the Land Rover while we followed the tracks on foot, a not uncommon action for rangers. We were gone for about fifteen minutes and were successful in finding the leopard's trail. I couldn't wait to tell Martin. When we got back to the Land Rover, I noticed that there was quite a lot of sand on the hood, but I thought nothing of it; I was just so excited to be able to get a leopard sighting for Martin. I'd been driving for about ten minutes when Martin announced, "I'm very angry with you! Take me back to the camp!"

"Why, Martin, what's wrong?"

"While you were gone, a bloody great elephant came along and threw sand at me! And every time it started to calm down, that bloody two-way radio would go off and get it all riled up again! I'm very angry at you—I was bloody scared!"

It's indeed very scary being that close to an elephant, and I know what it's like when they pick up sand and throw it at you; they don't do that when they're in a good mood. Small wonder Martin was frightened. I tried everything I could to win him back over the next couple of days, but he would have none of it. He'd decided to stick it out, but he refused to talk to us. Awkward silence prevailed in the Landi whenever we took him for a ride.

Eventually I tried a different tack, which was to get all the girls in the lodge to go up to him and tell him he was the world's greatest for having so courageously stared down a big bull elephant. This worked, and in no time Martin began to feel like he was the main man, even to the point where he began to expound on the story to any person who walked past the bar. By the time he left Londolozi, he felt like the king of Africa. His encounter with the elephant became his greatest memory; as always, nature provided the glorious send-off, not our efforts.

In the luxury safari business, we walk a line between making sure our guests have all the comforts they need and ensuring that their experience doesn't become cluttered with "stuff." We'll go miles out of our way to cater to sophisticated world travelers, but the more important goal at Londolozi is to provide a place where people can, from a comfortable surrounding, find a doorway into nature.

Occasionally, however, nature decides to visit not out in the wild but in the confines of the usually secure camp, and our best-laid plans come crashing down.

———

"A king is coming to Londolozi!" Bronwyn announced, her eyes wide with a kind of manic panic. "Their security people would like to come in and scout the area to assess the situation." We've had our share of visiting celebrities, dignitaries, and politicians—I have fond memories of tobogganing down a staircase with a certain presidential daughter—but handling this royal entourage would require an unprecedented level of coordination. For this, Mom and Dad were throwing me and Bron into the deep end.

A general sense of overriding hysteria developed in the village. The runway where our puddle jumper landed needed to be extended for the royal jets. Every single room would be taken up by the royal party; one whole camp would be reserved for the machine gun–wielding security guards. As the weeks wore on, Bronwyn fielded near-daily phone calls and faxes from the royal family's staff, who wanted to be sure the smallest details were attended to. Our small gift shop had to be hugely overstocked so that the royal retinue of twenty women accompanying the king could discover fresh merchandise should they choose to shop once, twice, or three times a day. Their royal chef—who would of course be traveling with them; our five-star chefs had been deemed inadequate to the task—required fresh herbs. Some we had; others had to be flown in. Silk sheets were shipped in to adorn the beds. Even a reserve of royal blood was flown in to be stored in our refrigerators, in the unlikely event of a mishap.

The king's staff insisted that we set up His Majesty's own personal exercise equipment in his suite. Many of the Shangaans were fascinated by the princesses' vibrating wobble plate, an oddly shaped machine with a flat base and long handles that one stood on as it jiggled. Apparently it was meant to have the same effect as running a marathon, except you did nothing and went nowhere. The speculation was rampant around the camp. "It's a flying device," opined one of the gardeners. "I think it's a mechanical dance teacher," I heard someone comment as I walked past the kitchen office. (Later, when one of the princesses actually used it, members of our staff walked past the makeshift gym extremely slowly, trying to catch a glimpse of this peculiar machine in action. Shrek swept the same spot outside the gym for an hour, utterly fascinated.)

The king's security detail requested a large satellite dish for the roof. The guards would use it for security communications and getting satellite TV. This brought on a new problem, as there were no TVs in any of the rooms. We had to truck in several TVs, work out where to put them in each room, and then run the required cables.

The demands seemed never-ending, but these are the sorts of problems a lodge that attracts high-profile guests feels lucky to have. The problem wasn't the guests but, rather, the group organizer, who'd arrived several hours ahead of the rest of the entourage to see to the final details. He was in a swivet, the Armani suit and tie he'd selected for a bush sojourn already soaked through from both the heat of the day and the pressure he was feeling, which translated to escalating demands.

"The prince will need some Clarins face wash. Please make sure it's in his room," he said.

"Absolutely, but it's going to take some time, as we will have to fly it in from Johannesburg," I pointed out.

"He needs his face wash immediately," the organizer reprimanded me, although the royals wouldn't be here for at least another six hours. Sure, I'll just go to the Clarins store by the warthog wallow, shall I?

Finally, after months of planning, the moment arrived. All that was left to be done was for me to run down the path to the Granite Suites and drop the final touch, a tray of cold facecloths, in the king's rooms. The suite features a spacious living room with suede couches and comfy chairs, a bedroom with a huge puffy white bed beneath a blizzard of pillows, a dressing area, and a grand bathroom with big glass panels framing the bathtub and shower that allow you complete privacy while you look out over the granite rocks to the river beyond. As I trotted down the path, I could hear via the two-way radio on my belt various reports from other staff members on where, when, and how the royal retinue would arrive. The ETA reports took on the urgency of a woman's labor contractions. "Boyd, six minutes." "Boyd, five minutes." "Boyd, four minutes."

I arrived at the king's suite out of breath, tray of towelettes in hand,

and was annoyed to discover that housekeeping had left the door slightly ajar. The radio crackled—"Boyd, three minutes"—as I zipped toward the bathroom. Standing atop the sink was a hairy little hobbit with long jowls, heavily padded feet, and close-set yellow-orange eyes. The baboon was chugging papaya hand lotion out of a glass amenities bottle. He glanced sideways at me but kept slurping away nonchalantly—and then at the same moment, both he and I realized that he was cornered. The radio informed me, "Boyd, the king has arrived in the car park."

The epiphany that I was blocking his way out—I was still standing, shocked, in the doorway—sent the baboon into an absolute state. He pulled his snout from the papaya lotion, the fur around his jowls rimmed in white like one of those "Got Milk?" advertisements, dropped the bottle, which smashed to pieces on the cement floor, then leapt off the bathroom sink, landing right on the shards of broken glass and cutting his feet. With a shriek of pain, he catapulted himself at a large floating pane of decorative glass above the tub. He slammed into it, creating a gruesome piece of modern art as his injured feet smeared it with blood. Terrified, he began to crap himself liberally, bouncing around the room like a furball on speed, leaving a garnish of blood and feces wherever he went. At one point he launched himself onto the ceiling and hung there upside down, gripping a light fixture, his white-streaked face set in an expression of annoyance and embarrassment, that "Oh dear, I just shat on the carpet" look your dog gets. I knew the all-too-human-seeming bloody prints on the ceiling would be hard to explain, much less clean, but not as difficult as the mass of shit that was now covering the bathroom floor.

Finally the baboon came to a decision and flung himself straight at me, his long canines bared. I barely had time to duck and let out an embarrassing Minnie Mouse scream as he flew over my head, hit the white bedspread with a final galvanic splatter, then shot out the door and hurdled over the high balcony.

Suddenly all was quiet, and I took in the room. It looked like Picasso's studio after they shot scenes for *The Texas Chainsaw Massacre* in it. My radio crackled. "Boyd, one minute to room."

"Stall him! Stall him!" I screamed. Months of planning had been undone by a metrosexual baboon with a love of moisturizer.

We couldn't move the king out of this suite for security reasons that we didn't understand. In minutes, Bronwyn arrived, armed with a large pair of yellow rubber gloves and an army of housekeepers. She surveyed the room. "Jesus, Boyd, this is a train wreck. Come on, ladies, let's get to work."

The royal party had been stalled by a snack on the deck and an obliging hippo, which had uncharacteristically strolled out onto the flat rocks in front of the camp in broad daylight. A scene straight out of *Fawlty Towers* started to play out.

Hailey, the operations manager, had begun the awkward delaying tactics. Although her glacier-blue eyes bought her a bit of extra time, it was an uphill battle. The king, despite having flown on his own jumbo jet, was tired and unused to waiting for anything. He never expressed any irritation—he had people who did that for him—but his personal assistant shot Hailey death stares anytime the king looked away.

"Some more snacks, Your Excellency?" Hailey inquired.

"No, thank you."

"Some wine maybe? Our South African wines are quite renowned."

"No, I would simply like to go to my room."

"Perhaps a tour of the park first, a quick game drive?"

"No."

"Would you like to see the Shangaan dancers? It's a remarkable cultural experience."

"No, take me to my room now."

"Certainly. We're just checking the path for deadly adders—oh my God, is that an elephant?"

There was a complex relay system between the staff doing the stalling and the staff cleaning the room, which now included guides, the general manager, a chef, four maintenance men, the housekeepers, and a mechanic. No one knew how the mechanic came to be there.

A runner between the room and the front deck passed us frantic messages:

"Bronwyn says that you should ask them if they would just like a full lunch now."

"Tell Bronwyn that's not an option; the group organizer just told me he wants me fired," Hailey relayed back. My job at this point was to make Bronwyn's job easier, so when she screamed for more bleach, I ran off to get it. Bron was fully committed to the old family maxim that volume helps solve a problem.

Eventually we could stall no more, and the procession to the room began. I ran back to escort the king. The royal party draped in silks made their way down the path in single file, followed by a herd of armed gunmen with rifles sticking in the air like quills. An exasperated Hailey led the way, sure that she would find a hazardous waste site. As the king stepped into the entranceway to his suite, Bronwyn and her crew, their hair frosted with baboon shit, slipped out the bathroom's sliding door. She led the team—buckets, mops, and all—into the bush, where all dove facedown into the tall grass as if dodging incoming mortar fire.

The king strode out onto his large front deck. A band of wood hoopoes flew by, piercing the calm with their raucous cackles. Then the stillness of the day descended. The king looked around, gave a satisfied sigh, and headed back into his room. As the door closed behind him, sixteen people arose from the bush with a wild look in their eyes and hotfooted it for the staff village.

"Bloody baboon!" Bron huffed to me as I caught up with her on the path. "What a royal cock-up."

The uncertainty of life in the bush was ever present, but encounters with animals were never malicious, even if they were sometimes bothersome. Looking back years later, I would miss a time when a baboon was the worst of my problems.

SIXTEEN

IN BATTALIONS

W HEN I WAS ABOUT eleven years old, the family took a trip through Zimbabwe. Dad signed us up for a white-water rafting experience on the Zambezi River. This was surely the most hostile commercially available rafting experience money could buy. The river down in the deep gorge literally roars at you, its thunderous call bouncing off the steep sides of the valley in continuous threading echoes.

Bron and I were too young to officially be going down the river, yet Dad had somehow negotiated for us to be allowed in. He hadn't wanted to be piled into a ten-man raft with generic overland tourists—he referred to such people as "Inge and Lars from Sweden"—so in classic Dad style, he'd decided unilaterally that it would simply be the four Vartys, two of them wildly underage, taking on the rapids with a guide.

Bronwyn was terrified. "I hate this sort of thing," she whispered to me. But the decision was made; down the river we would go.

In renting his own boat, Dad had overlooked one of the critical aspects of river rafting: weight makes a difference. When a towering wave comes at you, the idea is to dive headlong at it, so that as you meet white water, your weight holds the boat down.

Throwing slender Shan Varty at a Zambezi rapid is very similar to throwing a Ping-Pong ball at a tidal wave. Needless to say, when we hit the first rapid of the morning—called something like Death Trap—we capsized.

Dad came very close to dying. He told us later that it felt like a million invisible hands were pulling him down to the bottom of the river. By the time the current released him, he was low on air. When he finally scrambled back to the surface, he found himself trapped under the boat and still had to swim clear before he could catch a breath. Eventually all of us except the guide were able to reboard the boat, which had spun the wrong way around in the water but was still floating. This is the perfect metaphor for my family: count on us to be on the wrong side of a boat with no guide, going backward through a massive rapid.

Midway through the cascade of rapids, there was a single place where you could disembark. Bron got out immediately, but I stayed on. I liked the excitement, and I wanted to stay with my father.

That night back at the campsite, Dad described how his life jacket had gotten him trapped under the boat's hull. "All that was running through my mind," he told us, "was 'Jesus, I hope Bronwyn's okay.'"

"Well, thanks for worrying about me," I said.

"Aah, I knew you would be fine; you're always fine."

These words were mostly true; like my uncle, I had a way of getting through things, an instinct for how to slip danger.

The safari business is all about solutions. If you do it long enough, your whole psyche becomes about solving problems, solving problems, solving problems.

In Dad's world, you just get on with things. If there's a problem, you fix it. If you're underwater, just fight your way to the surface again.

"We Vartys, we're unshakable," my dad always says.

I didn't know it yet, but the truth was that we were very shakable.

———

"When sorrows come, they come not single spies, but in battalions," Dad told me once, quoting Shakespeare. That's exactly how they happened with our family in the next few years, in wave after wave. There were physical attacks—catalysts that forced change upon us. There were the deaths of beloved family members—one we could anticipate, one we could not, and both of which gutted us. And then the death of a stranger—an abrupt horror that undid me in a completely different way. All of these assaults were, at least, well defined. We knew how to deal with them, if imperfectly. And then along came a different kind of attack: vague, featureless, never-ending. And that was the one that pulled all of us under because we simply didn't know how to fight it.

When you're young, death is a faraway mountain at the culmination of a very long journey. I was faintly aware of it, miles out in the haze. And then I nearly died a few times and watched the people I loved come under serious attack. I don't think I was overly naïve, but in the space of a few short years, my rose-tinted glasses got yanked right off.

Over and over during that time, I went back to that boy on the termite mound with the black mamba sliding over his calves. If only I could stay still, even if I shook inside, the snake would crawl all over me but not harm me. *"Don't move, Dad, don't move."* I would be in some way in control of the outcome.

Over and over, I returned to the dry riverbed with the elephant in front of me, the wind of his breath on my face. Phineas was watching the elephant's every move; tracking his body language allowed an element of the predictable in what otherwise looked to be an unpredictable situation. *Never panic in the bush.* If you act correctly, you'll be fine.

The jungle of men does not have the same rules as the jungle of animals.

Here is the most complicated of simple challenges: to choose healing or bitterness, life or death, faith or dismay. My family and I ran that gauntlet for ten years. Ironically, while this kind of test takes your innocence from you, that sense of being bulletproof, it can also really teach you how to live.

SEVENTEEN

GUNPOINT

"MONEY," HE SAID. "I will kill you."

It was March 25, 2001. That night, Kate, Mom, Bron, and I were staying at our house in Johannesburg. I'd fallen asleep in my bedroom. Then, for some reason, I'd woken and gotten out of bed to put on a pair of shorts before falling back asleep. There are so many moments to which you can attribute meaning in hindsight; had part of me known what was about to happen?

Before that night, cricket, friends, and young love were the things that filled my mind while I finished up my schooling as a teenager. My parents had bought a small home in the outskirts of Johannesburg to ease the burden of constant commuting for business. Bronwyn had finished high school and was working at the Londolozi reservation office in Joburg. I was in my final year of high school, which I was completing from Londolozi through correspondence with a school in the city. Occasionally I would go into Joburg to get a new curriculum and take practical exams. The situation plucked me from my sheltered village life and put me smack in the middle of Johannesburg, where I could no longer remain ignorant of the aftermath of the long nightmare of apartheid in racist South Africa.

Growing up at Londolozi, Bron and I had been immersed in village life. Working side by side with people of all races, we had been largely sheltered from the truly horrific reality that had long since shattered the innocence of our country.

South Africa was a war zone in the early 1990s, particularly in the lead-up to our first democratic elections, in 1994. The elections had been a success; much to my family's delight, South Africa was finally a society—by law, at least—free from racial segregation. In reality, the divide between the haves and the have-nots remained.

After democracy defeated apartheid, a spree of violent crime gripped the country for ten years. The war in Johannesburg was largely an invisible one, taking place in the outlying townships of the city. In my parents' neighborhood, everything looked normal, all blue skies and denial. But cross over into the poor black townships, and people were getting "necklaced" with tires filled with petrol and set on fire, sliced to pieces with pangas. There was, literally, tribal warfare: Zulus against Xhosas, Afrikaners against English, black against white. The result was posttraumatic stress among a traumatized people. Even though we'd never officially been to war, the psychology of subjection to violence was there. People were dying, but for a great long time, I knew almost nothing of it. The journalists in the thick of it knew what was going on, but reportage to the general population was suppressed. All we'd hear back in our richer, mostly white suburbs would be a terse summary: "Another night of rioting in Soweto." We had no idea of the level of violence. It would be years before reporters from the Bang Bang Club broke the full story.

Every morning on the drive to school, at every social gathering in Joburg, Bron and I would overhear whispered talk among the adults about the number of deaths in places the whites never went. Speculation was endless: How soon before we'd be overrun and killed? Mothers walked their kids in the street during daylight but retreated behind ever-higher security walls as the sun set. Even in my teenage self-obsession, I had to face the cold fact that we'd become a fortressed society.

Whenever we were in Johannesburg, my family would expect trouble at night. We were always on high alert for Dad's "danger voice," which brooked no questions. Bron and I knew and respected that voice out in the bush, where the threat of lions and mambas loomed; it was so odd to hear it in "civilization." Dad would always circle the drive before pulling in toward our house, the headlights sweeping the grounds. He never drove directly through the gate; he rolled past it first, then quickly doubled back in case a would-be hijacker was waiting in the nearby foliage. Although Mom and Dad kept it secret from us at the time, hijackings, kidnappings, robbery, and murder were omnipresent threats. If Dad had to leave on a business trip, he'd always tell me, "Remember, you're the man of the house, Boyd. It's your job to look after your mother and sister."

———

My naïveté concerning the harsh realities of life in post-apartheid South Africa ended on that night in March. I woke up to find Bron sitting on me. She did this in an attempt to restrain my reaction when I saw that her hands were tied. Then the handgun appeared from behind the door, followed by the face of a young black man whose cold expression and flinty eyes suggested a life of violence and desolation. I could see it in his casual, threatening demeanor; I could feel his volatility and willingness to escalate. The air disappeared as if one collective breath had stolen all the oxygen.

As that man and two others walked in, I felt the most primal fear I have ever experienced. There was no shadow of a doubt that this was the worst moment of my life. I wasn't dealing with a familiar, measured risk with a set of principles and rules governing the dangers of the wild. These were humans, desperate humans. They weren't following any rule book I understood. I couldn't read their body language. I couldn't read anything. My body was shaking; I could barely breathe as I saw cocked handguns pointed at my sister's face.

I went back to my bush education. I was terrified, but I forced myself to remain calm.

I later learned that the invaders had already been in the house for two hours while I'd slept. Mom, Bron, and Kate had all been downstairs watching a movie. Dad was out of town. The assailants had found the women first and tied them up with their own shoelaces, the fine cords cutting into their hands and ankles so deeply that the limbs turned purple and the bruising remained for weeks after. They'd separated Mom from Bron and Kate, out of their sight, forcing her facedown on the rug. Bron heard her mother's whimpers and believed she was being raped. She was about to struggle to her feet—which could easily have earned her a pistol strike across the head or worse—when Kate threw her body across Bron's. "You are not going to move," Kate whispered to her. "Your mother is fine." Bron swallowed her scream.

Later the invaders untied the women's ankles and forced them upstairs so they could rifle through drawers for money and jewelry, which they took outside along with anything else they could lay hands on: linens, pots and pans, appliances, alcohol. Their English was limited but crystal clear. "Money. Money. We'll kill you." One of the men led our dog, Tatty, off to another room because she was barking madly. Suddenly, silence. The women were terrified that she'd been killed, and they all lost heart, thinking, "If they've killed the dog, they'll kill us." Bron told me later, "I accepted death completely. There were times when I knew this was now it."

After I was woken up, the robbers herded me and Bron upstairs into the living room and onto the couch, where my mother and Kate were sitting with their hands tied. The ringleader glared at me. "Guns. Where are guns?" I opened my mouth to reply, but Mom stomped down hard on my foot. "I don't know what you're talking about," she said. "We haven't got any guns." In fact, our one handgun was locked inside a gun cabinet in an obvious place. I was terrified that they would find it, realize that we'd been lying, and take their revenge. From my room downstairs I'd heard them going through the upstairs cupboards. I'd counted the bangs as each door swung shut—one, two, three. The gun was in the fourth cabinet, right at eye level. But they never found it.

Stress does remarkable things to the senses; smell, sight, and hearing become so acute. I realized that the four of us had become aware of each other's thoughts. Whenever the robbers were in the room with us, we couldn't speak out loud, but somehow we were all on the same wavelength, able to understand each other perfectly. If their backs were turned, we'd also pantomime. Mom decided that she was going to kick the assailants down the stairs; while they were distracted, ransacking some drawers, she pumped her leg furiously and mouthed instructions, getting ready for a practice run, before Kate and Bron stopped her with slicing motions across their necks.

A dance began as we tried to seek out threads of humanity, appealing to all manner of decency and stereotype. Mom tried cowering like a traditional Shangaan woman, whimpering, "Please don't hurt us." Then she tried being aggressive: "There's no money around here. Get out of here!" She assumed the mantle of an elder matriarch, a position revered among Africans, ordering, "No, just stop that. You can't do that." She collapsed into exasperation: "I'm telling you. We don't have anything." Bron tried misdirection, urging, "No, no, don't take that. Take this; it's much more valuable." *"Mfowethu"* I called them. "Brother."

The robbers began leading us off one by one, motioning us into rooms in the hope that we'd bring them to hidden treasure. "Money. We'll kill you." One of them had grabbed an old cowhide bullwhip from my room and shook it threateningly at us. "Tell us or we'll kill you." My greatest fear was that my sister, mother, and teacher would be raped. In a moment when the villains were out of the room, we agreed that if it started to go that way, the victim would call out, and the others would rush in and fight and to hell with the guns.

Thousands of years of evolution spoke through our actions. And then there was magic—or, rather, something divine. Hours into our ordeal, when Bron was near despair, as she was marched past a closed cupboard, her hands bound, the cupboard suddenly popped open and dozens of sympathy cards for the loss of our grandmother, whom Bron had loved dearly, poured out. Gogo Varty's photo fluttered down right on top of them. I felt sure that she was watching over us.

One of the invaders unloaded and reloaded his Glock in front of us, pointedly counting out the bullets—more than enough to shoot all of us. They took turns taking loot outside. We later learned they'd loaded it into one of our vehicles as a getaway car. At one point they took a break from their ransacking and went to the fridge, wolfing down that evening's Indian takeout. I was revolted by the normalcy of the one action combined with the menace of the other.

I'd become aware of something in me that made me even sicker. I'd weighed up my moment and knew that if given the chance, I would kill any way I had to. The knowledge of evil had reached the center of my being, where it could control my actions, where I would become the one without empathy and without mercy. I looked around the room, wondering what I could turn into a weapon that could induce blunt force trauma or a wound that would bleed heavily. Here was the perverse opposite of my bush training. Instead of saving a life, I was methodically and cold-bloodedly inspecting each object in the room for its potential to kill or maim.

Every time the robbers moved us around the house, I tried to position myself as a target. We were shoved into a small bedroom upstairs. Bron, Mom, and Kate hid beneath the bed. I sat on top, waiting. It had already been more than three hours, an eternity. We felt desperate, fearful that they would shoot us before they left, a common trend in these kinds of attacks.

One of the gunmen came into the room, grabbed me by the arm, and shoved me down a hallway. He pressed his gun's cold metal barrel against my forehead. And at that moment, piercing the deadness of my own capacity for evil, I felt a massive power protecting me, its only concern for the pain of others. The assailant then slid the gun into my mouth. A voice boomed inside my head and body; a knowing overcame me: *"You are always safe."*

It felt like a moment of divine clarity. I didn't stop to contemplate where this message had come from. In that instant, I knew only that it was absolutely true. I was loved and protected.

I looked up the barrel at the man with the gun.

And I winked.

It was a moment of silent connection. I was seventeen; he was perhaps only a few years older. But now I saw that he had become a boy, a scared little boy, with nothing else to live for and no other way to sustain himself. This wasn't some political throwback of blacks robbing whites; this was a desperate person doing what he had to do to survive. I saw him for what he really was under the paper-thin act, and I forgave him.

Downstairs, in the bar area, the robbers demanded the house and car keys, which I handed over. Then I handed them the panic button, which would send an alarm signal to a security company. "This is the gate remote," I told them. "Press it when you get close and the gates will open automatically." They led me back upstairs to a spare room, where Bron, Mom, and Kate sat mutely. One of the robbers was still brandishing my bullwhip. We heard the key turn in the lock, and the sound of their footsteps faded away.

A few moments later, our alarm started shrilling; the robbers had tried to get out through the gate. Armed security guards would arrive soon, although our assailants were never apprehended. Our ordeal was over. Tatty was safe and sound behind a closed door. Mom phoned Dad, who hopped the next plane from London to get home. Uncle John drove straight through the night for seven hours to be with us the next morning.

By the time we'd given our reports to the police, it was four a.m. and we were too wired to sleep. Mom lit hundreds of candles—her equivalent of cleansing the area with sage—and made each of us take a bath with sandalwood soap, for its calming effect. We told ourselves the story of what had happened over and over, still in the grip of terror.

We moved out of that house the very next day, never to return, but even so, we were shattered for months afterward, each of us in a unique way. If somebody slammed a car trunk at a shopping center, Mom would flinch or even dive to the ground. She had the head of lodge security put up a target, took out a 9mm gun, and just blasted that thing to smithereens. When she and Bron visited a trauma-release expert, he had them tell and retell their stories, then asked them to frame a new outcome for the robbery. "How do you want to finish it?" Mom conjured a vivid image of following the men and shooting them dead.

Various triggers could send Bron racing off at forty miles an hour: having to sleep in a big house, driving at night, when a guy—even a friend, sometimes—came anywhere near her. She couldn't breathe properly. It took months of breath- and bodywork before she could release the scream that had lodged itself so deep inside her.

Kate discovered a seething rage she'd never known. When Mom insisted that she do Reiki, the therapist gently touched her back and Kate broke down in racking waves of sobs.

Many months later, Mom decided that she no longer wanted to be frozen in fear. "Africa is my place, where I'm meant to be," she declared, "and I will accept it and make this thing pass. It will not have any power over me." She, Kate, and Bron wrote letters of forgiveness to the robbers, expressing gratitude for everything the incident had taught them. They believed that they had been allowed to survive in order to do some great work in the world. Then they released the letters into the sea.

I wouldn't—or couldn't—process the experience. "No, I'm fine," I told Mom when she pressed the point. I wasn't. We made a family decision to keep the whole thing quiet.

Dad was also shattered, but in a completely different way. For him, this was the third blow, following short on the heels of two other heart-breaks.

———

Four months earlier, I'd been with Dad and Mom when we got the news that Dad's mother had been in a car crash. We drove straight to the hospital. No one would tell us what was going on. I grew very suspicious. "Just come and wait in here," a nurse instructed, and stuck us in a side room. A huge bell rang for me. Sure enough, a doctor arrived a few minutes later. "Are you Mr. Varty?" he asked Dad. "I'm sorry to tell you that your mother died at ten twenty-five this morning."

Dad collapsed straight down into a chair and buried his face in his hands. I felt like I'd just seen someone blow up the base of a huge statue, so that it crumpled where it stood. My dad, the pillar of strength who would grab me by the shirt in the face of danger and guide me to safety, who tore holes in thorn trees, had now been leveled by one sentence.

"Do you want to see her?" the doctor asked. Gran was on the table in the operating theater with a sheet pulled up under her chin, lying there as if she were sleeping. Dad looked down at his mother numbly. Mom gently removed Gran's rings and necklaces so she could give them to us.

We all knew Gran as "the mother of Londolozi." When everyone else had urged her to sell the farm, she'd trusted that her teenage sons could make their dream of a safari business work. For fifteen years after my grandfather died, she hadn't gone back to Londolozi—the memories were too painful—but since then she'd become a regular presence. On every visit, she brought aloes for replanting along the pathways, a milk tart wobbling precariously on top of the box. She'd sit by Dad's side in the Land Rover, holding hands with him on long private game drives.

In that moment at the hospital, Dad became a small boy in front of my eyes. The knowledge that someday I would be a body on a slab hit me hard. But I stayed calm. My job was to support my father, to keep it together for him.

Two weeks after Gran died, Dad had flown to London to meet with the shareholders of CC Africa. It looked like the hammer was falling for him. The company was losing money, but Dad was confident that he could get it turned around with some adjustments. After all, he'd worked with these businessmen for ten years to launch twenty-three ecotourism operations, employ thirty-five hundred rural African people, and create a whole new park in Phinda. Dad was desperate for the corporation to wait out the losses and hold his vision for the long term.

When the home invasion came, a few months later, it really punched Dad in the gut. His family had been under dire threat while he was back in London, in a last-ditch effort to keep CC Africa on board. The shareholders had decided against him at that very meeting. He'd loved CC Africa the same way he'd loved Londolozi, but the corporation hadn't loved him back. It couldn't, by its very nature. And now he was out. He had no idea what he was going to do next.

On the small glass table next to my parents' bed is a black-and-white photo of Dad in his first boxing match, at age six; he's sliding under a heavy-looking punch from a bigger boy. On the back of the photo, written in faint pencil, the caption reads, "Dave's first fight, received a bloody nose but went on to win the fight." Despite countless bloody noses, he's gone on to win many fights since, but I didn't know if he had it in him to prevail over the three knock-down punches of his mother's death, parting from CC Africa, and learning that he'd left his family unprotected during a home invasion. He didn't, either.

How many times had my father told me the story of "the Rumble in the Jungle," the famous fight between Muhammad Ali and George Foreman in Zaire? He was obsessed with it. I wondered if Dad could make it to the place far out over the horizon, a place only the great boxers can find, where they receive that miraculous second wind. Dad and I must have watched that video dozens of times: after being punished for the whole fight, Ali found that second wind in the eighth round. There's an iconic moment where he hits Foreman and you can see the sweat explode off Foreman's head. In that instant, the whole fight changes. Ali starts to chant into Foreman's ear, "You shoulda never came to Africa!" A few right hooks, a few left hooks, a punch straight to the face, and Foreman hit the canvas. I'd always seen Dad as Ali. Suddenly he was looking like Foreman, down for the count.

———

He didn't talk to me about it, but I understood that Dad was profoundly disillusioned. Something had come into his eyes, a shadow I'd never seen before.

Something had come into me, too. Something I was too numb to truly acknowledge. After the attack, I knew that none of us would ever be the same; we had learned that security from violence is a fragile illusion. On that particular Sunday evening, sleeping in bed, watching a movie in our own home, we were being watched.

You can be sitting on your fat wallet when the market crashes. You can be sitting safely inside your beautiful home when it's invaded. From the bush I'd learned that the most dangerous animals in nature were mostly predictable; now I knew that the most ordinary human was not.

I felt poisoned by the complacent acceptance of crime, which dehumanizes victim and criminal alike. I hated that my experience had made me in some way a party to that kind of thinking. I hated the toll the invasion took on me, infecting my waking life with anxiety, my sleep with nightmares. And I hated the darkness inside me as I'd contemplated turning on our captors. You can't ever be young again once you've mentally rehearsed the details of a murder you genuinely intend to commit. There was a grim satisfaction in knowing that my bush education had served me well; I'd stayed calm throughout the ordeal. But that deeper, more sinister knowledge of myself as a cold-blooded murderer took a high toll. Unbeknownst to me, invisible shrapnel had found purchase in flesh and bone, where it would fester as a numbness that became so normal I forgot it was there.

"You are always safe." The cold numbness shrouded the memory of that comforting knowledge. It would be a long time before I could look back on that night and see that moment of light as well as darkness.

EIGHTEEN

SEEKING

"**H**AVE YOU THOUGHT ABOUT what your plans are going to be?" Mom asked. "You've got a good brain. I hope you're going to put something in it. Have you thought about going to university? It's a good idea to get something under your belt."

I didn't see the point. "I don't know anyone who's actually doing anything that they studied at university." Through my post-traumatic haze, I'd barely managed to finish high school.

"You're right in some ways," Mom said. "But it helps to have studied something."

Kate proposed a solution: "Boydie, why don't you take a gap year?" For most eighteen-year-olds, the gap year was an opportunity to cut loose before the rigors of college. By all rights, I should be getting a job on a tropical island, working for a year as a barman while drinking rum and sleeping with pretty girls. Yet I felt only faintly in my own life. What I needed wasn't mindless fun. The invasion had blown a big hole in my life, and I was embarrassed that it affected me so much. I thought that if

I could find something meaningful, I could fix it without anyone ever noticing.

Dad had always maintained that Bron and I should have an international perspective. He believed that travel was the best way to broaden your horizons. I was looking for who I was and where I fitted in. Sometimes you learn that by finding out where you don't fit. I decided to travel as a way of seeing myself out of the context that defined me; I hoped that journeying around the world would show me as much about myself as about other cultures. I was looking for answers to questions I hadn't even fully articulated yet.

———

After my adventures with Kate, I had a completely precocious idea of myself as a seasoned world traveler, but what I ended up with was a callow eighteen-year-old's reality of a trip: no plans, no money, no direction.

As a young boy, I'd pored over Julian Johnson's *The Path of the Masters,* a guide to spiritual enlightenment my father had brought home. It was one of the first books that tried to translate Eastern spirituality for the Western mind. Now I had a longing to meet a guru or to have a vision. I wanted an answer to show up, like a burning bush or a voice from the sky. I'd read about a certain master in India. Surely he'd have my solution.

Two weeks later, I was in New Delhi with a hundred thousand other people to listen to the master speak. There was a perfect order to the gathering; no one pushed or shoved, just endless line after line of people sitting in perfect stillness. Chants washed across the crowd like waves of energy passing across the audience.

The master arrived dressed in white, with a proud-looking turban. He quoted from different sacred texts, including the Quran and the Bible. "At their core, all the teachings are the same," he told us. "The journey is the same. Religious dogma and ritual created by men has obscured the simplicity of the journey." He urged us to seek peace within through meditation.

Perhaps this was the answer. I'd stay at the ashram, plant myself on a pillow, and find enlightenment. The next day I sat before the master in a private audience, waiting to present myself as his new acolyte.

His eyes were beautiful in their softness. "Don't join us," he told me. "Go and experience the world. Remember that the whole spiritual journey is internal. When you get a bit older and if you still have the longing, come back to me and I'll help you go on that journey." *The whole journey is internal.* I didn't even know what that meant.

Perhaps enlightenment lay at the mouth of the Inca Trail, the sacred valley that leads to Machu Picchu. I teamed up with Andy, a friend of a friend, to meet an authentic South American shaman. He likewise turned me away, with far less kindness than the Eastern master. He knew that we weren't prepared to journey with him. Then Andy and I headed deep inside the Amazon jungle to wrap ourselves in the lungs and immune system of the world. What we got instead was a grim slog punctuated by a heaving case of *turista*.

I was down in a squat, in great gastric distress, when out of nowhere a tree on the lip of the gully creaked and crashed down. I had to dive for cover to avoid being pulverized.

"Shit, Varty," Andy said when I told him what had happened. "I can't work out whether next to you is the most safe or deadly place in the world. You're a fucking magnet!"

Andy was right; I did feel like something inside me was suddenly a magnet for all the woe around me. It was in the lost, unsure places that I had always felt most alive. But here, in this most alive of all places, I felt lost and unsure.

After the jungle disgorged us, Andy and I went our separate ways. I kept taking aim at aimlessness, spending endless, monotonous hours on buses as Spanish movies blared through the night.

On a tour bus out of San Pedro, Chile, to visit the local hot springs, our guide warned us that when we arrived, we should walk very carefully and not go too close to the steaming pools, because the mineral edges there were very fragile and broke easily. We'd been there for about ten minutes, casually strolling around, watching the steam billow out of the springs in great clouds, when a scream broke through the morning stillness. To my horror, I saw a man who'd fallen in trying to swim in the boiling water.

All my years of safari lodge trauma training came back to me. I ran to him and, with a few others, managed to pull him out. But the boiling water had done too much damage, and his skin came off in great clumps in our hands.

It was one of the most terrible things I had ever seen. *"Soy muerto! Soy muerto!"* the poor man shouted. *I'm dead, I'm dead.* I will never forget the deep resignation in his eyes. If you were a believer, you might have said that angels were already there to carry him home. Or you might have said that his resignation was just the biological effects of shock. All I know is that when he'd woken up that morning on vacation, he'd had no notion that he would die horribly a very few hours later.

Not ten minutes after the ambulance sped away, I walked back to the tour bus and ate a sandwich. A ham sandwich, to be specific, flesh between bread. At the time I didn't even realize how bizarre this was, didn't understand how thoroughly my life had slipped away from its wild innocence. The problem with the numbness caused by trauma is that when you're feeling it, you don't know it.

You're a fucking magnet, Varty. Back at Londolozi after my trip to South America, more traumatized than when I'd left, I quietly fitted myself back into bush life, taking guests out on game drives, playing attentive host at dinners, telling stories and cracking jokes on cue. I told my parents about my trip, but I never spoke to them about how I was feeling.

On the surface, I probably seemed normal, but I'd begun waking in the night, my heart pounding, sweat pouring off me despite the dry air. On warm days after the morning game drive, I would leave the confines of the camp and wander like my ancestors had done down the lightly reeded footpath to a warm enclave of granite rocks where the cool Sand River flowed. The matumi trees stretched their knobby roots far into the depths, and I'd cling to them as the rapids flowed over me, giving me the sensation that I was being carried along by the current.

The Sand River had always been special to my family. Inspired by an old black-and-white photo of his family swimming in its crystal-clear waters, my father had long kept vigil over it. He campaigned with a kind of manic vigor to fight the destruction of its waters. He charted its ebb and flow, flew helicopters its entire length to the catchment areas with government officials to showcase damage upstream, and came close to physical fights with CEOs of multinational forestry companies that threatened to destroy these catchments by planting nonindigenous trees. Dad knew that the river was critical to the survival of the park and to our own sense of well-being in the world. He was also aware that his spirit wouldn't survive the death of something as magnificent as a river; none of our spirits would.

In December 2002, near the end of my gap year, my fellow traveler Andy and two of his friends came to visit me at Londolozi. We were all in the same space, coming off gap years, getting ready for university, but I didn't feel the same presence and lightness they seemed to exude.

The day was hot and humid. I decided to lead the group down to the Sand River, feeling slightly muted in the face of the others' exuberance. The clear, knee-deep water beckoned. I waded in while Solly, my ever-vigilant friend and tracker, wandered along the shore. I hadn't wanted to drag him on the trip, but Bronwyn felt otherwise.

"Boyd, if you go to the river, you take Solly," she ordered in her older-sister ignore-me-at-your-peril voice. The force of her insistence surprised me.

I was confident that there was no danger as I waded because I could see through the shallow water. I sat down where the sand dropped away into a small pool that skirted the bank. A large matumi tree cast a deep, inviting shade over me. My friends waded in the shallower water nearby as I leaned back into a small eddy created by a root that had been exposed by earlier floods. I stretched out until my legs were dangling in the water.

Key word: dangling.

A crocodile slamming its jaws onto your leg feels something like a pressurized vise clamp strapped to a grinding chain saw. "Get the fuck out of the water!" I screamed through the pain; my responsibility as a guide was ingrained.

The croc tried to yank me into deeper water to drown me, but my hand found the matumi root and grabbed tight. I began to kick furiously. I can't be certain whether my foot went so far down the croc's throat that he regurgitated it or whether he simply let go, but suddenly I was free. Somehow I climbed from the water up the root and into the branches of the matumi hanging over the pool. The attack was over in seconds.

I glanced down at my leg. *Shit shit shit shit.* It was lacerated beyond recognition. The entire back of my calf hung off in a great flap, exposing a silver-blue layer of flesh down to my Achilles tendon, stretchy white elastic with large holes torn from it. Blood poured from the huge, gaping wound.

I never saw Solly go into the water, but there he was, standing over me, rifle loaded. He'd run through the river, past the croc, to reach me. It was a huge act of bravery; even though I'd dropped from the tree onto the bank, I was still badly exposed. Crocs can return and attack a second time.

"Solly, get back! We have to get off this bank!"

With one arm pointing the rifle at the water, Solly used the other to hoist me up. Pure adrenaline propelled me up the steepest part of the bank and onto the flat part of the floodplain, where I collapsed. I could barely breathe, almost choked by the smell of my own blood.

Never panic. Never panic. My uncle's voice reverberated in my mind. I began to calm myself and called for the other guys, who circled me, wide-eyed. Solly took his shirt off, and I wrapped it tightly around my leg, as a makeshift tourniquet. By the time he'd carried me to the nearby Land Rover, my blood had soaked through the fabric, leaving a thick smear across the paintwork on the side of the car. I wrapped an old dog blanket from the Land Rover around the shirt, trying to slow the bleeding and contain the meat of the leg.

In a crisis, slow everything down. Now my father's voice, echoing the old bush principle, was coming through like an old cassette recording. Andy was driving, in his haste steering the Land Rover over bone-jarring ruts and bumps, trying to get me back to camp as fast as he could. "It's okay, Andy," I told him through gritted teeth. "Slow down. Just slow down."

It took me a while to raise the lodge over the Land Rover's radio. "This is Boyd. I've been attacked by a croc. I need a medevac organized." Through Solly's shirt and the blanket, my blood was still steadily gushing onto the gearshift. I wondered if I might die from blood loss. The shock had blocked out all pain; I felt strangely in control, albeit a bit light-headed. There's a profound difference between knowing that you will die one day and wondering if this is that day, not at the end of a robber's gun but as a result of your own stupidity.

The lodge managed to contact a plane flying overhead, while a group of other guides met me out in the bush to rebandage the wound properly with first aid equipment. As they began to remove the bloody wrappings, one ranger caught sight of the wound and began to gag. The smell of blood in African heat is potent indeed.

As the shock wore off, my leg started to throb fiercely, the pain escalating as if someone had cranked up the volume on a powerful stereo. Suddenly a chant sliced into my consciousness like a laser, one I'd learned from Karen Slater years earlier: *Amaram hum madhuram hum. I am immortal, I am blissful.*

The unspoken sound filled my mind. *Amaram hum madhuram hum.*

Back at the camp, they laid me down in my friend Alex's office. I could hear him speaking to my mother on the phone.

"Hi, Shan, it's Alex. . . . Yes, fine, thank you. . . . Yes, true, we had a bit of rain last night. . . . Ah, Shan, yes, well, everything is okay. It's just that Boyd got taken by a crocodile—no, no, I mean *bitten!* Bitten, not taken. He's lying on the floor here. Ya, he seems fine, but we're flying him to Nelspruit hospital." Alex had adopted the understated reportage style of a Shangaan, but Mom knew better; the worst thing to hear in the safari business is "Everything is okay."

They drove me up to the airstrip to make the seventy-five-mile trip to Nelspruit. Each bump we hit jarred my leg, sending a spike of agony through my body. Bronwyn's boyfriend, Simon, was holding my hand. I felt such warmth toward him; I'm sure trauma gives us a glimpse of others' true nature.

For some strange reason, the hospital staff kept calling me Charles, my great-grandfather's name. When they told me they wanted to X-ray the leg "to see if there are any teeth left inside," I had the fleeting thought that it would be very cool if there were.

The surgeon, Dr. Pansagrau, did a remarkable job of putting my leg back together. I spent the next few days watching my leg turn various shades beneath 260 exterior and 80 interior stitches and praying that drip after drip of antibiotics would ward off infection. Mom was by my side, but in usual Varty style, after it became clear that I was going to recover, her sympathy started to wane. By the first afternoon, the whole family was over the excitement. When Uncle John and Dad called the hospital, they offered no solace; after all, my carelessness had provoked the first reported croc attack at Londolozi. (A very experienced Kruger Park ranger later said, "When it comes to crocodiles, what I've learnt is you should check your bathwater at night.")

I didn't really want any visitors. People like to play up the machismo of surviving a croc attack, and it would be a lie to say that I haven't, on a few occasions in bars, promoted my assailant to a twelve-foot beast that I killed with a toothpick. But, really, the story embarrasses me. It could have been someone else in the group that got attacked. I'd declared the situation safe, and I'd been wrong. I'd gotten my ranger certification barely a year earlier, and already I'd screwed up royally.

The newspapers soon caught wind of the incident. Under the breathless headline "Croc Attacks Son of Conservationist," one newspaper reported, "The only son of South Africa's most influential conservation family . . . narrowly escaped death in a crocodile attack this week." Dad used the coverage as an opportunity to promote river conservation. The attack was actually a "good sign," my dad opined to the reporter: "It proves that crocodile populations are recovering from near extinction from the area in the 1960s. Water quality has improved, as have local conservation practices. We don't consider this specific crocodile a problem animal, and will therefore not shoot it." Uncle John figured that I'd escaped the croc only because my foot had accidentally kicked open his gular flap, a valve that seals the throat closed when the crocodile's mouth is open underwater. He therefore turned my travails into a hit fireside song, "Kick Him in the Gular Pouch," so he can torture me forever. That's the Varty attitude in a nutshell: No big deal. Save the animals.

I walked out of the hospital on crutches, with a calcified piece of bone under my right knee, a long scar down the back of my leg, and the family nickname of "Club Foot," since my right foot now sticks out a bit awkwardly. But there were deeper scars.

The very life of adventure that had once felt like a gift now seemed pointless and terrifying. The crocodile; the taste of gunmetal in my mouth; and the whisper *"I will kill you."*

I knew some things at the end of that year that I hadn't known when it began. But though I showed it to no one, I felt completely bewildered, even after a desperate surge of seeking as hard as any pilgrim.

Still, you wouldn't have known this to look at me. I was like any regular nineteen-year-old with unruly hair, a scraggly beard, and leather bangles. While I stood on a precarious bridge, Shakespeare's battalions rolled on.

NINETEEN

DEAD SILENCE

THE LION GRIPPED THE WARTHOG AWKWARDLY. It had failed to clamp its jaws over the warthog's windpipe, which allowed the hog to let out a squeal that was so close to a primal scream that even I was unnerved.

All around us lions were springing up and rushing toward the awful sound. The guests, Solly, and I had just been sitting in the Land Rover, watching the pride laze about in the shade of a torchwood tree, when one of the females had ambled out of sight—in pursuit of a shadier spot, we'd thought. Then we'd heard the squealing. The sound changed the energy of the game drive, as if some ancient part of all of us had been shocked into life, the part that understood hunting, killing, danger.

"*Famba! Famba! Famba!*" Solly screamed. "Go! Go! Go!" He wanted me to drive toward the sound so the guests could catch the action.

A guest seated behind me was so excited that he started to slap the back of my head, screaming, "Get us in there! Faster, man, faster!" In seconds we were witnessing the carnage.

Already the hog's piercing squeal was being smothered by deep, ferocious growls as the lions lashed out at each other to protect their piece of the prize, their ears flattened, faces bloodied, massive paws slapping. At a kill, it's every lion for himself.

The scene was gruesome. Although the hog was still squealing for his life, the lions had ripped open his stomach cavity and begun to feed. Guests were snapping photos wildly, the sound of shutters opening and closing a continuous hum.

I watched the guests closely, knowing that visually ingesting something like this can be challenging. After university, I'd gotten my ranger certification and had been back at Londolozi for three years. Part of my training had covered how to help guests handle the sharp end of nature when they come upon a kill. I was once again struck by our contrasting fascination with death and the horror of it. Sure enough, one woman's expression shifted from rapt to stricken, and tears started to roll as she leaned into her husband. The husband gave me a look that indicated they'd seen enough, but the other guests weren't close to sated, their cameras still humming.

I decided that I'd inflict no more suffering on the weeping woman that day. Ignoring all complaints from the other tourists, I drove away from the scene.

Now I know that we must always build space around real grief. We need to allow the pain to carve within us a deep knowing of what it means to live, to shape us as innocence never can. As Ram Dass says, "It is only in the dark night of the soul that you are prepared to see as God sees and to love as God loves." I found myself admiring the guest who hadn't blanketed her compassion for the warthog. I admired her for refusing to summon the false strength that robs us of our time to grieve. Grief should be treated as holy. When Gran died, I tried to give Dad all my spare emotional energy so I could make him okay. Later I understood that I could never dull his pain and should simply have let him feel it.

I saw with unsparing clarity how death arrives hand in hand with every birth. That December, when the impalas had hundreds of babies and I saw that every leopard at Londolozi had hoisted a baby impala up into its tree pantry, I mourned the end of innocence all over again. "Before you can know kindness as the deepest thing inside," says poet Naomi Shihab Nye, "you must know sorrow as the other deepest thing."

Then my mother's mother, Gorgs, was diagnosed with cancer and, after an initial course of radiation, refused further treatment. She moved to Londolozi a few months later and added herself into the rhythm around the house, although I sometimes felt as if our days followed a rhythm of her making. We all fell into a kind of slow motion.

The family had planned a December vacation to Zanzibar; we'd be taking a plane, then getting onto a Land Rover to bump along back roads, then onto a boat to ride the chop to a remote island off the coast, where we'd live in grass huts—rough going for the hale, a seeming impossibility for a woman harrowed by radiation. What should we do about Gorgs?

Dad called a family meeting. "Listen, I know she's weak, and I know Zanzibar is tough to get to, but I think we should just take her with us," he said. He'd always loved his mother-in-law.

"I don't know," I worried. "She's very frail."

"How will she get to meals at the hotel?" Bron fretted. "She's so weak."

Dad had a solution: "Well, I or Boyd will carry her."

"The doctors say it's not wise," said Mom.

"Doctors only know so much. I say we take her." This is the resolved magic of my father. He knew she was going out; we all did. But he was willing to defy all the high theory and just carry her himself. And he did. We carried Gorgs on and off the boats. We carried her to meals. We carried her to her hut as if she were a new bride crossing the threshold of her new home. She loved it, and she let herself be looked after. She played to the whole thing, sweeping her arm grandly. "Take me down to dinner, Boyd!" She had her first swim in the sea in thirty years. It was an unforgettable vacation.

Gorgs had been a timid woman all her life. Now she'd started to live again. One day back at Londolozi, Mom and I looked out the window to see Gorgs approaching the electric fence that keeps the elephants out. She'd had a lifelong fear of elephants. Now, bent over, she ducked under the fence and quietly approached a small herd beneath a marula tree. I was finally meeting my real grandmother, free from fear, just in time to lose her.

Phillip, our butler, tended to Gorgs with warmth and humility. He taught us so much about patience and the value of doing things slowly. He showed us how to take a dying woman to a sunny spot and just sit nearby until she wanted to move. "Ah, Gogo, I can do all things for you," he would tell her, employing the term of respect for elders. He taught me how to really hold a loved one's hand with no thought of your own pain until they slipped from this silly stretched-in-the-wash costume of a body. Phillip made the world a place of great care and love for my gogo as she sailed out.

I saw something in that dear dying woman's old, craggy face that was like a lightning bolt to something buried in me: an understanding that the life you are leading now is always defined by your choices and no other circumstances. Must we work this out so late, when we're old and too afraid to wear a bathing suit?

Gorgs would amble around the aloe garden my father's mother had planted, to make peace with the fact that she was going to die. I watched her take her last walks amid the sunbirds and aloes, eat her last few mouthfuls of food, and then finally subsist on just the warmth of the winter sun.

She asked to go back to her own home for a week. She was sitting in her small kitchen overlooking the Nelspruit valley, having her tea, when, with her usual dignity, she slipped from her body.

We knew that Gorgs's death was coming, of course; we'd started to prepare. But there was still that unfilled space from that ultimate part-ing. Mom was relieved that her mother was no longer suffering, but she was gutted by the loss. Her mother had always been her touchstone. I knew Mom was down and out when she softened enough to let us take care of her, allowing me to bring her cups of Earl Grey, Dad to run her baths, Bron simply to hold her.

As if that weren't enough, our beloved dog, Tatty, began to fail. We were supposed to be a pragmatic bush family; I'd thought that when the time came, we'd be like Farmer Bill—take her out back and end it right there. Instead, I'd find my mother spoon-feeding Tatty as she weakened, crooning, "You are my little darling." Tatty had been with us through a couple years' worth of harsh chapters. Her unconditional love and joy-fulness had reminded us that there was still good in the world. From a spiritual perspective, dogs get it so right (except for the annoying yap-pers, which get nothing right). When that little golden retriever ball of light died, we knew we'd lost a beloved family member.

Phillip was as deeply aggrieved by the death of Tatty as we were. To show his sadness and solidarity, he dug a grave so deep that in another two feet he might have hit lava. He didn't want a scavenger to smell the decaying body and dig it up—a not-unlikely scenario in the bush. This made placing Tatty into the grave a bit of a logistical effort, with me standing inside it and Dad lowering her down while trying not to throw his back out.

"Treat the body with dignity," Mom said from the side.

"I will, but she is bloody heavy," I replied with a grunt.

"Don't get sand in her face," Mom warned.

"Stop telling me what to do!" I shot back childishly.

We were all undone. Mom was clearly channeling her rage and grief over her mother's death into mourning Tatty. Dad began tearing up. We said prayers and gave thanks to the universe. (Some days I think we should just start a commune, we're such hippies, but we're too busy for that.)

We planted a tree in honor of our glorious pooch; she'd done well to

survive all those years in the bush. The next morning, my mother awoke
to see a nyala feeding on the tree. She found this most disrespectful, so
while all the other trees she's planted get broken and trampled by monkeys, elephants, baboons, and buffaloes, which thrash the trunks with
their horns, Tatty's tree is untouched, because in her sadness, Mom constructed such an impregnable wire fence around it that it could rival the
Great Wall of China.

––––––––

We are all being whispered to our death. It is the white noise hissing
softly beneath all other sounds.

All of this took place in the space of about eight months, and then the
final confusion arrived. My dad and uncle had gone into a project to create a sanctuary for tigers, so that when they went extinct in Asia, the
game parks could be restocked from the reserve. This had all the ear-
marks of a classic Varty Brothers project. It was outlandishly ambitious:
vast in scope, freighted with complicated logistics, and therefore irresist-
ible. If they pulled it off, the project could stem the extinction of the wild
tiger, of whom only about three thousand or so remain in the entire
world. It drew on the brothers' unique skill sets: Uncle John could apply
everything he'd learned from raising Shingi and Jamu to reintroducing
zoo tigers into nature and helping them raise future cubs in the wild,
while Dad could apply his knowledge of restoration to bringing tracts of
overgrazed land back to life. JV's expertise as a documentarian would
bring the tigers' plight to international attention. By this time, Phinda
and Londolozi had become big successes as restoration projects, so Dad
and Uncle John were excited to tackle a new challenge. After the way
Dad had been hammered by the loss of his mother and CC Africa, Mom
was thrilled to see him excited and hopeful again.

Dad and Uncle John threw themselves into this new venture, but
in their eagerness to make the project happen, they went in too fast. As
the project was finding its groove, one of the investors became disgrun-
tled and accusatory and lobbed a lawsuit at us. The claims were endless

and confusing, launching a legal battle that would drag on for years. The litigation exhausted us emotionally and financially, especially on the back of all that had already happened.

For the first time, Bron and I saw our father truly beaten down. He and Uncle John had always been so sure of everything they did. Now every belief that said we lived in a protecting universe was completely erased. Our operating philosophy had always been: You stand together and you fix the problem. But here there was nothing we could fix; the process was complex beyond our understanding. I'd watch Dad take a call from his attorneys and hang up, drained. I'd come home to find him sleeping on the couch, curled up into a deflated ball, as if he'd been punched. It broke my heart. Often when I was near him, I could smell faint wisps of adrenaline on his skin—something you only really know if you've been near serious danger often.

Once again I thought of "the Rumble in the Jungle." Maybe Dad had somehow known that he would face a similar battle in his own lifetime. Without him asking, I became his cornerman. I was in the fight with him, even if I wasn't throwing the punches.

But how do you punch a cloud? In many ways, I wished it were a proper fight—at least there'd be something I could do. Here there was no physical action I could take—no robbers to outwit, no crocodile to outrun. The opponent was an ill-defined shape-shifter, impossible to corner.

As the weight of the threat and the seeming insanity grew, the stress fell onto the entire family. The litigation stretched into a second year, then a third, a fourth. The family tried to keep up appearances—we had a game reserve to run, guests to greet, a village of employees to support—but there was no hiding our grief and panic. Bron handled every bit of lodge business with ferocious intensity, often starting at six in the morning and finishing at midnight. She worried that missing the smallest detail might manifest a grand disaster.

I thought that if I could just do the right thing, be the good son, it would take some of the pressure off Dad. I was determined to give him emotional life support. So each morning, I woke up and took my warhorse off to plow the fields. I was there physically, animatedly pouring guests tea, taking people out on safari, fixing water pumps, but the wildest part of my spirit had fled.

Our lives felt under threat, so we did what we knew how to do: we started drinking. We became piss-cats, hammering three bottles of wine in an evening.

———

My sister was wrangling a roasted chicken out of the oven. With Fleetwood Mac blasting, she used her oven-mitted hand to pour herself a second or third glass of wine.

"Can we turn the music down a little?" said Mom, already lowering the volume. She was on her second glass as well.

This irritated Bronwyn, who felt that the chef should have ultimate control in the kitchen. She twisted the knob back up. By now, Fleetwood Mac had become a musical thermostat indicating the tension in the room.

My way of dealing with this was to attack another beer and say, "Mom, just relax, we're cooking in here. Go sit in the living room."

Saying "relax" had the opposite effect. "I *am* relaxed. It's just bloody loud," Mom shouted.

"I'm in here, I'm cooking—just leave me to cook," Bron said. Now we weren't fighting about music. We were fighting about cooking.

"Just calm down, everyone," I said.

Mom and Bron turned on me like angry lionesses. "Shut it, you. We *are* calm!" Bron bashed down pot lids to add to her point.

"Don't attack me! I'm just saying be cool!" I said.

Dad walked in on cue. "Jesus, don't shout!" He'd been asleep for half an hour. Between six and eight in the evening, he couldn't stay awake; from eight to three A.M., he couldn't sleep. It had been like that for months. The next song roared to life, and Bron clanged another pot.

"What's going on in here?" Dad wanted to know. No one answered.

"Just carve the chicken," Mom snapped.

Dad started to bellow along with the music. "Dad, bring it down a notch," I said, trying to keep the peace.

"If it's too loud, you're too old!" Dad unleashed a slogan he'd heard on the radio, unwittingly pissing Mom off completely. "Did you order those curtains for the camp?" he asked her. At eight o'clock at night, Dad was starting a lodge operations meeting.

"I ordered them from Johannesburg, but they screwed up the order," Mom told him.

"So are the curtains coming or not?"

"They are, but a week late."

"Well, what should we do till then, have no curtains for the guests? They must fucking get them here!" Dad grabbed the wine and poured himself a generous glass. He slammed the bottle down next to the empties on the counter.

"You don't have to tell me that! I know that!" Mom growled.

Dad winced. "Let's not talk about it now."

"Then why did you bring it up?"

Bron let out an exasperated snort. "I'm going to bed."

"Everyone, please, let's be civil," I pleaded. "Everything is fine. We're having a conversation, not invading Russia."

"Everything is *not* fucking fine, and you know it!" My sister was now crying. I went silent, trying to be the calm and rational one. "Ya, I'm also going to bed," I said, and stalked out of the kitchen, leaving Mom and Dad and an uneaten roasted chicken.

I walked out of the house, toward my cottage. I was screaming inside. The night seemed so still, like it was holding its breath. We all were.

———

Indhawu yi nwanyani. It's gone to another place. This term is used by Shangaans to describe the utter destruction of an inanimate object or the demise of a person. In true understated Shangaan style, you might be told that the tractor "has gone to another place" when a better description would be "the tractor lost control while crossing a steep section of the riverbank, resulting in it crashing into a particularly deep hippo pool, where it now lies like the wreck of the HMS *Lusitania* at twenty fathoms." If something has gone to another place, it's truly broken.

I'd gone to another place.

Being depressed is one thing when your life can be seen by outsiders as justifiably hard, but it is a whole different shameful story when you have everything and still feel like you can't bear to get out of bed in the morning. People can't really be sympathetic to you when they can't begin to fathom what you could be so upset about.

The fear of losing everything, including Londolozi, was paralyzing for me. I spent as much time as I could alone, ashamed that I was lost among plenty. God, I was so tired of being tired all the time, and I felt like I had no right to be. I wanted my hair to mat into one gnarly, twisted dreadlock so I looked as haggard as I felt. Every night, while the others started singing around the fire, I would slip away to be by myself with the stars, even though their presence now made me feel insignificant whereas before I had felt part of the grand harmony of this world. It's said that depression is undiagnosed homesickness, but where was home for me?

One night I drove to a staff party that was taking place on the tiny airstrip where the puddle jumpers ferried guests from Johannesburg to Londolozi. Airstrip parties were renowned as fertile ground for madness. We would make a fire on the apron and under the stars something part tribal stomp, part native ceremony, part mating dance would ensue. I'd always been among the most enthusiastic participants, leading the charge with a bottle of Jack Daniel's permanently welded to my hand.

This time I cut the lights and steered the Land Rover towards the gathering. The roosting water thick-knees lined the airstrip, their high-pitched contact calls piercing the night air. Beyond them I could see the shadowy silhouettes of the assembled crowd laughing, dancing, singing around the fire. I turned the Landi around in the moonlight. Unsure why I couldn't be there and dreading equally as much being alone, again I swung the car back towards the gathering. The instant I faced the fire, I just kept the wheel locked and again swung away. The revelers in the distance were completely unaware of my manic loops. Part of me wished that someone would break from the crowd to find me. I was afraid that I was mad, that no one would understand. Eventually I turned the engine off. It was suddenly very silent; then the thick-knees called their eerie faint whistle. My life had become an endless loop to nowhere.

One day I dragged myself to a game of touch rugby with my fellow guides. One of the guides accidentally ankle-tapped me. In the seconds after I hit the dirt, the white-hot weight of year after year of litigation landed. The lights went out: I rushed the guide and started to punch him. I was lined up to kill him. "Leave it alone! Leave it alone!" another guide yelled, grabbing me. Everyone pulled us apart. I couldn't say anything.

I stalked away from the field and then to my cottage. I went into my room and then into the bathroom and then into the shower, pulling the sliding door closed behind me. If there had been another door to lock behind me, I would have pulled it tight. I wanted to be shut away—for myself, yes, but more for the good of others. I felt I'd brought disharmony to Eden. The only noble option in my mind was to cast myself out, but how could I leave when my father was depending on me? I didn't want him to have my madness to worry about, on top of all his other problems.

The years of litigation had taken their toll on Bron, too. One day she and I went out for a hike. What we thought would be a casual walk up a gentle hill turned into a five-hour forced march over steep terrain. Eventually we were within sight of the summit, with about three hundred yards to go, when Bron stopped suddenly and declared, "I'm done." Her skin seemed very pale, almost anemic. But her jaw had that strong, set frame, and the skin between her eyes had crinkled into a sharp furrow.

"Are you joking?" I said. "The summit is right there." It was cold on the hillside, and as I stood there dripping with sweat, the wind suddenly chilled me.

Bron glared at me. "Listen, Boyd, I'm done. I'm over this. I'm going to sit right here. You go where you need to go. This is my summit."

So much frustration boiled inside me. All the unspoken anxiety could spill out when I least expected it. "What the fuck are you doing? There's the summit *right there*!" I jabbed my finger toward it. "Why won't you just go the last bit? We've come all this way." I needed badly for her to want the real summit for herself. "Don't do all the hard work, then sell yourself short so close!" I was shouting now.

"Boyd, I'm not going! I don't care if it's Mount fucking Everest—I'm not going any farther." Now Bron was shouting, too. "I don't need any more shit in my life . . . not *one more step* of struggle. I am *not* going farther. I am done done *done* with feeling like the sky is going to fall on my head. I'm done being pushed, I'm done with courts and lies and fearing I'm going to lose it all. I am *done*." Tears were rolling down her face. She, too, had gone to another place.

After all we'd been through, the litigation was a final act of violence that had shredded in me the desire to do anything. From within the storm that blew up in my own teacup of a life, I had to find my way back to a sense of vitality.

———

To seek the wellness in the soul we've lost, we return to what we know best. For me, that place was nature. Nature as a physical space that reframes and recasts one's inner space. Nature as an outer world that, like no other force, facilitates the journey to the inner world. Nature as healer.

TWENTY

THE VAV

CHEVAVANE ARRIVED AT THE gate to Londolozi with an old duffel bag slung haphazardly over his shoulder. His T-shirt and jeans were ragged, but he sported a worn yet stylish Stetson drooping on his head and a huge, obviously fake Rolex on his wrist. He was a wiry Shangaan man with scarred arms, clearly uncomfortable in the presence of whites. His eclectic clothes hinted at an underlying contradiction. Somehow, beneath his roguish edge was a profound humility.

Chevavane was the most famous outlaw in the area, and from the moment I heard his name, I knew we had to meet. I wanted to find someone who lived off the land, who still knew all the old-school secrets of hunting and gathering in the bush. For hundreds, if not thousands, of years, people in that area had lived off the land. Then those areas were declared national parks, effectively turning hunters into poachers overnight.

I want to make a clear distinction here. Yes, Chevavane was breaking the law. But I couldn't see his crimes the same way I saw those of poachers who hunted for black market profits. These poachers will kill rhinoceroses just to take their horns, ripping through an already declining population. Chevavane hunted for bush meat; he killed only what he and his family needed to eat. He had a skill for living off the land that was hard to come by, and it was this knowledge that I wanted.

I called in a favor with the Mhlongo family, the leaders of a nearby village, and they convinced the Vav, as I'd come to think of him, that I had no intention of arresting him. In fact, quite the opposite; I wanted to hire him to teach me everything he knew. My message traveled by bush telegraph, like a faint song on the breeze. He agreed to come, but only under major duress.

Two weeks later, Chevavane appeared.

We gave the guard a false name—after all, Chevavane was a wanted man. On the drive toward the game reserve, I turned to him. "Thanks for finally agreeing to meet me." He simply nodded his head and gave me a wry, crafty grin.

For three months I lived alone in the bush with the Vav. We shared a love for silence and slingshots. We drank out of the river, hunted birds, and followed lions to sharpen my tracking skills. His style of tracking was to string together a broad concept of where the animals were and then walk a brisk zigzag, picking up the quarry's trail here and there. The Vav had a homemade spear, an old fence pole with a sharpened end, that he could fold into his duffel bag. He was a surgeon with that spear; he handled it with a grace and precision that made it an extension of himself. He claimed to have killed Cape buffalo with it. The Vav seemed to have no concept that wild animals might be dangerous; the first time we encountered a snarling male lion, his response was to unleash a penny-sized pebble into the lion's rump with his slingshot and then laugh thunderously. Everywhere we went he found something to snack on: date palms in the river, milkberries on the bank, sour plums inland on hot days.

The Vav was a master tracker. He recognized the alarm calls prey animals made when predators went in for a kill. He taught me how to follow up on those calls. The birds' trills became songs to cheer me, the impressions in the sand a language I could read, an opening to a new world in the same way that a foreign language can initially isolate you and then suddenly make you feel perfectly at home. At first the Vav acted as an interpreter, but then in staccato bursts and finally in fluent harmonies, the voice of the bushveld started to talk directly to me through the tracks and sounds.

Maybe that's why all the mystics went to nature. Maybe Buddha, Jesus, and Muhammad wanted to hear the Creator speak through his creation.

During those hours out in the bush, we communicated only with hand signals and subtle sounds. When we were tracking an animal, the Vav would hold his hand flat, palm down, to indicate that tracks were old and cold. His hand palm up, fingers poised to snap, was a sign that we were getting close. If we lost the track and then one of us rediscovered it, he would snap his fingers and point at the discovered spoor. Two snaps meant "freeze"; there was some potential danger. Tapping his ear meant "listen," and slicing his hand across his throat, in that universal gesture for "cut it," meant "Let's leave the track; we're not making any progress." We'd make a knocking sound with our mouths like a woodpecker hitting a hollow tree to get each other's attention. Eventually we had so many snaps and knocks that we were like a walking Tourette's menagerie.

During those silent hours of tracking out in the bush, I felt a sense of purpose and power seeping slowly back in. Every day was a balm, and our shared comfort in silence deepened our bond.

Sometimes in the middle of the day I would do a training routine that involved a run through the bush followed by a series of calisthenics: push-ups, sit-ups, and squats. The Vav was amazed that someone would intentionally burn extra energy. "You're a *byzaan*"—a madman—"to be running around like this," he'd say. Still, he became an eager participant in the midday training. He certainly brought his own style to it. Not wanting to sweat up his clothes, he would strip down to his underpants—a ragged pair of tighty-whities—don his walking boots, and run off like a gazelle. We cut quite a sight for the afternoon game drive, the Vav in jockey shorts and boots and me shirtless and bearded like a wild man.

On a cold winter morning, we discovered a wildebeest a poacher had trapped in a snare, its tongue engorged and purple. I called it in on my two-way radio; the anti-poaching team was on its way. Much to my surprise, the Vav had us wait in ambush with the anti-poaching team until the poacher returned. Amid the gunfire, which made me dive for cover, Chevavane ran the poacher down. It seems he ran as well for the anti-poaching rangers as he did running away from them. He was whatever he needed to be in the moment. The rangers were impressed; of course they didn't know it was the notorious Chevavane who'd aided them.

After a while, I started to move like the Vav, think like him, see the world from behind his eyes. I'd grown up learning to track, but the Vav took me to a far deeper level. Tracking put me in the system the same way hunting did, but without having to kill something. It required the same level of immersion and alertness; it was like stringing together a series of clues, and it had all the thrill of pursuit.

———

The Vav and I sat around a small wood fire as the dawn broke into gold and the first sounds of the morning resounded a wild call to prayer. On the other side of the hill, a male lion roared. I felt such a deep mixture of emotions. The Vav was a wonderful, uncomplicated person to spend time with, but it was still lonely out in the wild.

When my time with Chevavane was over, I moved back in with my family. The ongoing litigation was continuing to take its toll. Mom proposed a new family motto: "Love many, trust few, be discerning, paddle our own canoe." "From now on, we are gonna call ourselves the Canoe Company," she told us.

One day Janet, our maid, approached me shyly. "I can help you," she murmured. It turned out she was also a village *sangoma,* or medicine woman. She urged us to gather the whole family, including Uncle John, on the deck. This quiet, reserved woman, who normally wore a powder-blue dress with a frilled white apron and a traditional white cloth *doek* head covering, suddenly appeared before us in full *sangoma* regalia: a bright red wig, her neck circled with dozens of plastic beads, her legs wrapped in a traditional *shwe-shwe* skirt. Rattling her beaded wildebeest tail to chase away bad juju, Janet urged us to slip some money under the mat as an offering to the ancestral spirits. She began to shake and twitch, allowing herself to become possessed by spirits, ranting in such rapid Shangaan that we couldn't even translate it.

"Bring me a razor blade!" she suddenly demanded. I jumped up, ran to my room, dug out a safety razor, and smashed the plastic to break out the blade. Janet grabbed it from me and started waving it around wildly as Mom blanched. Our maid's body jerked with convulsions as she danced around the deck, spitting at us and whacking us with the wilde-beest tail. Then she danced up to each of us in turn, using the razor to nick us between the eyes, on our wrists, elbows, knees, ankles, and the backs of our necks—everywhere the bad spirits needed to be let out. Into each of the nicks she rubbed black powder, or *muti,* calling in ancestors from the spirit world to heal us. Bron leaned into me. "We've totally lost it. We are off the reservation."

Another *sangoma,* this time a white medicine woman, told us to lay giraffe bones a certain way in front of our house. "This will help you see beyond the trouble. Giraffes give you vision." We were fully aware of how unhinged it seemed, but there was no reason not to go for it; we were that desperate. We trolled the land until we found the necessary bones and arranged them in a pyramid in the front yard. There was no visible effect from the giraffe bones, but who's to say it didn't help?

An astrologer told Mom, "Look, this is really weird, but I want you to see a specialist. There's a guy I know who deals with people who have been cursed by black magic." That seemed utterly ridiculous, but by this time, our attitude was *Why not?* We'd try anything once.

A few days later, Harold arrived with his wife. A kinesiologist trained by Edgar Cayce, the "sleeping prophet," Harold was so far out on the fringe that suddenly the giraffe bones seemed normal. He closed his eyes and sank into deep contemplation. "There's a tear in your energy," he pronounced solemnly. "You've had a Chinese voodoo put on you. I can clear it." He did a kind of energy healing on each of us. Then he gathered us into a circle, what he called a "clearing ring," where he declared he was "working in the energy field."

Two days later, Harold died.

"He's crossed over to do spiritual work for us on the other side, to right the scales," his widow told us. Such was our mood that we found this a comforting thought. Meanwhile, each of us privately nursed a different belief: "Shit, our problems are so bad, we just gave Harold a fatal heart attack. What's going to happen to us?"

As word of the litigation spread, a slow parade of packages began to appear, unbidden, on our doorstep. Statues of Ganesh, the Hindu elephant deity—lord of success, destroyer of evil, remover of obstacles—began to arrive. We got packet after packet of *vibhuti,* sacred ash, from a famous guru called Sai Baba, considered by some to be the "highest vibrating" person on earth. A steady flow of universal support was coming to us from all over the world, even if we were too locked in fear to see it.

———

Uncle John moved to a much smaller farm and, even with the lawsuit, kept the tiger project going. But I started to see him less and less. He didn't come to Londolozi as much, and when he did, he tended to stay alone. The only people he liked being around were his children. When Savannah was five, Uncle John and Gillian had had twin boys, Sean and Tao. They were full of energy and curiosity, just like their father, and JV lavished as much love and attention on them as he had on me, Bron, and

Savannah. Being a parent—a job he was brilliant at—was the one thing that brought him unalloyed joy, perhaps the only thing that kept him from unraveling completely at this time.

The years of litigation piled up like boulders. After five years, it seemed endless. Even at a haven like Londolozi, the pressure crushed us all. Uncle John was hurting so deeply, but he didn't know how to express it. So he did what men like him do: he stayed away.

He would show up at court in full JV couture, unhappy that he'd had to leave his .44 Magnum in the car. Often he'd get so mad during the proceedings that he would shout out, "This is bullshit!" and one of our lawyers would ask him to leave the courtroom.

The pain of a lost dream, the constant attacks, and the endless courtroom appearances and lies drained him and Dad. They started talking to each other only in short, clipped sentences, as if saying too much would lead to feeling too much. A space developed between them.

It made me afraid.

———

Dad looked so haggard all the time.

"What can I do to help you?" I asked.

"Just keep trading." Meaning, just keep making Londolozi go. We needed the money. We feared that the cost of litigation would drive us into bankruptcy and we would lose everything.

I didn't know if I had it in me.

TWENTY-ONE

THE FLAMING SHAMAN

THE ZULU SAY, *"Utshani obulele buvuswa wumlilo umame."* The dead grass is awakened by the fire mother.

The flames hissed through the bush like an adder's warning. In the darkness they looked like a sunset painted in slashes of orange and red against the earth. Backlit clouds of smoke rose into the black sky, plumes of dancing orange cotton candy spun by the heat and rage of the fire below, a work of anger and artistry.

Bush fires can start spontaneously, particularly at the end of the winter, when the first rains are threatening. The storm builds, with all its lightning and thunder, but no rain arrives. A single bolt touches down and detonates a raging fire. This one had broken out in a thick patch of brush south of the Londolozi lodges. All around me was a coordinated madness: tractors hauling water and fire-fighting equipment, and men with beaters trying to contain sections of the blaze. The radio crackled nonstop, while francolins by the dozens burst out of the long grass in front of the flames, as if shot from cannons. Caught suddenly on the rising heat, for a brief moment they realized their eagle aspirations, until they got beyond the temporary thermals and their short wings began to flail in the face of their true terrestrial nature.

My grandfather always said, "Men should be in harm's way together." We were designed to work together and face hardship together. We don't go out and fight wars now in South Africa. Instead, we seek that huge sense of bonding and meaning in booze and women, bar fights and extreme sports. Then a fire touches down, and something in us comes out.

I was trying my best to coordinate the effort to start back burns all around the racing blaze in an effort to contain it. At times this took me to remote edges of the fire where the crews hadn't yet arrived. I must have run at least fifteen miles, and it was only one A.M. As I was standing alone on the fringe of flames, downwind so that the smoke led the fire in my direction, I felt the earth shake and jumped aside as a rhino ran past me. And then, in the midst of the fiery furnace, I saw the leopard.

A strange thing happened. For the first time in years, I felt calm.

The leopard walked out of the firelight wearing a veil of orange smoke, as if his air of mystery had manifested ectoplasmic dancing spirits around him. There were sparks on his coat, glowing jewels studded among the rosettes. In many ancient cultures, the solitary cat is heralded as the animal that walks between the realms. This was a shaman, a master soul dressed as a beast of the field. A leopard in a fire should have been frantic and alert. But this leopard was as calm as if he were lying in the morning sun. Regal as a king, he looked straight into the depth of my soul. *Come with me. I will take you to another place.*

And then, as if approving, he walked past me. Close.

You are always safe. Amaram hum madhuram hum. I am immortal, I am blissful. Utshani obulele buvuswa wumlilo umame. The dead grass is awakened by the fire mother.

I just stood in the smoke and chaos, watching the trail of smoke the leopard left behind. My memory flashed to a long-ago moment when my father's mother, Gogo, described seeing my grandfather's parents appear in the fire like apparitions the day before he died. She had known then that they had come to carry him away. Fire marked the boundary between worlds, for the first Boyd Varty, and now for me.

In the clarity of those few seconds with the leopard in the fire, I had a glimpse of peace. To the mystic in me, it felt like the leopard was calling to a place inside me that knew deep stillness. Maybe my subconscious was looking so hard for meaning that I saw it in the leopard, but I truly felt like the message came from nature: *There is a place inside you that is as healthy as the day it was born.*

Then I heard my own voice. "I want that."

TWENTY-TWO

TRACKING

DOWN BY THE RIVER on a winter morning, the water ran clear and shallow over the coarse sand, and the mist rose as if heated at some unfathomable depth by the earth's heart. Lions had congregated. I could see their clear tracks damp with the dew of the reeds; the water had run down their muscular forelegs, wetting the pads of each paw and leaving a drop of moisture in each pawprint. The tracks approached the water and then turned away. The length of the stride told me that the animals were moving fast; the change in direction spoke to a kind of frustration. The lions wanted to cross but, like most cats, were uncomfortable going into the water.

Then the tracks headed right to the edge of the water. Here they were deeper, as the sand was soggy where the alpha female had stopped. Her weight had created clear impressions in the sand. In my mind's eye, I saw her lifting her paws high out of the water as she crossed it awkwardly on tiptoe, her ears pinned slightly back and a wincing look on her face.

On the far bank I could see where water had splattered down onto the powdery sand; this was where the lions had exited the stream. I've followed this pride on this crossing many times. Ahead was the winding path to the tamboti grove at the edge of the clearing, where the shade might have tempted the pride to lie down, unless they could muster the will to push through the heat and head for the deeper shade on the banks of the Manyaleti River. I saw all of this in my mind's eye as I stood amid the pugmarks in the sand. I am connected with every animal as I track it. The warmth of the sun on me is the same warmth on the lion's skin.

In my experience, when you're tracking, the mystical derives from the practical. You get really good at the practical aspects of seeing tracks, listening to birdcalls and the alarm sounds of animals; then a mystical intuition begins to flow into it. With yoga, you get on the mat and do the positions and the breathing, and then something else arrives. It's the same in life. You've got to go and do the work. You have to get good at following the feeling, practice following the rhythm of life. Then it starts to look like magic.

After I saw the leopard in the fire, when my soul realized, despite all the grief and trauma, that it wanted to heal, it became like an animal that instinctually knew how to find its way out of the wilderness. It began to conjure imagery of better times as tracks to a healed place. It began to pace, looking for a fresh scent on the breeze. There was the slightest glimmer of intentionality; I cared about finding my way home. I did what my animal brethren did in that situation: I began an inner and outer pacing.

When I'd first started tracking, as a boy, I was hopeless. Elmon would point out a sign—"Look, a leopard slept here"—and I'd see nothing. Eventually, I got so I could detect those faint clues. The other hazard was following the wrong track. Once when I was ten, we were stalking a rhino in long grass, the three-leaf clover of its gigantic, bucket-sized track. But a hippo had followed the rhino and crossed the path, and suddenly I was following the hippo's pie-plate prints instead, just similar enough to lead me off course. "Go back to where you started," Elmon told me. "Go back to where the track is freshest."

So, where was my track the freshest? What was the last time I'd felt as healthy as the day I was born? The night after the fire, I spent hours sitting on the front lawn daydreaming, my soul pacing. Then I remembered. It was a few years earlier, with Jen and the lions.

———

Jen, the daughter of a family friend, sat beside me as I poked at the embers of the previous night's fire. Although she was tired, her eyes sparkled in the dawn light. With her stick-straight hair, she was beautiful in a sixties folksinger way. We'd been up all night "kicking logs"—that's where two people are just talking but at least one of them is thinking there could be a vibe. You're not sure; you're kind of keen, but you wonder, is she keen or is she just sitting up because you're interesting to talk to? Every time you become uncertain about what to do or say, you stand up and kick a burning log deeper into the fire. I knew I was keen because I'd been getting her boyfriend's name wrong the night before on purpose. It felt good to get a jolt of that playful chemistry, particularly in the midst of the family's legal troubles.

A lion roared across the river, the sound starting almost lethargically, then beginning to find its groove, the deep *rooo-a-a-a-r* blasting into the cold winter air. I could see him in my mind's eye, his stomach a giant set of bellows inflating and then compressing, the condensation of his breath fogging the early morning air like dragon smoke.

Jen's starlit blue eyes brightened with a mixture of excitement and concern. We now had something to work with. I gave her a half grin. "That's how lion tracking starts," I told her, trying to sound casual.

We drove out for a few miles, to where we estimated the roar had come from. By the time we got there, it was getting light and faint tracks were beginning to become visible on the road. I spotted the saucer-sized pugmark of a male lion.

"Okay if we go on foot from here?" I asked, swinging out of the Land Rover and unslinging the rifle from the rack. "Jen, your job is to keep looking around for the lion. I'll be watching the tracks." Jen nodded.

We began to follow the tracks, me crouched over and walking ahead, Jen behind me, scanning the area. I looked like an old Vietnam vet with my boots, rifle, and camo winter jacket three sizes too big. Bob Dylan and Joni Mitchell tracking lions.

I noticed that one of the giant pugs had a smaller track faintly superimposed onto it. A nocturnal white-tailed mongoose had walked across these tracks. At first I'd thought the tracks looked so fresh, but now I realized that the lion had walked down this road hours before, in the middle of the night. Lions can travel twenty miles in a night of hunting; there was no telling how far away he might be now. I was feeling a little despondent when I heard a lion roar about two-thirds of a mile away. Then a second roar started. Two lions! This was such a lucky break.

I grabbed Jen by the wrist and began to trot in the direction of the roars. Three minutes later, the lions roared again. I could tell they were moving fast—and directly toward us. I spotted a game path—a byway through the bush created by animal traffic—leading into the clearing where we were standing. I was certain that the lions were walking along that path. They'd be on us in a matter of minutes.

"They're heading straight toward us. Are you ready for this?" I asked Jen.

The look on Jen's face suggested that the reality of the situation was only now landing, but she also had a spark of excitement in her eyes. "What will they do?"

"Don't know. Just do exactly what I tell you," I said, squeezing her hand. I'd have to make a split-second assessment of their body language to gauge what kind of mood the lions were in. When a lion comes at you in a warning charge, its body is tightly coiled, it moves unbelievably quickly, its tail lashes from side to side, its lip curls up to reveal its powerful canines, and the sound of its growl makes you think it has a dirt bike in its belly. Often it will stop only yards in front of you. On these occasions, you must under all circumstances stand your ground and face up to the lion. "It's afraid of your courage," my uncle always used to say. Lions aren't used to other creatures staring them down. It's a good tactic for life, too; even if you're terrified inside, stare it in the eye.

Jen and I ran about thirty yards to a spot safely back from where the game path entered the clearing and dove into the dewy grass. Jen was still holding my hand, both of us panting with fear and excitement.

Suddenly there they were, two huge adult males, black-maned, their deeply pronounced muscles bunching as they glided fluidly into the clearing on massive paws. As they came into view, they began to roar again, setting the ground shaking.

The lions were now twenty yards away. Jen and I were still holding each other tightly. I could see by the speed they were moving that the lions had no interest in us. They passed right by us, most likely in search of the rest of the pride. With each step they took away from us, a little more electricity drained out of the air. I discovered a grin on my face I couldn't get rid of. My heart was still pounding. This was what lion tracking was all about.

Suddenly we were laughing hysterically, and neither of us knew why.

"Oh, my sweet Jesus, can you believe that?" was all we could say, lying on our backs in the damp grass.

That was the track to my right life. That feeling of aliveness would not always reach the intensity set by the lions, but it was the direction I needed to head in. Tracking is like putting together a puzzle with no idea of what the picture is—faith in an as yet undefined future.

You don't know who will change your life. You can't foresee the circumstances that will connect you with your helpers. One thing I do know: even out in the middle of the African outback, the right people will show up if you are open to their arrival, if you allow yourself to ask for help. I now understood what I wanted and how to track it, even if I wasn't quite sure how to get it.

One day I found myself standing in front of the allocations board full of guests' names; each name had beside it the initials of the guide who'd be taking that person on safari. In the silence of the game rangers' room, I committed the ultimate breach of guiding etiquette and rubbed a colleague's name off and placed my own initials—a tiny "bv"—next to the name of a guest another guide had told me about. "There's this woman who asks you really interesting questions," he'd told me. "She's quite cool. She's gonna come back here sometime. You should meet her." My body seemed to be operating independently of my mind. This was how I met the master tracker who would help guide the next steps of my journey.

Martha Beck arrived on my game drive when I most needed her. Life has a greater imagination than I do: if you had told me, in the depth of my dark, silent time, that a twenty-something, beer-drinking, meat-eating, rugby-playing farm boy from South Africa would find his mentor in the form of a wispy former Mormon Harvard PhD, I would have called you an idiot.

Martha's neck looks like it works hard to hold up her head, partly because her intellect is so big. Despite her fragile frame, however, you shortly start to see her as immensely strong. She fills a room in a way you cannot imagine. She is one of those radiant people who become more beautiful with each moment you spend with them. She'd written a memoir about having a son with Down syndrome and some books on life coaching that were bestsellers in South Africa, but I didn't know that then. I only knew that she was someone gifted with incredible intuition and that I felt deeply drawn to her.

That afternoon, I took Martha out on a game drive. We came upon a small herd of elephants foraging in the waning light. Toward the back of the herd I saw Elvis.

I'd first come upon Elvis five years earlier. A herd of elephants were drinking from a deep hollow in the earth where some rainwater had gathered. In the middle of the group stood a tiny, deformed female elephant whose back knees were inverted and fused, so that her hindquarters were a bow of sloped discomfort. Another ranger had dubbed the little lady Elvis—playing off Elvis "the Pelvis" Presley—because of the way her pelvis swayed when she walked. This poor, undersized elephant would probably be dead in a couple of days, I thought; the herd would leave her behind, and she'd soon buckle under the weight of her own body and perish.

Suddenly the matriarch turned and led the herd up a steep bank toward a clearing. Elvis pivoted to follow. For a second she seemed to psych herself up, and then she attempted the bank. Her back legs buckled, and she tumbled down the slope. She tried a second time, and again she lacked the strength. On her third attempt, an amazing thing happened. A young teenage elephant walked up behind her and, propping her trunk and forehead against Elvis's flanks, very gently began to shovel her up the steepest part of the bank. I was astonished; I'd never seen this kind of behavior among elephants.

A few days later, I watched the matriarch plucking branches from a tall tree. She placed every other branch on the ground so that Elvis could get it, feeding herself with alternate mouthfuls. The entire herd was caring for its little invalid.

Remarkably, Elvis returned to Londolozi with her herd every winter. It was always thrilling for me to be out in the bush and come across her unique track, a backward bracket drawn in the sand by the strange drag of her back legs. I would follow it, sometimes for hours, to see this special little lady who was so full of pluck despite her deformity.

On that game drive, I shared Elvis's story with Martha.

"My son has a disability, too," she told me. "Elvis has a similar carriage to Adam's. That is officially my favorite elephant ever." I immediately liked that about her: where others saw only deformity, Martha saw kinship.

It's strange how we find our own lives reflected at us in nature. I felt a kinship with Elvis too, but for a different reason. I felt as vulnerable as Elvis looked.

Martha was a guest, so I tried to remain professional, but when you get to know her, you see that it's pretty impossible to hold back in her presence. I couldn't believe that anyone could be so unconditionally kind to a relative stranger. After the game drive, we sat on the front deck of Tree Camp, the vervet monkeys surrounding us. Soon I found myself telling her, "I know this is sort of strange, but could I ask you about some stuff?"

Martha looked at me with her calm, bright blue eyes. "I've been waiting for you to ask."

"I'm really worried about my family. They've been under so much pressure." I gave her a run-down of the litigation. How everyone was locked in fear, our emotions so volatile that we could suddenly find ourselves in a screaming match over the color of couch cushions.

"And what about you?" Martha asked. "How are *you* doing?"

"I'm fine. I just think what's happening is so unjust."

"It sounds horrific." She seemed to pin my attention where I didn't want it to stay, then waited for me to speak.

"Everyone has their challenges," I told her. "If we just keep positive, things will go right."

"Mm-hmm," she said. Then: "Have you tried just acknowledging that something terrible is happening to you?"

"That's not what we do. We don't talk about the problem. We just keep shooting for the solution. We just keep going. That's who we are. We're bush people."

Martha chuckled softly. "And how's that going?"

"Not so well, I guess."

"You have to accept what you're going through before you can get anywhere better," she said. "The only foundation you have is the truth. You're all acting like nothing's happened. You're playing parts in a giant act, and acting leaves you exhausted and frayed and angry. Offer your parents your best—that's all you can do. Do your best—that's all you can do. Trying to do more just sacrifices you on the altar of being supportive. That isn't going to help anyone. If you want them to heal, *you* work out how to heal. If you want them to feel joy, *you* work out how to find joy. The best you can do for your dad is be happy. That means you go where the tracks send you. You need to learn who you're becoming, and then teach your parents who you've become."

The whole interaction with this woman from miles away had taken no time. You can know someone for years, and they have no effect on you. You can know someone for five minutes, and they change your life forever. I felt like Martha was talking the most sense I had heard in a while. In this brief encounter, the light had been switched on in some way. I had the simple realization that life and strife are not the same thing, that the only way I could help anyone else was first to help myself.

At that very moment, the elephants walked into the clearing, pausing right in front of us. They stopped and extended their trunks, exploring our scent; or maybe they were saluting—who can say? The herd parted, and suddenly, there was Elvis again. "You can't really understand care until you give it to yourself," Martha had just told me. In the simplicity of that moment, it felt like Martha was the elephant matriarch gently placing branches on the ground for me.

As Martha continued to speak, I felt a tug in my center, a pull I was learning to respect as an inner track. Something inside me was telling me to travel again, even if it meant absconding from the post of the good son and my self-imposed obligation to stay and support my family. It seemed crazy and selfish, but I decided to keep following that path, no matter what. It was time to leave Londolozi again.

———

But where to go? I began lunging toward every thought that occurred to me. For a while I was obsessed with the Lugenda River, in the most re-mote part of northern Mozambique. I decided I was going to paddle down it because there's no one there, no one to help you. I wanted it to be possible that I might not come back. Maybe, my mind said, *this* adventure would make it all okay. Or maybe I'd join the French Foreign Legion. Yes, that was it: I'd be a soldier.

Or maybe I'd sail a boat from Cape Town to Brazil, put myself in the hands of the elements. My mind loved the story. Nothing else within me leapt at it.

I paced and paced, pelting Bron with a different great idea every day until she said, "Fine, you can do any of these things if you think you need to do them. But before you do that, do me a favor. Shut up for a while."

So I did. I shut up for about ten days. I stopped trying to think of what I would do with my newfound time and freedom. I stopped thinking I should do anything. I just shut up. And that's when I heard the first real directive from within. It said: *Go back to India.*

TWENTY-THREE

THE MEDICINE

"So WHAT'S THE DEAL when I see this guy?" Dad asked.

"I don't know," I told him. "I guess you just lay it all out."

Dad wasn't used to meetings with enlightened types. But when I'd told him that I wanted him to join me for an audience with the master in India, he hadn't hesitated. It was a sign that he, too, was searching for resolution.

Seven years earlier, the master had told me to experience the world, to come back to him when I was ready to seek within. Now that a longing for reconnection to my spiritual side had been reawakened, I was sure he would help me find my answers. I hoped he'd help Dad, too. Although he was essentially a practical man, Dad had always been open to examining all approaches to the spiritual path. Every year, he would ritually write the core principles from *The Path of the Masters* into the front of his work diary. "These guys are on to something," he told me. "Wish I had the discipline to meditate." He was closer than he thought.

It had taken three days, two plane rides, and assorted trains and taxis to get from Londolozi to the ashram. We made a beeline for the master's home, weaving our way through the dense New Delhi traffic, millions of scooters darting around the car like a school of remoras around a shark.

We met the master in the living room of his estate house. Dressed all in white with his immaculate turban, he projected a powerful presence that commanded respect. Dad told our story. When he finished, the master simply looked at us and said, "Know your truth, stick to the process, and be free of the outcome."

I waited for more, but he was finished. I could feel the love in the master's gaze, but I didn't want love, I wanted a solution. Part of me was screaming silently, "Do a goddamn miracle!"

A three-day journey for a twenty-minute audience? I walked away sick with disappointment, the deadness back in my mind, no solution to enforce. "Know your truth, stick to the process, and be free of the outcome." So simple. So obvious. "I could have gotten that from a fortune cookie," I snarled to myself. The yoga teacher at Londolozi was probably telling a batch of guests the very same thing right now. Why the fuck had I dragged my father all the way to India to hear it?

As we drove back to the airport, I could see that Dad was disappointed in the audience, too. "Well, that's a long way to come for a sentence," he said. He was being kind. I'd made all the arrangements and had asked him to run a three-day gauntlet and now had so little to show for it.

"Yes, I'm sorry. I guess with all that's gone wrong, I was just kind of expecting a lightning bolt," I said. "Something has to give—something has to bounce our way."

Dad stared out the window at the New Delhi traffic racing around us.

Dad went back home to Londolozi, and I stayed behind. I wandered down to the south of India. I had reached a point where I needed space from the people closest to me so that I could concentrate on my own reclamation. An element of selfishness is a required part of healing, but if you get right, it ultimately leaves you with more to give.

For months I paced, suspended in a place of complete uncertainty, trying to find the next track. I had no idea of what I was meant to be doing, but that was all right for now. Then Martha called. "Come to Arizona," she said. "There's someone here I want you to meet."

———

Arizona in August was like the set of a cowboy movie being baked in an oven. During the middle of the day, the earth was bleached by the sun; the buildings quivered and floated on a mirage. Cactuses burst out of the earth like upside-down taproots, appearing simultaneously out of place and perfectly positioned. The bushveld and the desert share a common witching hour through the middle of the day; nothing moves in that kind of searing heat.

The desert reserves its magic for the late afternoon, when the light fades from white to gold and washes up against the jagged towers and rocky outcrops that lift out of the earth like rising swells. The heat calls to clouds that will not give water without the anger of lightning. Watching the clouds build from miles away, you might catch the faint hint of rain on the air, and the scent of it is the smell of respite. The desert wants to sit you down, hold you down, and then baptize you. The desert is the definition of harsh beauty, the home of silence and the keeper of stillness. It is a challenging friend.

Martha had guided me to friends running a Navajo sweat lodge, and a ceremony was scheduled to take place in the desert town of Guadalupe. Something in me wanted to face this.

The ceremony was surrounded by festivity. Firecrackers illuminated the still desert heat. A whole pig roasted on a ragged front lawn as stray dogs sniffed the perimeter. Guadalupe was poor and marginalized, with high levels of unemployment and alcoholism—an unlikely stage, I thought, for a sacred ritual. I was nervous, not knowing what was coming—the heat, song, and spirits, and the sacred medicine of peyote—but I sensed that it would change me.

The ceremony began in an odd way because the elder leading it was late getting off from his job in construction. When he finally arrived and everyone jumped up to make a fire, Darryl, a Navajo medicine man with long raven hair and a huge presence under his gentleness, took me aside. Under his guidance, I gave praise for the fire by sprinkling cedar into it. I set an intention, crouching down as Darryl fanned tobacco smoke over me with an eagle-feather fan. Each of a series of football-sized stones was praised and blessed before it went into the fire, where it baked until it glowed red-hot.

"I want you to think about what you want to leave behind," Darryl told me.

"Leave behind?"

"You can give the things inside you back to the earth if you want."

"Um . . . okay."

"Everything is good, brother. How it is, is okay."

As we heated the rocks that would warm the sweat lodge, fear began building inside me. When Martha had first told me about the sweat lodge, I'd felt my heart float upward in my chest with hope. Now I was reconsidering. I'd heard reports on how intense the heat could be. I was afraid of being locked into a hot, dark hole. I didn't know what would come up inside a burning oven designed to rip me open. I'd spent almost every day of the last seven years battening down emotional hatches.

I breathed out as far as I could, trying to still the fear. The ancient cultures knew the value of falling apart. They did it regularly, on purpose. The Aboriginal Australians had ceremonies for men and walkabouts in the penetrating heat of the desert. Native Americans had the sweat lodge. I knew that my falseness and fear needed melting. I knew that I couldn't keep up my defenses and tolerate the physical extremes of the ceremony at the same time. This was a startling thought, but not a pleasant one. I wished I were more like Dad or Uncle John; this shit wouldn't scare them.

We offered blessings, then drank the bitter, oily, earthy peyote brew. I was afraid that I'd trip out in some psychedelic way. "What's it going to do to me, Darryl?" I asked, trying to look relaxed.

"The medicine only gives what you need," he told me gently. "There is nothing to fear."

The sweat lodge was a shallow dugout covered with heavy blankets. We had to crouch down and crawl inside on our hands and knees. It was pitch-black inside, a safe cradle of the earth just the right size for me and my demons. Packed closely together, ten of us awaited the arrival of the first rocks, the "grandfathers." There was no place to go; just my own body and the heat.

The elders described how the blanket-draped sticks over the earth's womb were the ribs of the Great Mother. "In our way, we honor the Mother," the leader said. "In the sweat we go back to her and we let her hold us again. When you emerge from the hollowed ground, you are reborn." Everyone was invited to give thanks; like all Navajo ceremonies, the ritual of the sweat lodge is first and foremost an act of gratitude.

"I want to give thanks for this fire and this gathering, for this earth, for my wife, Pam, and her beautiful way," said Darryl softly. In the darkness, his words created an image of light.

In the sweat lodge, we all sat on the same ground. We all expressed our gratitude to the wood for birthing the fire; everything was honored. I listened to the medicine men speaking their thanks to the consciousness of everything, every object, space itself. We are the earth's thinking children, and our thoughts can bless or curse. These people, I realized with awe, know what it means to be keepers of the garden.

The rocks arrived into the blackness, glowing red from their time in the fire. They hissed and spat as water was ladled onto them. The temperature climbed. The elders broke the sweat ceremony into four sessions; between each one, they lifted up the Great Mother's skirts—the blankets that sealed the lodge's sides—to give us a brief respite of cooler air. The sessions had no set time; the lead elder moved as guided by the ancestors.

The experience was, in a word, intolerable. I kept squirming around, sometimes sitting, sometimes kneeling and putting my face into the earth, trying desperately to find a cooler place. Soon I couldn't remember how many sessions there had been, only that the one taking place right now felt as if it would never end. The elders sang and chanted, somehow finding oxygen in the fire-starved air. Every time water hit the rocks, a fresh wave of heat filled the space. It just kept getting impossibly hotter. A desperate war raged inside me—I wanted to run for the door; I wanted to fight the heat with all the willpower I had, push it back, feel better. I wanted to flee this hell. I sought the most resilient bush guy parts of me; I ran to every hatch I'd ever battened—it was the response that had gotten me through every trial so far. "I'm strong," I thought. "I don't want to relent." But I was burning up, losing my resolve against the relentless heat.

As the ceremony went on, interminably on and on, I felt my last defense disintegrate in the heat. Every idea that told me who I was caught fire, burned away. I realized that "being strong" wasn't an idea worth keeping. No idea of self, no fleeting creation of human pride, was worth keeping.

As the heat built, so did a crescendo of singing, sobbing, and screaming. The demons were finding their voices through the people sitting around me; the heat absorbed the sharp notes in their cries. When the elders lifted the lodge's skirts to let in some air and light, it was odd to see the regular people sitting around this circle, knowing they had made those primeval sounds.

I felt as if I'd lost a gallon of fluid; everything was pouring out of me. The heat had to win. It had burned its way through my self-concept; now it was heating the barriers to memory, turning steel into liquid, and I wasn't strong enough to resist it. In my mind, fueled by the peyote, a slow slide show of horror began to click forward. I saw the look on my father's face as the litigation dealt him another blow. I saw my darling mother trying to shore up her family against the effects of all we had been through. I saw my uncle losing part of himself with every yard of earth that was robbed of its original nature, hurt so deeply by the evil of men. I saw how we had always tried our best, and how our strength held us apart from each other.

Then suddenly, I was far away from the sounds in the sweat lodge. It was absolutely quiet. I saw myself sitting alone in an African clearing. It was late afternoon, and the sky was pale pink, peaceful. A leopard was walking toward me with white butterflies floating around her paws, silent in the fading light. It made me so happy to see her sleek, gentle beauty. She walked right up to me and rubbed her head against my shoulder. Then she lay down next to me in the summer grass.

I was pulled from my body, floating up above Londolozi. The leopard watched my spirit rise. I saw zebras, wildebeests, and a herd of impalas. I floated toward the river, where hippos blew great funnels of mist into the air as I glided past. I saw the granite dome where my grandfather's ashes had been scattered. I felt like a piece of heaven was pasted down here, that the great ebony trees were in fact pegs connecting this canvas of God to the ground. The bateleur eagle was gliding next to me, my constant guide. I was at such peace.

Then the vision was gone and I was back in the sweat lodge, lying on the ground, my face in the dirt.

I submitted to the heat. I submitted to everything. I submitted to my own weakness. All the hatches gave way, melted, vaporized. The slide show began again, now rapid-fire: the mamba climbing up my leg, my father's mouth bleeding as he bit the inside of his cheek in fear, my shredded calf after the crocodile attack, the blood on Uncle John's Masai bracelet after the helicopter crash, the pistol thrust into my mouth, the man boiling to death, Tatty going into the ground, Gogo's small cancer-ridden frame, my father battered to prostration on the couch by litigation, the fights about curtains, the endless nightmares and morning fear. Sweat. My body began retching.

Then it was all quiet. Everything I was had burned up, leaving empty space. And I realized that this clear openness, space itself, was the only real strength, the only thing that could not be destroyed.

I awoke on my belly outside the lodge, on a large pile of sticks and leaves. A Navajo brother with long plaits was trickling water over me. My body was covered with dirt and twigs. I could feel the hum of the earth, the great vibration; I could smell the faint smoke of the cedar wood. I felt merged with the earth. I was still retching.

The brother was singing Navajo incantations over me. "Lie still, brother," he told me. "You have been to the other place to fetch the medicine."

Come with me, that other leopard had commanded as he walked past me, cloaked in that other fire. *I will take you to another place.* He had honored his promise.

"I feel like I might die," I whispered.

"No, brother, that's what being born feels like. You will see."

To restore ourselves, we must surrender everything that is not ourselves.

———

I took my tender, new self to visit my friend Ashley and her husband, Rob, at their home on a lake in Connecticut.

I did lots of solitary kayaking, watching the parade of my thoughts, noticing the calm that had largely replaced the turbulent waves. Some days, though, I still woke from anxious dreams, sweating.

It seemed nothing less than miraculous that though I had once felt that there were parts of myself that couldn't be trusted and feelings that might never return, I found myself coming back to my true nature. It had been there all along, but I had grown so disconnected from it under the stress of everything that had happened. There I was, in a scene from a movie: sitting on a bleached gray dock on a sunny summer day, the green sea before me—an endless cliché. Ash's son, Gates, and his cousin Megan stepped onto the dock behind me. Gates was a skinny boy of ten with big brown eyes, curly brown hair, and an animated face that looked like it held a hundred goofy schemes. Megan, a year or so older, was deeply tanned, with freckles across her nose and coquettish green eyes.

The children pranced down to the end of the dock like the stars of a Hollywood movie, their exuberance uncontainable. Their faces shining with sunscreen, they grabbed hands and sprinted along the dock's boarded length. Behind them the sparkling sea flashed like the cameras crowding a red carpet, if the red carpet had a crab pot tied to its end. They were the actors and this was the movie of their life, one only I could see because I was sitting in the theater, watching the sheer joy of jumping into a cool sea with your best friend on a warm summer day.

That night Ash called me from the living room with a finger over her lips in the universal sign for "Be quiet." We crept down the hallway and lingered outside the bedroom where Gates and Megan were singing songs to each other. As I listened to those soft, confident voices, all my raggedness vanished. Yes, right there in the hallway, I *felt* again. And I knew I was back from the wasteland.

For a long time, I didn't think I could recover a sense of faith in life. I'd felt so washed out; all the colors were faded versions of what they had been, a picture left too long on a bulletin board that catches the afternoon sun in a forgotten part of the kitchen. Now the color was back.

Being jaded, feeling you've been down the wrong end of the barrel too many times, seeing your fortresses crumble, is something we all go through. I accept that. Innocence is really just presence at its simplest. It's what Gates and Megan had shown me: play and laughter for their own sakes. I hadn't known if I could recapture that part of myself, until the tracks had led me there.

The next morning, I woke up missing home with an intensity that surprised and delighted me. I missed the francolins' morning call, the scent of the sweetgrass at sunrise, the bushbucks and nyalas grazing outside my window. I wanted to eat ice cream, I wanted to walk for hours in the bush, I wanted to lie on my back and stare at the sky all night with people I loved. I wanted to live.

More than anything, I wanted to go home to Londolozi.

TWENTY-FOUR

THE LEOPARDS BY THE WATERING HOLE

S UMMER HAD ARRIVED. In the glades and gardens around the camps, butterflies cut the air in flashes of orange, white, and yellow. The rejuvenation of nature was spread over the landscape in thick concentrations of life. Dried earth became swaths of grassland.

Every morning I woke up having come home a little bit more to myself. I'd been away for ten months. I tried to coax the cells of my body to lose the frantic buzz from all my travels, to reconnect with the gentle, lilting hum of nature. While all the guests went out on their afternoon safari drive, I took myself out, powered by my own legs, into the bushveld. I sat around the puddles, my feet soaking in the sunlit warm water. Frogs patrolled the shores, while all around me dragonflies swarmed like a squadron of nimble jet fighters around a lumbering airship. I was as fascinated by the dragonflies as I was by a lion. The rain-rinsed air highlighted the complex striations of lichen and bark on the knobthorn trees.

The physical journey I'd taken thousands of miles away from home had allowed me to finally see the entirety of where I'd come from. Now

I felt so elementally linked to my physical home that becoming aware again of the beauty of the wilderness was like seeing the truth about what was still inside me. I thought of how the bushveld goes dry and dormant in the winter while life thrums below the surface, waiting to be liberated by rain. I thought of a woman who'd once ridden on my safari truck; she'd looked at me as a herd of elephants surrounded us and said, "I never knew how much I loved them until right now!" We are all filled with an ocean of latent love for parts of life that lie yet undiscovered. Within this regeneration was the seed of everything that had become important to me: the art of death and rebirth, restoration from the inside out.

Mom, Dad, and Bron didn't rush me to do anything. In realizing how truly barren I had been, they'd also realized that it was true for them, too. While I had gone looking for healing, it had been happening naturally at home for everyone else in my family.

Dad had been spending time every afternoon under the big ebony tree in the garden, trying to meditate. "It's bloody difficult," he told me. Stillness was not a natural state for this man, who'd spent his life making reserves, building lodges, working in the physical realm, but he was committed to trying.

I told Mom about all the things I had seen in my vision.

"I've been on that same path, Boydie," she told me. "I've set out to heal myself, too. I've started a little vegetable garden. Every day I turn the soil, and that's my meditation."

The real balm of life resides in such simple things. I saw how one journey to healing can open doors to others' healing.

My parents left me to heal the final parts of myself in nature. Mom would see me and say nothing more than "I'm here if you need me."

My walk one day took me farther into the woods around the house. I walked barefoot so I could feel the moistness and warmth of the earth. In the thick riverine of the drainage line, the grass had been flattened by hippos making their way to the nearby dam. I could see their four-toed tracks slipping in the wet mud as they waddled back to their daytime resting pools. Around me, peering silently from the grassy banks, was a herd of nyalas. Their ears pressed forward in curiosity; the softness of the skin around their mouths made me notice the simple gentleness of their carriage and manner. I felt like Adam in the garden, alone in the warm silence with the animals.

I walked out of the grove, into a clearing with a watering hole. On the hole's far side, in the shade of a short acacia tree, I saw two young leopards, about ten months old. They saw me at exactly the same time. The leopards, doubtless waiting while their mother hunted, were already sizable. Normally, they would be shy of a human on foot; I expected them to sprint for safety into a thicker patch of bush. At the very least, I thought, they'd keep me firmly fixed in their gaze, their bodies coiled and twitching in case they needed to move quickly.

Instead, one lay down and dozed, while the other turned his attention to a yellow-billed hornbill hopping awkwardly from branch to spiny branch in the acacia above him.

Over the course of the next hour, I edged closer to the cubs, close enough to see that one had a pink nose, his brother a black one. Black Nose snapped at flies buzzing around his face, while Pinky fell into a deep sleep. To my amazement, I wound up sitting three yards away from them, on the other side of the pan. The day was perfectly quiet except for a cackling flock of wood hoopoes floating past. A starling landed and hopped around me quizzically, as if puzzled by this strange scene of a half-naked man and two wild leopards relaxing by a pond together.

Eventually I stood and backed slowly away. When I was behind some brush, out of the leopards' sight, I began jogging. Then something inside me started to build, an astounding wave of energy that flooded through my legs, pushing me into a sprint. The pent-up joy burst out of me.

I ran for miles, sweat mixing with tears of elation I couldn't hold back: the great-grandson of a leopard hunter who has leopards for friends, passing through a land that was once farmed into bankruptcy, then healed to a thriving wilderness. A bateleur eagle flew overhead. I could feel my grandfather and great-grandfather running beside me. I think they understood why we don't hunt or cull or kill the animals anymore. They understood that a great change was occurring. They were with me to help my generation restore the earth for my children and my children's children.

I felt I could run forever. I passed herds of impalas and zebras, feeling their springy energy, the towering gentleness of giraffes, the wisdom radiating from a herd of elephants. These were my family, my kin. I'm not ignorant or innocent; I know full well that this is a dangerous and damaged world. But I'd found safety again in nature and in my own heart in the cathedral of the wild.

———

Suddenly I felt reengaged with a vision that had animated generations in my family, a vision as clear as the one I had seen in the sweat lodge. Simply this: I, too, wanted to reconnect people to our kin in nature.

I remembered the male leopard who'd appeared in a veil of orange smoke, the shaman who connects humans to nature, who had come to teach me that I could walk through fire. I remembered his mate, the female who had come to me in the earth's womb and opened me to gentleness, play, and nourishment. Those magical masculine and feminine powers, both sent as emissaries from nature, were healers. I knew they could heal others. We should all walk with butterflies floating by our feet, and we can. In that moment, I knew that my work was in Africa with my family, with nature and with the animals.

———

I drove to see my uncle, who was living out in the wild central part of South Africa called the Karoo. The man who'd been such a huge part of my childhood, always my icon, had become distant. Driven by the depth of his rage over the litigation, he kept more and more to himself. His children were in boarding school; he and Gillian lived amicably apart. He focused on running his tiger project. As he'd always told me, "Nature doesn't lie, buddy."

A barn and an L-shaped house came into view, the back window frosted with a thick layer of red dust. In front of the house were some old Land Rovers with bashed-up hoods and roofs. Off to the side was an area enclosed by an electric fence at least twelve feet high. After driving all day, I'd arrived at Tiger Canyons.

The barn door burst open and out strode Uncle John, wearing a jacket mauled ragged by the bush, packing more heat on his hip than Dirty Harry. The years of legal battle had taken a toll on his body; he looked older, weathered, but in his eyes was that same fire and that same passion for conservation and, more than anything, for big cats.

When the litigation had started and everything had fallen in a heap, a lot of people would have packed it all in and given up. Uncle John had downgraded the scale of the tiger project and kept going.

He showed me around the sanctuary. Julie, the original tigress he'd started the project with, walked up to the fence and chuffed at him. He chuffed back at her. Uncle John had added cages to the backs of his trucks so he could drive them inside the enclosure and visitors could sit inside the cages to watch the tigers safely. Since the terrain of the Karoo is so flat, the tigers would sometimes jump up onto the trucks for a higher vantage point. Occasionally they would mark this higher territory, with the result that Uncle John would sit quietly inside the truck's cab while his passengers in the back got sprayed.

"Do you think I could charge people extra for getting peed on?" he asked me.

That night we sat in his candlelit house and ate a guinea fowl he'd shot for dinner.

"Buddy, success and failure are brothers," he told me. "If this stupid litigation hadn't come, this would be the most innovative tiger conservation project in the world. Instead it's my one-man crusade."

It was dark in the room except for the candlelight, and Uncle John seemed cast in shadow and in light. "Living with tigers, teaching them to hunt, walking with big cats has been the greatest experience of my life after my children," he said. "I would take ten more court cases if it meant being able to help these cats." After all these years, he remains a role model. I envy his resilience.

As I left, he said a strange thing to me out of the blue: "Buddy, remember, if anything ever happens to me, I want you and Bron to help look after my kids." Was this man with nine lives finally feeling his own mortality? Uncle John had been mostly alone day after day, month after month, and the last few years had been hard. When I visited, perhaps he saw an opportunity to lay down some kind of plan for the future. This was his way of telling me that he saw me now as an equal, that he loved me and trusted me.

A few weeks later I got an email from him:

Buddy—

If I die, please bury me down at Plaque Rock. At my burial, please make sure there is lots of singing and dancing. People must feel free to express themselves. Songs and poetry. Stories.

Look after your Dad.

Tread lightly on the earth. JV

Uncle John's whole life had been about survival and triumph: malaria, a brush with paralysis from the helicopter crash, the wear and tear of the court case. Perhaps my uncle felt his life of adventure was catching up with him. Part of my growing up was seeing the people I loved, once so vital and invincible, now with more life behind them than ahead of them. The nature of adulthood is realizing that you're not immortal. At the end of my twenties, I already understood that I didn't have infinite time. It seemed it had taken Uncle John deep into his sixties to get there.

"Look after your Dad." This was how he said he loved his brother. In taking a moment to think about his death, my uncle had expressed a lot about who he is in life.

From an original pair of tigers, JV has overseen the birth of several litters. Those tigers have all learned to hunt and are living wild in the large fenced-off area. To see a tiger strolling across the grassland changes everything. People from all over the world make pilgrimages to the middle of nowhere to visit Uncle John's tiger project, and they're always blown away by the sight of these exceptional cats. But what they don't see when they drive off in the late afternoon light is a man completely solitary for hundreds of miles in every direction, playing Bob Dylan songs on his guitar, alone with his commitment to his cause and the stillness of the Karoo night.

TWENTY-FIVE

IN THE FRONT GARDEN
OF EDEN

MOM WAS USING HER SECRET WHISTLE to hail Dad. From my cottage I heard it shrilling over the call of the orange-breasted bush shrikes that were inspecting the flowers in the large weeping Boerbean tree. Mom and Dad have had this secret whistle for so many years that it has developed into a very complex code, blasts and hoots of such intricacy that only they can understand them. They can whistle things from the simple "Where are you?" to "Meet me down by the lower deck. There's an elephant that's just been born and the mother is trying to remove the amniotic sac."

All I could decipher from the string of tootles was "teatime." This is the simplest pleasure of our routines out in the wild.

"Where?" I shouted from my doorway toward the general direction of the sound. Mom fired back a series of tootles that only R2-D2 and Dad could decode.

"Front garden under the knobthorn because it's in bloom," Dad shouted from his vantage point on the cool of the front steps. Thank goodness, because all I heard was "Wooooo-whooo."

I arrived at the top of the stairs that lead to the front garden to find Mom crossing the lawn with a tray of tea fixings. Behind her Phillip, the family's butler, was bearing a puffy granadilla cake on a footed platter as proudly as if it were King Arthur's sword.

The knobthorn was beautiful in full bloom, as if the tree's fingers had been wrapped in pale yellow cotton wool. A pair of chinspot batises flitted from branch to branch, unleashing their shrill whistling call, which makes them sound as if they're singing "Three Blind Mice" to each other. These two were a couple—the male with a macho black breastplate, his bride with a warm chestnut streak—and I suspected briefly that my parents were part bird.

It was warm, but heat is never a deterrent from tea, in my mother's view. "It actually helps," says Mom. "You heat up, and then when you go back to normal, it feels cool." She inevitably delivers this line through a thick glowing sheen of perspiration as she sips from her smoldering cup. As some nyalas fossicked among the lacy blue flowers of the plumbagos, a faint breeze plucked dead leaves from the nearby ebony and sent them spiraling down around us like whispering confetti.

My parents, strangely, looked younger than they had during my inner exile. They seemed to have drawn vitality from the plants, trees, and animals they nurture and love.

I could see how Mom has let go of trying to control everything. She's learned to enjoy her life instead of relentlessly steering it. My father's not much for travel these days, while she always wants to go voyaging. In the past year, like me, she's stopped waiting for circumstances to set her free and simply headed around the world, taking herself off to the Arctic and India, joining us for a fund-raising bike ride in Namibia. I'm not sure one ever quite recovers from the sight of one's mother in spandex biking clothes, but we did raise half a million rand for the white rhino.

"Bloody Elphas Ntuli!" fumed Bronwyn, arriving as if by magic from the Land Rover car park and flinging her Ray-Bans and straw Panama hat onto the table in disgust. With these elegant words she officially opened the ceremonial meeting we call afternoon tea.

"Who's for what?" asked Mom, hovering over the tray.

"Giraffe piss for me," said Bronwyn briskly. "Giraffe piss" has been our name for milky weak tea ever since the day Dad flung a cup off the porch, saying, "This is weaker than giraffe piss." "So you know, Elphas had to be bandaged up last night after getting knocked over by a 'buffalo.'" Bron used her fingers to rake savage quotation marks around the final word. "Well, today I find out a whole different story from the trackers."

"Here's your tea," said Mom, handing Bronwyn a cup of the brew at its weakest.

"Thank you. Does it have sugar?"

"Not yet."

"Oh, good. I've decided to give up sugar."

"I think I'll give up sugar, too," said Dad.

We all give up sugar weekly.

"Boydie?" Mom asked, looking at me.

"Ya, giraffe piss first," I said.

Bron and I like weak, milky tea, so Mom pours ours first. Dad likes his tea the color of what's left in a water hole during the hottest days of summer—a murky deep brown. We all have to remind each other daily of our preferences, and occasionally we still get it wrong. It's part of the ritual.

Now the vervet monkeys, having seen the granadilla cake, a confection made of the sweetest passion fruits, were edging closer, the whole time pretending not to be interested. Every time I glanced at one of the troop, they looked away and began to conspicuously play with a nearby twig or leaf, in an "I don't care about the cake; I just walked over here to inspect the hose pipe" kind of way.

"So the trackers go to where he was 'gored,'" said Bronwyn (again with the finger quotation marks), "and what they found in the soft river sand of the *boma* was an empty bottle of whiskey, an Elphas Ntuli–shaped sand angel with a pool of blood where the head imprint was, and a sharp corner to the barbecue." Bron's voice crescendoed. "Now, you don't need to be Horatio Caine to work that one out! The buffalo story is a complete fabrication that he made up when he realized in his drunken state that he was bleeding out the head."

In these parts, "A buffalo gored me" is an excuse on par with that old high school classic "The dog ate my homework." The habitat team once told me that the reason a tractor had crashed into a fence was "because a ghost tried to drive it out of the shed."

Bron's sneakers were spattered with dried blood, and she was smiling as she mock-raged. "I know that Elphas drinks, and I have tried to help him and I will *keep* trying, but he'll lose his life if he bleeds on my voetsek takkies and then lies to me!" Bronwyn looked down fiercely at her *voetsek*—pronounced "foot sac," the word basically means "bugger off"—takkies. (*Voetsek* is also a favorite curse word of Uncle John's; he uses Afrikaans words to frighten off all manner of game. *"Voetsek! Voetsek!"* he once screamed at a charging elephant.) Bron's always dressed immaculately and fashionably. The besmirched takkies were an affront to the rest of her pure white attire.

"Take it easy, Bron," I said. "If you put mielie meal on your takkies, I'm sure they'll go white again." Bleaching was just one of the endless properties of the cornmeal staple we enjoyed as breakfast porridge, polenta, and in a thousand other dishes. "Now calm down and tell me if anything interesting is happening at the camp."

"All is well. Mike and his guests went out after dark last night to follow the lions hunting, and they got back at three A.M. after watching the pride kill a big buffalo bull. So they were all blown away. Exhausted, but you should have seen them—ecstatic!" She smiled. "And Duncan did a Champagne stop for the honeymoon couple. He said it looked amazing: lanterns everywhere, a Bedouin bed, snacks and Champagne set out in the clearing at sundown, with some giraffes feeding nearby. When the guests arrived, a hyena was circling the table. They loved it."

"Don't forget we've got to go over the new video for the website," I told Bron.

"Right," said Bron. Was that a blush I saw? Londolozi had a new videographer-photographer, a rather dashing sort. Bron certainly seemed to have had a resurgence in her interest in wildlife filmmaking since his arrival. I'd noticed that she went out after work in the afternoons to make sure we were capturing the best imagery possible for our next marketing campaign. Her newfound diligence was truly commendable.

My dad watched Bron as she moved around the tea party. He had a distinct glow as he studied his little girl all grown up. When she sat down next to my mother, they looked like pictures of the same person taken twenty years apart.

Our friend Alex used to call Bronwyn "Tugwana" after a very unpredictable leopard that roamed near our house. My beloved Tugwana charged everything she faced like she'd charged that elephant with the Land Rover as a child. Somehow, Bron had taken all that had come at her these last years and used it as fuel. Like me, Bron had felt too much responsibility for the world. She's as hard charging as ever, but now she feels that the world also has a responsibility to her. She's much more relaxed, more able to enjoy things. She's the one who gins up silly drinks parties or dresses the staff in funny masks or brings a photo booth to a New Year's party in the bush. For Bron, peace has meant becoming a powerhouse in the business, while remaining that girl in the pink tutu twirling in the front garden.

"The pookies are back," said Dad, as wings rustled overhead. When we were kids, Dad used to read a book to Bron and me called *Pookie and the Swallows*. He'd read to us on his bed while we watched the swallows building their nests under the roof of the front veranda. Those swallows were summerhouse guests to be honored and welcomed.

And now the swallows had returned. I loved seeing them arrive back at their summer breeding grounds. Overnight there were suddenly flocks of them dogfighting through the sky like mini Spitfires. They skimmed the earth, snatching up any insect that leapt into their path. When they found mates, they began to build their nests, mud igloos glued upside down to the roof of the front porch, dive-bombing in under the eaves and plastering in more mud as carefully as stone masons.

Some other swallows had built their nests in the apex of the A-frame roof that covers the public area of the Granite Camp. They were very welcome to make this their summer home; the only problem was that during construction of the nest, flecks of mud fell down onto the beautiful cream sofa guests liked to loll on as they watched the baboons play and forage on the thick slabs of granite in front that had given the camp its name.

Mom had devised a cunning plan. She'd gotten the maintenance team to cut her a piece of plywood, stained it black, and had it installed in the roof beams under the swallows' nest, with the words "Swallows' Loft" stenciled in graceful italic at the base. The guests could still watch the breeding pair flit in like jet fighters and disappear into the nest, but the plywood protected their heads from any mud or discarded insects that fell out of the nest. Word got out via the bush telegraph that we had added a special room at the private Granite Suites, and we soon had folks calling to ask if they could reserve the "Swallows' Loft Suite."

"Come, come, come, my fat friends," sang Mom, who had spotted a family of francolins clucking in from the wild bushy fringe of the lawn.

The phone rang inside. Recently, I'd heard Dad hanging up on the lawyers after saying, "I know my truth. Same shit, different day—it doesn't even bother me anymore." I got to my feet. "Shall I get that?" I asked him.

"Nah, Boydie," Dad said. "They are just gonna have to wait. It's only got the power I give it." He leaned back against the ebony tree and closed his eyes for a little nap.

After tea, Mom drifted off toward her garden, Bron down to her room, and I headed over to take up Dad's previous position on the cool cement of the front steps. Suddenly a shrill blast from down near the vegetable patch sliced the air. A monkey that had stuck its hand into the sugar bowl had panicked, knocking the bowl over, and the nyalas had given flight.

At the sound of Mom's whistle blast, Dad immediately popped awake, shooed the monkey off the table, and headed for the veggie garden, an organic wonder that represents Mom's triumph over marauding baboons and hyenas and the source of much fresh produce in the Londolozi kitchen. As he walked past, he glanced at me and muttered, "I swear she waits till I'm asleep to give me an errand. She wants a rake."

————

I walked around to the back of the house and stood on the porch overlooking the Sand River. I watched the great fronds of the palm trees flap and shake. Down below, the elephants were feeding on reeds and palm leaves, but I couldn't see them. Elephants have a way of being around but unseen. Many times on game drives, we'll pause in the Land Rover to survey the landscape. Suddenly the shadows will shift and we'll realize that a six-ton elephant is mere yards away; incredibly enough, it had been there all along, massive yet invisible.

Now I could hear the grumbling of the elephants' stomachs and that deep vibration they use to talk with one another. I knew that those sounds were in fact a sliver of the full extent of their low-frequency communication, which occurs at a level that my ears can't hear. Even so, I could feel the invisible net of frequency the elephants cast around themselves as a tingling in my own body. The unseen awareness of a giant presence. The *om* of the ambassadors of peace. *You are always safe.*

I remembered that same feeling the night the gun was put to my head. Horrible things give us the opportunity to feel and sense the bigger powers in our life. Now I realize that "Know your truth, stick to the process, and be free of the outcome" are the only operating instructions we will ever need for a right life. These are the pegs I have put into the ground, and at age twenty-nine, I feel clear and peaceful.

Sometimes, just as a bonus confirmation, the elephants will walk out from beneath the palms, into the clearing, and I'll be aware that my sense of them was true. I'll watch the young ones running under their mother's feet, flailing tiny trunks that don't quite work yet, and I'll know that my sense of God is also true.

TWENTY-SIX

THE *OM* IN MOTION

O N SOLO DRIVES THROUGH the park, I sing to myself, rambling songs that flow perfectly into each other. I grin, catch myself finding myself funny. Let's face it—there's something innately amusing about rocking out in your Land Rover with only the impalas to witness it. These songs are so much more than songs; they're the sound of a healthy soul, and to someone who'd lost the joy of singing to himself for so long, each song becomes a sacred chant.

There is a gift for those of us who have grown up with all the fear, uncertainty, and wonder of the African bush, a moment that God created just for us as compensation for all the years of worry. It's the moment you come to the end of a long journey, down the final dusty stretch of road where you learned to drive. You catch sight of the big marula tree at the end of the garden and are struck by how unchanged it is, still marking the end of the garden. Home is timeless, in the heart, near love, close to a river. Where the animals are.

The Intention Circle at Londolozi is set on a piece of high ground near the lodges, where there's a clear view as the land falls away to the faraway mountains miles off to the west, along the path of the ancient elephant corridors, long since destroyed. Two twenty-foot elephant tusks made of twisted wire—from the old apartheid fence that once separated Londolozi from Kruger Park—frame the entrance to a circle of river sand about fifteen feet in diameter. Around the circle are stones from different parts of South Africa: large chunks of fading pink rose quartz for unconditional love; amethyst for protection; serpentine for releasing negative energy. Scattered around these larger crystals are thousands of smaller ones, so that the flat surface of the circle sparkles like a sequined sky. The circle is a quiet place outside the confines of the camp, the tusks a doorway into a sacred space where visitors can set an intention for their lives.

The Intention Circle was designed by Simon Max Bannister, Londolozi's artist in residence, my friend since we were babies and fellow costar of Uncle John's *Bush School* series. Even then, he was an artistic visionary. Just after he finished building the installation, Simon asked Dad and me to jot our own intentions on pieces of recycled paper. He sealed them in a jar and fixed a small piece of wire from it to the larger of the two tusks, so that the intentions might be broadcast into the sky.

There was a time when all of this "intention setting" sounded like rubbish to me, a lot of New Age bunk that had nothing to do with the gritty, practical realities of my life. But that was a naïve perspective. Hemingway said we heal stronger at the broken places, but I've found that where the heart is concerned, we also heal more tenderly, more open to the miraculous. Because of the medicine our troubles brought us, my family is unable to deny the possibility that miracles exist.

One evening, as the sun began to set directly between the tusks of the Intention Circle, I sat inside it with Dad, Mom, Bron, Kate, Kate's mom, Mo, and a few other staffers.

Kate bounced her sleeping daughter, Maya, on one hip. Maya is a preternaturally gorgeous little girl with huge, warm brown eyes. Her new pink outfit glowed against her dark skin, her eyelashes curling glamorously even in sleep. She clutched a stuffed bear with a shredded pink blanket for a body, which Kate claims is so covered with food stains that in an emergency we could boil it and feed thousands from the soup.

After enduring grueling evaluations from authorities, Kate had been set to adopt a baby from a pregnant teen mother. In a cruel setback, at the last moment the girl disappeared from the hospital where she'd gone to give birth. Kate was crushed. Then the social worker said, "There's another child here at the hospital, a baby who's been here for four months." She'd been put up for adoption by her schoolgirl mother. Kate walked into the room, saw tiny Maya, and it was game over. They've been a unit ever since. As always, the right people show up if you're open to them.

Kate's adoption of Maya is more evidence that miracles can strike anywhere, anytime, in any of our lives. Maya could easily be an impoverished orphan instead of having one of the most amazing mothers in the world. I think the universe guided her and Kate to each other, partly for their own happiness, and partly to help, in some small way, erode the racism that still infects the small backwater towns of South Africa. I love the shocked look on villagers' faces whenever Kate introduces a new acquaintance to her daughter.

Maya brings magic to our family, signified by the praying mantises that seem drawn to her (one even crawled out of her baby clothes the day Kate adopted her). In certain African cultures, praying mantises are very powerful, incarnations of the gods.

We've been given a hint of how Maya plans to share her magic. Later, at age two, she announced to Kate, "Mommy, one day when I am big, I am going to teach all the children in Africa."

This evening, we settled ourselves inside the circle. Simon broke the seal on the jar and removed the papers on which Dad and I had written our intentions a year before. We all noticed that the words had faded away, as if drawn off the page and absorbed into the universal airwaves. Inside the jar, a plant had miraculously started to grow. We'd written about the return of nature, and now our words had been replaced by this small, beautiful living thing, growing against all odds in an airtight container. What better symbol of our intentions' manifestation could there be?

Down the hill by the dam I could hear a hippo honking, as if another hippo had just cracked a hilarious joke. I couldn't shake the feeling that maybe they knew something we didn't.

The sun dipped below the lip of the jagged mountains. "Boyd, Dave, it's time for you to renew your intentions," Simon told us. Without saying a word, Dad and I began to scribble away. Meanwhile, Mom and Bron dozed on the warm sand. Kate made a few lethargic attempts to corral Maya, who'd decided it was much more fun to explore the Intention Circle while tossing sand on her mother and chuckling to herself. Gogo Mo just laughed; she always thinks whatever her granddaughter does is wonderful, no matter how naughty. Eventually Maya tired of her mischievousness and lolled in Kate's lap. It was a wonderfully casual ceremony, light-hearted and playful.

Once Dad and I were done, I stood up and read out what I'd written: "It is our intention to support Boyd in his quest to date every supermodel now living." A murmur of mockery rose up. "Okay, okay, seriously," I said. "Our intention is to create corridors of wildlife for animals, to advocate and fight for more land to be returned to its natural state. We wish to create a model for restoration that the rest of the world can replicate. We commit to this in love."

As I finish reading my note, I noticed Dad looking at me quizzically. "We have written *exactly the same thing*," he said, smiling. I looked over at his note; the wording was indeed virtually verbatim. There was so much that should have pulled father and son apart, yet even with all my time away, we'd arrived at exactly the same spot. Those who'd known my father earlier would have been shocked to see that he'd written, "We commit to this in love," but I'm no longer surprised by these sorts of occurrences. I don't believe this was a coincidence. Dad and I didn't create this intention; it simply came through us.

The next morning I found Dad on the veranda, practicing his medita-tion. "Well, Dad, I have a bit of an idea," I said when he was done, feel-ing a little nervous. Dad's not one for arrogance, and I didn't want it to come out that way. "I want to re-create the original elephant corridor," I said, "and I want your help. I want to see elephants walk again from Kruger to the mountains. I want Kate to build learning centers along the way. We've already got two up and going." I felt like I was babbling as I laid it all out. "Everywhere you go, people talk about how we need to save the planet, and we're the people who actually know how to do it. We've restored land, we've restored our connection to the animals, and in a way, we seem to be learning how to restore ourselves."

I dreamed we could create a protected piece of wild land that would connect Londolozi to the mountains west of us, the mountains framed by the tusks in the Intention Circle. This land would allow the elephants, the *om* in motion, to safely walk the sixty miles from the reserve to the high-rainfall areas on the mountains. The learning centers for rural peo-ple in the villages along the way would be beacons of hope. The ele-phants would give the villages a source of income as well as a source of pride.

As a boy with Phineas in the riverbed, I felt I had been visited by a mountain. Now I wanted the elephants to be free to go to their moun-tains.

Dad grinned. "Everyone will tell you it's impossible"—for a second I was taken aback—"but they said that to me when we started Londoz, Phinda, and CC Africa. Okay, the tiger project was a glitch—I admit that—but one glitch isn't going to stop us, is it?" He smiled, his blue shining eyes bright and young beneath his graying hair. "Listen to your old man, my boy; everything is a gift. The things that test you can move you into a new state."

I've learned that nothing is worth doing if it cannot be done from a place of deep peace. If we want to restore the planet, we must first restore ourselves. I believe that you find your way to your right life, your mission, the same way you find an animal. First, quiet your heart and be still. Then find the fresh track and be willing to follow it. You don't need to see the whole picture; you only need to see where to take the next step. Life isn't about staying on track; it's about constantly rediscovering the track.

As I write this, my restoration proposal includes a thicket of details on building the elephant corridor, a speaking tour, and, in conjunction with Bron, an online arm that will carry stories of restoration all over the world. Dad, Mr. Logistics, has been working to get high-level government support. Kate has discovered her gift and passion for building learning centers; her dream is that every single African child will have access to a world-class education. That's why she and Mom created the Good Work Foundation. Kate has already been working at centers at Londolozi and in a little town called Philippolis and has just finished building a new learning center at Hazyview, a village near the proposed corridor. Our plan is mostly still pie in the sky. It might not get off the ground, or it might go down in flames. Or, hell, it might even work; we've pulled off madder schemes. The important thing is to dream big.

The first twelve thousand acres have been tentatively scheduled to become a part of the elephant corridor. It's all been happening without struggle. The more we all come toward peace, the more things flow. The court case rages on, but the outcome doesn't matter. We're sticking to our process and putting our energy and focus on what does.

The outer healing of the land will always be my and my family's work. But our inner healing is even more important. We see the world through inner frames. Healing ourselves is as much a part of the restoration of the planet as building a place for elephants to walk to the mountains as ambassadors of peace.

Maybe, like me, you also need to heal but you can't walk out into the wilderness this afternoon. But you can look up at the sky or that tree poking through the concrete and know that there are thousands of other people who feel equally disconnected from their inner and outer worlds. You can, from where you stand, make a decision to restore from within, even if your mind screams that it is not possible. Whatever feels unresolved, the animal part of you is already tracking the healing you need. Follow that trail; the medicine will feel like freedom. In that moment, you'll become a part of restoring Eden.

———

Last night, I lay down on the earth at Londolozi, its red warmth exuding comfort into the marrow of my bones.

Lying on my back, watching the stars emerge, I was struck by how they'd been there all along, invisibly lining my day even when I couldn't see them. Sometimes the darkness reveals, its ways more mysterious than light's. Sometimes the darkness gives a gift of stars by which we can navigate our way home.

ACKNOWLEDGMENTS

S O MANY SPECIAL PEOPLE have helped me write this book; to them I owe a huge debt of gratitude.

I would like to thank my mom, my dad, and Bron for the amazing support they have given me, not just in the writing of this book but through everything. It has been an amazing and intense journey, and I'm grateful that everything that has happened has served to make our bonds of love stronger.

I would also like to say a huge thank-you to my mentor and friend Dr. Martha Beck, who has played such a significant role in not only getting me to write but also in shaping so much of my outlook. Without her, I would never have had the courage to undertake this project.

Then Betsy Rapoport! I cannot say enough about how exceptional her support has been. Without her, this book would never have happened. She has provided immense editorial as well as emotional guidance. And that was before she let me move in with her and her family and made me feel so welcome and at home. I have been astounded by her amazing love and her belief in this project. I am so grateful to you, Betsy, and to Ken, Sam, and Kate Weiner.

I would also like to thank my agent, Tina Bennett, who championed the creation of the narrative from its earliest iterations. Her insightful editorial eye was critical to birthing this book. I'm likewise grateful to her amazing team, Svetlana Katz and Dorothy Vincent, for all their help.

I owe a big thank-you to Susan Kamil, publisher of Random House, who was instrumental in shaping what was a very big and unruly manuscript into this book, and for believing in its message from the very beginning. I also appreciate the assistance of Kendra Harpster and Sam Nicholson, Susan's wonderful editorial team.

Ashley and Rob Jansen opened their home and heart to me and let me hang out on their couch for hours. Thank you, Ashley and Rob, for your love and support.

I would also like to acknowledge my uncle, John Varty, who had an immense influence on me during my formative years. My time in the bush with him as a child was very special to me.

Our partners, the Taylors, were instrumental in the creation of Londolozi. Together we have built a professional bond and friendship that is special in today's world. I am very grateful to Alan Taylor for his wise counsel and his unwavering support of my father and uncle.

I need to thank Kate Groch for her support and passion. She has been an inspiration to many, most particularly me. Kate's continued work as the CEO of the Good Work Foundation brings profound change and hope to many people in the often forgotten parts of South Africa. An educator truly does shape the lives of individuals, and no one works harder at this than Kate. She and her mother, Gogo Mo Groch, are changing our country one person at a time.

My aunt Beejay has been with us through so much and is always so full of love and fun. I am thankful to have her in my life as an ever-present source of joy.

Finally, I would like to send great thanks to the entire Londolozi family, all of whom have had such a big influence on me. It's a very special place, and we are very lucky to live there.

———

If you'd like to come see us at Londolozi, additional information is available at www.londolozi.com.

Additional information about my amazing uncle, John Varty, his films, and Tiger Canyons is available at www.jvbigcats.co.za.

Additional information on Martha Beck and the retreats she leads at Londolozi is available at marthabeck.com.

Additional information about the Good Work Foundation, founded by my mother, Shan Varty, and my teacher, Kate Groch, and the learning centers is available at www.goodworkfoundation.org.

ABOUT THE AUTHOR

BOYD VARTY was raised on Londolozi Game Reserve, in South Africa. By the age of eight, he'd shot his first impala, driven his first Land Rover, and acted as a principal photographic assistant for his uncle, a world-famous documentarian. He currently lives and works at Londolozi, where his most recent projects include advocating for the restoration of an ancient elephant corridor, helping the Good Work Foundation create more learning centers in South Africa, and adventuring across the African continent on his motorbike.

ABOUT THE TYPE

This book was set in Granjon, a modern recutting of a typeface produced under the direction of George W. Jones, who based Granjon's design upon the letterforms of Claude Garamond (1480–1561). The name was given to the typeface as a tribute to the typographic designer Robert Granjon.